Major League
Expansions and

Major League Baseball Expansions and Relocations

A History, 1876–2008

FRANK P. JOZSA, JR.

with a Foreword by Larry Schroeder

McFarland & Company, Inc., Publishers

Jefferson, North Carolina, and London

LIBRARY OF CONGRESS CATALOGUING-IN-PUBLICATION DATA

Jozsa, Frank P., 1941–
    Major league baseball expansions and relocations : a history,
1876–2008 / Frank P. Jozsa, Jr. ; with a foreword by Larry
Schroeder.
        p.   cm.
    Includes bibliographical references and index.

    ISBN 978-0-7864-4388-8
    softcover : 50# alkaline paper ∞

    1. Baseball—Economic aspects—United States.   2. Baseball
teams—Location—United States.   3. Baseball teams—United
States—Marketing.   4. Baseball teams—United States—History.
I. Title.
GV880.J695   2010
796.357'640973—dc22   2009050085

British Library cataloguing data are available

Cover images ©2010 Shutterstock

Manufactured in the United States of America

*McFarland & Company, Inc., Publishers
    Box 611, Jefferson, North Carolina 28640
    www.mcfarlandpub.com*

To Frank Chance and
Michael Utsman

Acknowledgments

While I was organizing and writing this book in late 2008 and early 2009, several people contributed in different ways. Some of these individuals also helped me when I wrote other sports books including *Baseball, Inc.* in 2006 and *Baseball in Crisis* in early 2008. Without their dedication and support these books might not have been published.

With respect to the manuscript's development, Frank Chance provided me with articles, books, and other readings in sports topics, especially the game of baseball. As the director of Information Support Services at Pfeiffer University's campus in Charlotte, North Carolina, Frank made a special effort to expedite my requests for materials. His evening librarian, Theresa Frady, also forwarded me many relevant scholarly pieces that were incorporated in the book. I am very grateful to them for their commitment and interest in my research of the business and economics of the sports industry.

Lara Little, the library director and reference and periodicals librarian at Pfeiffer's campus in Misenheimer, North Carolina, efficiently furnished me with different types of demographic data, names, and locations of urban places and metropolitan areas, and other basic information reported in government periodicals that applied to the history of baseball leagues and teams in the United States and Canada. I appreciate Lara's expertise and willingness to mail me materials I requested. It is fortunate that Pfeiffer has these three individuals as librarians to meet the needs of the university's faculty, staff, and students at each of its campuses.

Professors in institutions of higher education also contributed to this book. Thanks go to Syracuse University professor of public administration Larry Schroeder, who wrote the Foreword. I am grateful to University of Michigan professor of sports management Rodney D. Fort, who advised me to discuss the motivation for expansions and movements of teams and also to explain the role of baseball leagues in facilitating the establishment of new franchises, and in hindering those that did not receive an expansion team or were not allowed to relocate. Retired economics professor James Quirk, who coauthored with Rodney Fort such insightful books as *Hard Ball: The Abuse of Power in Pro Team Sports*, was of welcome assistance. Winthrop University professor of economics Gary Stone suggested some topics for me to consider involving leagues, teams, regular seasons and postseasons.

During August 2008 at a downtown hotel in Atlanta, Georgia, I was interviewed for a PBS documentary titled *Milwaukee Braves: The Team That Made Milwaukee Famous*. While in the interview, the film's executive producer, Bill Povletich, asked me several complex but intriguing questions about the movements of the Braves from Boston to Milwaukee in 1953 and then from Milwaukee to Atlanta in 1966. Since I was writing a manuscript then of Major League Baseball Experiences and Relocations, this interview motivated me to learn accurate, relevant, and specific information about these two relocations of the Braves franchise and why they had occurred. Thus special thanks to Bill for including me in his production of these events that were scheduled to be broadcast on public television sometime in the spring of 2009.

Two friends of mine made comments to me regarding the business of professional baseball. That is, subcontractor Bill Focht of Charlotte, North Carolina, and orthodontist Dr. John Roshel, Jr., of Terre Haute, Indiana, each stated their views about what professional baseball meant to, and how it impacted, communities and sports fans in various consumer markets of America. Their insights into the game and its popularity and effect were interesting, provocative, and thoughtful. I thank each of them.

As a special acknowledgment, my girlfriend, Maureen Fogle, understood how important it was for me to finish my manuscript and then submit it to a book publisher. Maureen left me alone to spend numerous hours on our computer for several months even though she was writing a dissertation for her Ed.D. in healthcare education. In the end, Maureen and I each achieved our goals.

Table of Contents

Foreword
by Larry Schroeder

Frank Jozsa is, on the basis of his many publications including seven books, obviously an expert on the business and operation of various professional sports leagues and the economics and performance of franchises in baseball, basketball, football, ice hockey, and soccer. Major League Baseball Expansions and Relocations constitutes another important contribution to this impressive list.

During the mid–1970s, I served as chair of Jozsa's dissertation committee while he was a doctoral student in the Department of Economics at Georgia State University in Atlanta, Georgia. After studying the professional sports industry and successfully completing his dissertation on that topic, Frank received a Ph.D. from the university in 1977. The current book constitutes an extension and impressive update of his dissertation work.

Here he traces the history of when, where, and how the American League and National League in Major League Baseball—and other prominent major leagues in the sport—had expanded and also, which teams within these leagues moved from ballparks in their home areas to sites in other sports markets of America during the nineteenth, twentieth, and twenty-first centuries. Based on my knowledge of topics in professional sports, this is the only book that includes a scholarly and comprehensive analysis of expansion and the relocation of clubs in the majority of major professional baseball leagues for the years 1876 to 2008.

Each of the five chapters contains tables of raw data, descriptive statistics, and other information regarding the demographics of small, midsized, large, and very large metropolitan areas in the United States and Canada. The analysis also reveals how competitively expansion teams have played within their respective leagues, how the performances of clubs varied before and after they had relocated, and how cities ranked from the least to most popular as locations of prior and current baseball franchises. In short, Jozsa's book incorporates and applies different types of criteria and measurements to explain the decisions of various baseball officials to increase the size of their leagues and of team owners to vacate an area and move their enterprises into another place.

1

In addition to the Preface, Introduction, supporting tables, and Index, the volume includes an extensive list of readings in the Bibliography. Of particular interest to serious students of the game are pictures of baseball league presidents and former owners of franchises, and of famous baseball teams who in some way were involved with a topic. Thus fans will remember those who had played important roles in the emergence and development of leagues, especially with respect to their expansion and redeployment.

I admire Frank Jozsa for his accomplishments as an author of sports books and respect him for his career as a college teacher in economics and business administration. I'm certain that Major League Baseball Expansions and Relocations is a title that will inform, impress, and reward you by reading it.

Larry Shroeder is a professor of public administration at Syracuse University and has co-authored several books and written articles about the problems associated with financing the construction and maintenance of public infrastructure.

Preface

To conclude my doctoral studies as a graduate student in economics at Georgia State University in 1977, I completed a dissertation titled "An Economic Analysis of Franchise Relocation and League Expansion in Professional Team Sports, 1950–1975." Then 22 years later, I co-authored with John J. Guthrie, Jr., a book named *Relocating Teams and Expanding Leagues in Professional Sports: How the Major Leagues Respond to Market Conditions*. That volume, in turn, analyzed the expansions of various leagues and movements of their teams from 1950 to 1995. The book highlighted the strategies of such American-based professional sports organizations as Major League Baseball, the National Basketball Association, and the National Football League. I have continued to research and study many topics about team sports, and I authored seven more books during the early 2000s (including, for example, *Baseball, Inc.: The National Pastime as Big Business* in 2006 and *Baseball in Crisis: Spiraling Costs, Bad Behavior, Uncertain Future* in 2008).

During the summer of 2008, I travelled to Atlanta, where I was interviewed on camera for a future television documentary—scheduled to be telecast on the Public Broadcasting System—that discussed the relocation of baseball's National League Braves from Boston to Milwaukee in 1953 and then from Milwaukee to Atlanta in 1966. To adequately prepare for the interview, I read several detailed accounts of why and how these movements occurred. I learned many interesting demographic, business, and economic facts with respect to the Braves' two relocations—that is, from a relatively large city on the East Coast to a smaller one in the Midwest, and subsequently to an attractive and booming metropolitan area in the Southeast.

I was inspired to further examine the business and economics of expansion and relocation in professional baseball as I had initially discussed in my dissertation and then in *Relocating Teams and Expanding Leagues in Professional Sports*. I restudied league expansions and team relocations in organized baseball from the seasons of 1876 to 2008. These were the circumstances that compelled me to forward a proposal for this book to a publisher for their approval.

My efforts to study and comprehend expansion and relocation in organized baseball led to some intriguing questions. For example, why did the National League become established and perform as a unit 26 years before the American League? What were some factors that caused professional base-ball teams in America to fold during the late 1800s and early to mid–1900s? How did expansions in the American and National leagues affect the busi-ness of this team sport? Which teams became more competitive and finan-cially prosperous after they moved to another city. These and many other questions were worthwhile to evaluate and in part, to incorporate in chapters of this book.

This book is written for several kinds of readers, among them the man-agers, owners, and executives of—and investors in—major league and minor league teams. Because of the historical data and other facts in my book, these and other sports entrepreneurs, leaders, and officials will better understand when and why some professional baseball clubs had to move their operations to other cities in order to effectively compete against their rivals in a league or a division of a league.

People working with the local, regional, national, and international orga-nizations that have licenses, partnerships, sponsorships, or marketing contracts with major and minor league teams: this book is also written for them. The critical events and trends that have propelled the sports industry continue to affect the future economics of baseball. These factors are each thoroughly dis-cussed in the chapters to follow. Some reasons are revealed for the amounts of cash flow, overall revenues, and profits of teams, for the passion of their ballplayers, coaches, fans, and proprietors, and for the support offered by the broadcast networks and print media.

This book should prove useful as a reference and bibliographical source for university professors who teach undergraduate and graduate courses in sports administration, economics, history, management, marketing, and strat-egy. Sports fans who read this book will, I very much hope, appreciate the foundations and complexities of baseball markets—how they emerged, devel-oped and matured, and whether other teams nearest the new arrivals survived and prospered or failed within the short term or over decades in the long run.

For those interested in various aspects of the commercialization, eco-nomics, or globalization of professional baseball and other sports the fol-lowing books, of which I am the author, should prove useful: *American Sports Empire: How the League Breed Success* (2003); *Sports Capitalism: The Foreign Business of American Professional Leagues* (2004); *Big Sports, Big Business: A Century of League Expansions, Mergers, and Reorganizations* (2006); and *Global Sports: Cultures, Markets, and Organizations* (2009).

The contents of this book are based on the research I did for my dis-sertation and books and the articles I wrote for academic journals, popular magazines and local newspapers—and also on my experiences as an amateur and semi-professional baseball player while being a kid, teenager, and adult. My wish is that you will experience as much pleasure reading this book as I did conceptualizing and writing it.

Introduction

Since the early 1900s, at least one professional baseball organization in America has successfully operated for more than several decades while others failed and then disbanded within a few years. Each of these leagues was established for various business, cultural, economic, and social reasons. As typical baseball groups, they mostly consisted of some outstanding, mediocre, and weak performing teams whose field managers had coached their players to provide competition at the ballpark and also entertainment in their respective markets for sports fans during months of early to late spring, an entire summer, and throughout the fall of each calendar year.

While they developed, matured, and prospered or floundered, a large majority of these baseball leagues had teams that were operated for profit as franchises. As such, some of these clubs co-existed in cities and within regions of the United States and Canada. Therefore, they had to share their markets in metropolitan areas with other local amateur, semiprofessional, and professional basketball, football, ice hockey, or soccer teams. However, as a result of different game schedules but somewhat overlapping regular seasons, America's baseball leagues occasionally but strategically adopted reforms and implemented changes to keep the game exciting, fun, and interesting for hometown spectators. As a result, some of these leagues created both a short- and long-run demand for baseball and its teams among sports fans and the general public who may or may not have interacted with, or participated in, the entertainment industry.

Between the late 1800s and early 2000s, among the most popular and prominent of the U.S.-based leagues in each of five professional team sports were the American League (1901 to 2008) and National League (1876 to 2008) in Major League Baseball (1901 to 2008), and also the National Basketball Association (1949 to 2008), National Football League (1922 to 2008), National Hockey League (1917 to 2008), and Major League Soccer (1996 to 2008). Besides these different sports organizations, there were other important professional baseball, basketball, football, ice hockey, and soccer leagues that existed more than one year in the United States, but because of economic, financial, or sport-specific factors had folded. These groups included, respectively, the American Association (1882 to 1891) and Federal League (1914 to

1915), Basketball Association of America (1946 to 1948) and American Basketball Association (1967 to 1976), American Football League (1960 to 1969) and US Football League (1983 to 1985), American Hockey Association (1926 to 1942) and World Hockey Association (1972 to 1979), and American Soccer League I (1921 to 1933) and North American Soccer League (1967 to 1974).[1]

Throughout their histories, many of these and other professional sports leagues in America varied from being traditional and conservative to very creative, flexible, and innovative as business organizations. As such, the latter leagues were compelled to adopt and undertake risky projects. Thus their leaders decided to realign and restructure them in order to continue operating and also to become even more well-known and successful in a team sport. Indeed a few of these sports organizations benefitted by merging with others while some changed the composition of their conferences and divisions over the years by decreasing or increasing the total number of teams. Finally, there were sports leagues in America that also reformed by approving or rejecting the movement of one or more of their clubs from one metropolitan area into another within the U.S.

In short, these were a number of the important methods, tactics, and strategies that sports league officials and the various owners of teams had jointly initiated and implemented to be more competitive and improve their performances in regular season and postseason games, to expand the boundaries of their respective market, and also to generate additional revenues and an increase in profits, or inversely, to reduce their financial losses. Nevertheless, some clubs in these leagues had failed to perform effectively in their divisions or conferences during one or more regular seasons. Consequently, they did not attract enough local sports fans to fill or nearly fill their arenas, ballparks, or stadiums. As a result, a number of them ceased to operate in a league after a few or several seasons and then vanished as sports enterprises because they were unsuccessful at providing entertainment to fans within their home cities and surrounding areas.

Sports Markets

Despite their peculiar circumstances, unique characteristics, and contrasts in styles and structures, all professional sports leagues are basically groups with various members who have a common mission. That is, each of them essentially consists of profit-maximizing franchises that exist as teams to the best of their ability in games at home and away sites during regular seasons and perhaps in postseasons. As such, it is crucial for officials of leagues to select and then assign an appropriate number of their clubs each season to a specific division or conference. Furthermore, all sports leagues attempt to have each of their members located—and entertaining spectators—within areas that attract the greatest number of fans and generate enough revenues for them to continue operating from year to year.

For sure these metropolitan areas are unalike culturally, demographically and geographically, but also commercially since as markets, they have been the homes of different businesses and industries. In fact, the majority of them have experienced strong, average, and weak economic development during various years, decades and centuries, contained ethnic and racial populations and adjusted to the population growth of these groups. Meanwhile, others have been engaged in and impacted by various historical factors.[2]

Being the home site for one or more franchises of a professional sports league or leagues, these metropolitan areas are extremely important for professional teams to study, exploit, and penetrate, especially from a marketing perspective. So as prior and current sports markets, all metropolitan areas—which once were identified as urban places—have gradually changed over time with respect to their cultures, economies, and populations. Therefore, each sports league and its respective coalition of teams must be aware of how these markets in areas had been developed and will be transformed, and accordingly then adapt by reforming their brands, images, and strategies. If these changes are not completed, then some professional sports teams will no longer be competitive against their rivals, lose goodwill and support among local fans in their areas, and fail to expand their operations and popularity in the new and challenging business environment of the twenty-first century.

Since the sport was originally established in the U.S. and tended to grow and prosper from the mid to late 1800s, and because its teams were organized and initially grouped into a professional league beginning in the early 1870s, baseball is the focus of this book along with two types of historical actions within each of two separate but interdependent baseball organizations. As such, the latter groups are the American League (AL) and National League (NL), which had combined in 1901 to form one of America's most elite, popular, and prestigious professional sports league: Major League Baseball (MLB). Indeed during the late nineteenth and then early twentieth century, baseball became known as America's pastime. Meanwhile, major league teams continued to emerge, establish policies, schedules and rules, compete in home and away regular season and postseason games at their ballparks, and geographically locate themselves to co-exist among small, midsized, large, and very large urban places across the United States.

EXPANSION AND RELOCATION

To exist and then gradually succeed as a group in professional baseball, and also to effectively operate as a business and entertainment organization for more than a century, MLB was compelled to realign its structure during years when new franchises had joined the AL or NL in cities of the US and Canada, and also when some of the existing AL and NL clubs had to move their operations from one urban place—now metropolitan area—to another within the United States or from Canada to America. Based on these reorganizations, *Major League Baseball Expansions and Relocations* identifies and then thoroughly discusses two interesting but extraordinary and strategic phenomena that have transformed the sport.[3]

First is the expansion of franchises in the AL from 1901 and the NL since 1876, and second is the extent to which teams in these leagues have or have not relocated by moving from their sites within sports markets—which geographically are identified in the literature as metropolitan areas. In fact, by applying demographic and economic data and also baseball-specific information, the five chapters in this book are formatted and organized to highlight them and also address several key issues about the years, numbers, and consequences of expansions and team relocations within the AL and NL of MLB and other professional baseball leagues.

Expansion

With respect to the former leagues' previous expansions into occupied and unoccupied U.S. and Canadian sports areas, a few questions are interesting to ask and also are relevant to topics in this book. A list of these questions includes, for example, the following subjects. First, when did the AL or NL expand and increase their total number of teams during years of the nineteenth, twentieth, and twenty-first centuries? Second, what was the business, demographic or economic factors that caused these baseball leagues to approve the entry of new franchises in each of the expansion years?

Third, where did the two leagues' new clubs base their operations in areas within the U.S. and Canada? Fourth, how well did these expansion teams perform against others in their respective league and then after 1968, against rivals in their division? Fifth, why did some expansion teams fail to exist after one or a few baseball seasons while others continued to operate and play games for years and even decades? Finally, since the early 1900s, should MLB or should it not have expanded and thereby increased the number of teams, and agreed or disagreed with franchise owners to place them in distinct markets within the U.S. and Canada?

Generally the decision by a professional sports league to expand or not expand in size is a complex, tedious, and time-intensive issue because of differences in the economic interests, financial commitments, and other business and personal relationships between and among each franchise owner or a syndicate of owners in the group. To be sure, an expansion of one or more teams in a sports season has several implications for current members of a league, which in turn, operates as a business cartel according to sports economists. An entry fee, for example, totaling tens or even hundreds of millions of dollars must be determined by members of a league which, after it is paid, will be proportionately allocated among the current clubs. Furthermore, a league must approve who owns, controls, and manages an expansion franchise by evaluating their credentials, experiences in professional baseball, and also the amounts of their financial assets and debts, and wealth.

Another issue to consider in a decision is that an expansion team's owner or owners will eventually receive an equal share of the revenues from a league's national television contract(s) and that sum usually amounts to several million dollars each year. Besides that distribution of money, the gate receipts collected from ticket sales at home and away games may also be redistributed between the respective clubs. So it is reasonable to assume that each owner of a franchise in a sports league must measure these and other potential benefits and costs, and then determine whether an application and plan from an individual or group—to purchase and operate an expansion team— should or should not be approved and also implemented in the following or a future season.

Relocation

With respect to the relocation of AL and NL clubs since the late 1800s to the early 2000s, the following are a number of important issues that researchers should think about and which will also be of interest to the readers of this book. One, when did any of the franchise owners within each of these two baseball leagues decide to move their teams from one urban place (or metropolitan area) to another that was nearby, or to an area hundreds or thousands of miles across North America? Two, what were a few of the business, economic, and sport-specific reasons that caused any relocation to occur within a league during a given year, decade, or century? Three, which AL and NL teams moved and where did they relocate to play their home games?

Four, did more movements occur among AL or NL teams prior and subsequent to 1901? Five, which clubs in each league were the most and least successful before and after their relocations into other metropolitan areas? Lastly, why should NL officials have encouraged and approved the movements of more clubs since the late 1800s, and the AL from the early 1900s to 2000s? In short, these and other questions were worthwhile to research by this author and in part, to discuss in one or more of the five chapters presented here.

From a theoretical perspective, a group's or individual franchise owner's decision to move a team from its current location is an all-important and perhaps long-run business strategy. The goal, of course, is to put the club into an area (or urban place) where its after-tax profit and present value as a com-

mercial enterprise will each be maximized. Indeed the drawing potential and
financial worth of a club are expected to be greater at a new site—in contrast
to the former site—because of such demographic and economic factors as the
differences in the two areas' total population, average population growth and
household income per capita, the boundaries of the local and regional radio
and television broadcast markets, and also the existence of a new or renovated city ballpark whose construction cost was paid by a government.

As a result of these and other matters, the current members of a league
will approve any move of a franchise if it will increase the net benefits and
economic interests of their club(s). That is, the planned relocation of an existing team is expected to generate more revenue and profit for them and also
add value to their respective franchise(s). Otherwise, an overwhelming majority of members will reject a proposal to move and will maintain the league's
current structure until another existing franchise owner or ownership group
decides to relocate their team(s).

Besides the influences of previous issues, other important concerns of current franchise owners to evaluate are the short- and long-run effects, if any,
of an expansion or team relocation on a league's future competitive balance,
rivalries within divisions, and business strategies. Furthermore, each expansion team's and relocated club's entertainment role, image, and value within
its new home area—which consists of the local community and includes sports
fans, government and business organizations, and perhaps other professional
sports clubs—are expected to change after it arrives, performs in regular season and any postseason games, and competes for consumers in the marketplace.

Because of potential problems, risks and uncertainties, and also the traditions and successes or failures of existing clubs in the AL and NL, there
have been relatively few expansions and relocations of teams since the late
1800s to early 1900s. Nevertheless, those that did occur have been identified,
reported, and analyzed in the baseball literature by various historians, practitioners, scholars, and officials in sports and other kinds of organizations. So
in part, this book is a contribution to an increasing body of literature that
had somewhat examined and exposed these phenomena and their impact on
communities, sports fans, and the history of baseball.

In the next major section of this Introduction is a review of the different types of publications that were used to learn some basic facts and statistics, and other historical information about the expansions and team
relocations that have occurred since 1901 in the AL and 1876 in the NL.
When that section concludes, there are a few paragraphs which discuss this
book's organization. Finally the notes at the end of the Introduction contain
the names of authors, and titles and dates of readings that were used as references in earlier pages and also are listed in the bibliography.

BASEBALL LITERATURE

For several decades, many historians and other scholars have researched and studied various business, cultural, and economic aspects of team sports being played in America. As a result of their efforts, these academics, analysts, and practitioners in total have authored numerous articles and different books on topics that concern the conduct, operation, and performance of professional baseball leagues and their respective teams. In fact, such diverse topics in big league baseball as broadcast rights, federal antitrust laws, labor-management relations, and teams' attendances, revenues, and ticket prices have been documented and thoroughly discussed in the literature from both qualitative and quantitative viewpoints. Because of this research, a typical sports fan and also the general public are well aware and more knowledgeable about professional baseball's origin and development, and the sport's business, cultural, and economic role in American society.

Within various publications of the literature, there are specific chapters, essays, and stories about the establishment, history, and success of the NL since the early to mid–1870s and AL since 1901. Indeed some of these readings also include dates, events, names of officials, and data and statistics that emphasize the expansion of major baseball leagues and furthermore, the movement of one or more of these leagues' teams during years of the nineteenth, twentieth, and twenty-first centuries. Here are samples that highlight and represent these different publications. Accordingly, there is a brief review of a few books and articles that fully discuss, or at least mention in some way, any expansions in the AL or NL, and also the relocation of teams within these two baseball leagues.

Books

One of the most relevant and recent publications with respect to the contents in this book is Frank Jozsa's and John J. Guthrie's *Relocating Teams and Expanding Leagues in Professional Sports*. Published by Quorum in 1999, this title examines the business of sports leagues and their teams in professional baseball, basketball, and football. More specifically, the book applies an assortment of demographic, financial and economic statistics, and also some government data on population and other reports to explain the market conditions for when and why leagues in these three sports had expanded between 1950 and 1995, and to identify and analyze the metropolitan areas where these leagues' teams moved from and into within this 46-year-old history of sports seasons. Furthermore, the book discusses topics and other related issues such as the business strategies of sports franchise owners, government subsidies for the construction and renovation of new ballparks, arenas and stadiums, performances of many professional sports teams during regular seasons and postseasons, and the economic impact of professional sports in various cities, markets, and regions.[4]

In an early part of their publication, Jozsa and Guthrie reviewed some other sports books. These volumes included economist Roger G. Noll's *Government and the Sports Business* (1974), Paul Staudohar's and James Mangan's *The Business of Professional Sports* (1991), Charles C. Euchner's *Playing the Field* (1993), Kenneth Shropshire's *The Sports Franchise Game* (1995), and Mark Rosentraub's *Major League Losers* (1997). In short, *Relocating Teams and Expanding Leagues in Professional Sports* is the primary title and best source in the literature from which this book was derived, organized, and portrayed.[5]

A first-rate, scholarly, and well-researched book about the business of professional team sports was published during the early 1990s. Entitled *Pay Dirt*, it was authored by a retired California Institute of Technology professor named James Quirk and current University of Michigan faculty member Rodney D. Fort. Their book, in part, reveals and examines the economics of such topics as the market for and value of professional sports franchises, emergence and development of rival sports leagues, and the financial returns and economic risks from investing in professional teams. For sure this is an excellent, provocative, and useful title because it separates popular myths from realities in professional team sports, relies on these authors' solid and objective analysis, includes a 150-page technical and data supplement, and contains an extensive bibliography of publications and a detailed index of names. In total, *Pay Dirt* exposes the complex and entrepreneurial side of team sports and also combines factual and entertaining anecdotes with economic laws, models, and principles. Indeed Quirk and Fort wrote the standard reference for those—who like me and others—have devoted years to examining, researching, and comprehending the business operations, finance, and economics of the sports industry.[6]

Since the present work focuses primarily on the histories, demographic profiles, and geographic locations of sports markets, and the performances and successes or failures of teams that had previously expanded or relocated within the AL and NL, some other books were also consulted by me to research the emergence, origin, and development of these and less popular professional baseball leagues. For example, one of them reviewed was David Pietrusza's *Major Leagues*. Published by McFarland in 1991, *Major Leagues* examines the formation and demise of 18 professional baseball organizations beginning with the rowdy and undisciplined National Association, which was formed in 1871, and ending with the disintegration and collapse of the farcical Global League in 1969.[7]

Being then a member of the Society for American Baseball Research (SABR), Pietrusza profoundly discusses when, why, and how a number of major leagues had failed such as the American Association and Union Association in the late 1800s, the Federal League and United States League in the early 1900s, and the Continental League and Mexican League in the mid–1900s. Because of its fascinating storylines, historical legends and detailed facts, and an extensive appendix, bibliography and index, some editorial reviews of this book describe it as being authoritative, first class, heavily illustrated, spectacular, and also fun to read. Even so, my principal interest in *Major Leagues* was reading and learning about the genesis, early years, and crucial issues of the National League in Chapter 2 and also the American League in Chapter 8.

Besides the former three titles, there were additional sports books that provided me with even more data, facts, and historical information about the establishment, growth, and development of different professional baseball leagues and their teams while they were based in the US during various years of the late 1800s to early 2000s. To illustrate, in 2007 a sports historian named Warren N. Wilbert authored *The Arrival of the American League*. Published by McFarland, Wilbert's book concentrates on the circumstances, events, and personalities that paved the way for the creation of a new and major American professional baseball league in 1900 and 1901. He explains in concise and clear detail how Charles Comiskey and Ban Johnson had made critical decisions and also planned the groundwork to successfully launch the AL from its origins as the Western League of the 1890s. Furthermore, Wilbert convincingly explains how and why the new league challenged the 26-year-old monopolistic National League during the early 1900s. Basically, *The Arrival of the American League* is an important contribution to the history of baseball and a core title that this author referred to in analyzing and discussing the numbers, roles, and consequences of expansions and team relocations in the sport.[8]

In contrast to reading more about the origin and early development of the AL, two prominent books were published that described the formation and establishment of the NL. These titles were Tom Melville's *Early Baseball and the Rise of the National League*, published in 2001, and Neil W. Macdonald's *The League That Lasted*, published in 2004. The following is a short but introspective overview of these two baseball books.[9]

With regard to the emergence, growth, and popularity of the NL before the 1900s, the former book provides a chronology of events and some historical information about the social forces that influenced these events. More specifically, Melville contends baseball was shaped by its existence and development in New York City among sports fans who demanded high achievement and success of their teams. Also, he highlights the role of NL founder William A. Hulbert of Chicago, discusses the problems of the Cincinnati Reds and other professional teams of that era, and emphasizes in the book that during the late 1800s competitive social forces replaced fraternal ones. This transition, in turn, spawned championship games, professionalization and promotion of the sport by the media, and national standards for professional baseball events. In other words, by grappling with such issues as gambling scandals, crowd outbursts and spectator abuses, Hulbert attempted to inject moral accountability and responsibility into the game and for the league's teams to recruit the best athletes and sports coaches in America to make baseball exceptionally competitive and also entertaining for the public.

In *The League That Lasted*, sports editor and reporter Neil W. Macdonald describes how white, post–Civil War owners of early baseball teams and their players—who were Germans and Irish sons of immigrants—preferred to avoid any contact with black people in America. Nonetheless, several of these owners and many ballplayers had jointly participated in professional baseball's first league, the National Association, during the early 1870s. However, when that league failed in 1875 because of teams' attendance, financial, and scheduling problems, one year later the NL was established.

Although this newly-formed national baseball organization had consisted of a number of underfunded and inconsistent clubs whose ballplayers were often brawling, alcoholic and corrupt athletes, the league's early history depicts when and why American business entrepreneurs invaded the sports industry, and how a few visionaries realized that people within markets would actually pay their money as an admission price to watch men perform in a game of hitting a hard ball with a stick, and also of catching, fielding, and throwing a ball among them. According to Macdonald, it was the leadership of the NL's president William A. Hulbert who stuck to and enforced his beliefs in ethics, honesty, and integrity, and who gradually had reformed his new baseball organization by prohibiting games on Sunday and stopping the sale and consumption of liquor within any team's ballparks. Moreover, Hulbert expelled the New York Mutuals and Philadelphia Athletics from the league when the owners of these teams refused to make a Western trip near the end of the 1876 season. In short, *The League That Lasted* was a good reference because of its history about the early NL and also to learn the nicknames, locations, and performances of the league's teams.

For detailed information about specific franchises and their players in seasons of the AL and NL, two books edited by Peter C. Bjarkman were reviewed. Published in 1991, these titles were *Encyclopedia of Major League Baseball Team Histories: American League* and its companion text, *Encyclopedia of Major League Baseball Team Histories: National League*. With the assistance of other sportswriters, including some who were also SABR members, Bjarkman presents an excellent history of several big league clubs in each of his books. Furthermore, he provides listings of such facts as year-end standings and season summaries of baseball teams and the all-time career and season records of their ballplayers. And at the conclusion of each book's chapters, there are some interesting notes and an annotated bibliography.[10]

As a useful source for topics to be included in the present work, Bjarkman's books contributed data, statistics, and background information about such AL expansion teams as the Kansas City Royals, Seattle Mariners and Toronto Blue Jays, and about such NL clubs that had relocated as the Boston–Milwaukee–Atlanta Braves, Brooklyn–Los Angeles Dodgers, and New York–San Francisco Giants. Moreover, these two titles provided me with insights about the different emotions and eccentricities of baseball's ballparks and also the fates of these two leagues' franchises. Based on his research findings, Bjarkman contends that the NL has been more innovative than the AL in making the game entertaining, and also, the NL has contained more of the sport's most colorful and exciting teams. Although there is little information in each book about the financial aspects of MLB franchises, these titles were helpful in my analysis of when and why the two baseball leagues expanded, and where and why some teams had moved from one metropolitan area to another within the United States.

To increase my knowledge of how various MLB teams had performed and their seasons of success or failure, parts of Peter Filichia's *Professional Baseball Franchises* were scanned. Published in 1993 by Facts on File, Filichia's book lists almost every city or town in Canada, Mexico, and the United States that had hosted a professional major and minor league baseball team between 1869 and 1992. Within the book's contents, readers are given each team's full identity including its nickname, the league or leagues and years in which it had operated, and a brief note about whether or not it survived. This title has more than 1,100 entries and these include such unique clubs as the Staunton Hayseeds and Zanesville Flood Sufferers, and also the names of teams in the Negro Leagues and women's U.S. professional baseball leagues. Although it was of marginal use for me in the research and study of topics for this book, *Professional Baseball Franchises* is a comprehensive, practical, and authoritative reference that gives information about numerous teams in the world. Thus it is recommended as a primary source for sports historians.[11]

Besides these publications in the literature on baseball, some facts that pertain to the issues of league expansion and team relocation are also included in such books as Lee Allen's *The American League Story* and *The National League Story*, David Nemec's and Saul Wisnia's *100 Years of Major League Baseball,* and Dean A. Sullivan's *Late Innings.*

Articles

Within a section of the Bibliography, there are several interesting readings regarding the history, development, and reform of professional baseball and also about the decisions of major league officials to increase the number of teams and of franchise owners to move their clubs from a ballpark in a city to a site in another urban area. Although a majority of these articles are incorporated in one or more parts of this book, three of them are especially important because they discuss the economics of professional team sports and that relates to topics included in various portions of this book.[12]

In "An Economic Analysis of Team Movements in Professional Sports," James Quirk summarized an economic structure of a professional sports league and then presented a survey and analysis of those franchise relocations that had occurred in MLB between 1946 and 1972. To justify and support his survey and analysis, Quirk constructed a total of ten tables which included such statistics as the regular season finishes, home attendances, and before-tax profits of AL and NL teams for selected baseball seasons. Furthermore, there were tables in the article that denoted the television and radio revenues of franchises for the years 1952 through 1956 and 1960 through 1973, and also the populations of metropolitan areas and a distribution of professional sports teams among them in 1972.

After analyzing this information and briefly discussing the rules structure of organized baseball, Quirk concluded that franchise moves are only a temporary expedient to correct imbalances of playing strengths and differences in the revenue potential among teams in a sports league. Moreover, the results from evaluating these tables of data suggested to Quirk that relocations were not a long run solution to the problem of large market teams being able to dominate this professional sport. Consequently, he recommended, in part, that government officials apply antitrust laws to big league baseball as a remedy to control any abuses when franchises move from one area into another that is elsewhere.

Since the early 1970s, the AL and NL have each adopted an amateur draft, free agency, revenue sharing, and a competitive or luxury tax on teams whose payrolls exceed pre-established thresholds, and also other policies in order to redistribute money from franchises in very big and large midsized markets to those located in small metropolitan areas. To some extent, these reforms have marginally improved the competitive conditions within each league during some of the previous baseball seasons. In 2008, for example, the low-payroll Tampa Bay Rays won the East Division and an AL pennant, while the small-market Milwaukee Brewers were a wild card winner in the NL. Based on organized baseball's reforms to improve the competitive imbalance within each league, and because of business and economic conditions in America, there has not been a recent all-out attempt by the US Congress to revoke MLB's exemption from the antitrust laws.

The second paper of interest and also relevant to this book is Martin B. Schmidt's "Competition in Major League Baseball: The Impact Expansion." As published in *Applied Economics Letters* in 2001, Portland State University professor Schmidt applied a conventional or traditional measure of inequality named the Gini coefficient to examine the effects of expansion on the degree of competitive balance in MLB. To accomplish that task, his sample consisted of 14 total expansions, or seven in each league, which had occurred during 1961 to 1998 inclusive. Then, based on estimates and plots of various Gini coefficients for the 1901 to 1998 seasons in baseball, Schmidt displayed some graphs in his article that showed the behavior of time-series representations of competitive balance for the AL and NL.

So rather than declare that establishment of the amateur draft or introduction of free agency were the two most significant reasons for increases in competitive balance among teams in each league, Schmidt concluded that inequality in baseball began to diminish from when the leagues had started to expand during the early 1960s. That is, after that period of baseball seasons the estimated Gini coefficients of each league tended to decline in value and deviate less on average than in earlier years of MLB. Consequently, Schmidt's application and interpretation of Gini coefficients in 2001 denoted that expansion better explained and influenced the increases in equity between each group of teams in the AL and NL than did the introduction of an amateur draft or free agency.

In contrast to the quantitative methods applied—and findings reported—in the previous two articles, St. Norbert College professors Kevin G. Quinn and Paul B. Bursik in 2007 authored "Growing and Moving the Game: Effects of MLB Expansion and Team Relocation 1950–2004." Mathematically, they constructed and tested some time-series regression models to estimate and detect the effects, if any, to trends in professional baseball's average game attendances, within-season competitive balances, and also the balance between defense and offense as a result of expansion and the relocation of teams. Their data set was assembled from numbers from the Baseball Archive and a few other sources to include 55 years of teams' performances. Also, the authors' regression models controlled for changes in MLB's population coverage, effects of teams' new stadia, and the consequences of players' strikes.

Given their types of models and the control of certain variables, Quinn and Bursik discovered from their empirical analysis that expansion had no effect on trends in MLB's average attendance over time or on the balance between defense and offense. However, these researchers also determined that expansion depressed the growth in home attendances of the leagues' incumbent teams and furthermore, reduced within-season competitive balance. Alternatively, team movements depressed the trend of increases in average MLB attendances that occurred from 1950 to 2004, but then had no effect on within-season competitive balances or the balance between defense and offense. Based on these results about the consequences of expansions and team relocations in MLB, this study implies that existing franchises in those 55 years would have been freer to move from their sites in metropolitan areas to others without the league's antitrust exemption. And moreover, elimination of the exemption may also have reduced the incentive and likelihood of MLB to contract a number of its franchises that were located in their respective sports markets.

Besides these analytical articles about the game, the following are several readings listed in the Bibliography that discuss the business decisions of leagues and their franchise owners in baseball or other professional sports groups to expand in size, and of teams within these leagues to move their operations out of an area into another one. For articles on expansion, there is Paul Attner's "How Professional Sports Governs Expansion Will Mean Success or Failure for 21st Century," Joe Gergen's "Is Global Expansion the Wave of the Future?" and Skip Rozin's "Growing Pains: The Evolution of Expansion." For a series of readings on team relocation, see, for example, Glen Gendzel's "Competitive Boosterism: How Milwaukee Lost the Braves," Cindy Stooksbury Guier's "When the Home Team Leaves," and Arthur T. Johnson's "Municipal Administration and the Sports Franchise Relocation Issue."

THE ORGANIZATION OF THIS BOOK

The main portion of *Major League Baseball Expansions and Relocations* consists of five chapters. The first and second chapters discuss, respectively, all expansions in the AL from 1901 through 2008 and all expansions in the NL from 1876 through 2008. Chapter 3 examines the number of team relocations in the AL from 1901 through 2008, while the fourth chapter analyzes the movements of teams in the NL from 1876 through 2008. Chapter 5 then explains the markets of expansion and relocation within both leagues of MLB and other sports leagues. The following paragraphs are a brief overview of the contents within each of these chapters.

Since Chapters 1 and 2 discuss when, why, and how the AL and NL have each increased in size during several decades of baseball seasons, these chapters complement each other and thus, they are very similar in format, organization, and style. That is, they reveal what expansion has meant to the development, growth, and prosperity of baseball among various metropolitan areas and regions of America and Canada, and also what the sport has accomplished for the big leagues and their mixture of very large, large, mid-sized, and small market franchises throughout the twentieth century.

In each chapter there are tables that denote such information as the nicknames, locations, performances, and total seasons of expansion teams in each league, some that show population characteristics of these teams' market areas, and some giving profiles of metropolitan areas that have hosted the leagues' non-expansion (or incumbent) franchises. Based, in part, on the data presented in these tables, the two chapters describe the early histories of AL and NL expansion teams and provide cultural, demographic, and economic reasons for their temporary or permanent existence as competitors in MLB. The Appendix contains some additional tables about the performances and population areas of expansion teams that are identified and discussed in sections of chapters 1 and 2.

Because their contents resemble those in the first two chapters, chapters 3 and 4 were also organized alike since individually they explore when and why some AL and then NL clubs had moved from ballparks in urban areas to sites in different places. Tables within each of these chapters indicate teams' names, number of regular seasons played, and types of postseason results, and also the population ranks of their areas before and after the year they moved.

These kinds of data and historical facts are discussed in detail to provide some insights into what factors motivated the owners of major league franchises to vacate an area after one or more years and then choose a potentially more lucrative site to play their home games, whether within a relatively close or distant city. Chapters 3 and 4 expose the history and success or failure of team relocations, respectively, in the AL from 1901 through 2008 and likewise in the NL from 1876 through 2008.

The final chapter relies on the information in Chapters 1 through 4 and this author's previous articles and books to indicate when, where, and why future league expansions and team relocations will occur in MLB—whether the AL and NL will most likely decrease, increase, or remain constant in size after 2009 and 2010. Chapter 5 examines whether there will be fewer or a greater number of movements of big league franchises from and into different or similar metropolitan areas of America and in cities within one or more countries abroad.

1

American League Expansion

Prior to the 1903 regular season and a World Series that was held between the Boston Americans and Pittsburgh Pirates in Major League Baseball (MLB), a few innovative, prominent, and professional leagues were established in organized baseball, and they operated for years in various cities east of western Kansas. Besides the National League (NL), which had formed in 1876, some others included the National Association of Professional Base Ball Players (NAPBBP) in 1871 to 1875, American Association (AA) in 1882 to 1891, Union Association (UA) in 1884, and Players League (PL) in 1890. After one or more seasons, however, the NAPBBP, AA, UA, and PL folded while the NL became increasingly popular and continued to exist as America's premier professional baseball league before 1900. In fact, such cities on the East Coast of the United States as Boston, New York and Philadelphia, and in the nation's midwest as Chicago, Cincinnati and St. Louis, had each established a fan base in their metropolitan areas and thus, they became markets to host their NL team or teams.[1]

Although the Western League of Professional Baseball Clubs (WL) had originally formed as a minor league during the late 1870s, it struggled and then failed after a number of years because of low attendances at regular-season games and teams' financial problems. Then in 1893, the WL reorganized and one year later, its franchises played a schedule of games. After this event occurred, the WL's president, Bancroft "Ban" Johnson, realized that the NL might eventually reduce the number of its clubs from 12 to eight or less. So he devised a plan to immediately place WL teams in some of the cities that were abandoned or not invaded by the NL.[2]

Anyway, to avoid competing for baseball fans against clubs in the NL, most WL teams tended to initially locate in small midwestern cities like Grand Rapids, Michigan; Sioux City, Iowa; and Toledo, Ohio. After some of the league's teams in these and other cities disbanded or were reorganized, replaced, or transferred to different locations during the mid to late 1890s, Johnson decided to rename his organization in 1899 and refer to it as the American League (AL).

Meanwhile in that year, the NL eliminated each of its teams in Baltimore, Cleveland, Louisville, and Washington, D.C. Consequently Johnson decided to place AL clubs in Chicago and Cleveland. Furthermore, in 1899 and 1900, he declined to renew the WL's membership in the National Agreement, publicly declared the former WL to be a major—and no longer a minor—league in professional baseball, and by ignoring the reserve clause, he and his group of officials proceeded to raid NL teams and sign contracts with their players in order for them to perform on clubs in the AL. Despite being condemned as an outlaw league by the NL, the AL had immense success among fans in baseball's 1901–1902 regular seasons and especially with respect to attendance, exposure, and popularity.

Six years after he reorganized the minor Western League in 1893 and became the organization's president, former sports editor Ban Johnson renamed it the American League. In 1900, Johnson pulled out of baseball's National Agreement and challenged the rival National League in the players market. Because of his dispute with Baseball commissioner Kenesaw Mountain Landis, Johnson was forced to resign as the American League president in 1927. [National Baseball Hall of Fame Library, Cooperstown, N.Y.]

Rather than continue losing their teams' players and local fans to its rival, and being influenced and even threatened by the entry of AL clubs into or near one or more of its current markets, in 1903 the NL franchise owners jointly agreed to recognize the AL as an equal partner in the sport with no exchange of compensation being offered or demanded by either of these baseball organizations. In retrospect, the primary reason for the AL's early success was the NL's confusion and public relations problems, managerial mistakes, and flawed decisions. First, there was a conflict of interest among a few owners of NL teams because of their joint ownership of clubs in the league. This controversy, in turn, created intraleague disputes, high turnover because of trading players between strong and weak NL franchises, recurring power struggles, and a questionable proposal to reorganize the league as a business syndicate.[3] WHO?

Second, the NL failed to meet consumer demand in its markets and thereby disappointed the nation's baseball fans when it reduced the number of franchises from 12 to eight rather than expand into various eastern and midwestern cities where populations and commercial activities were booming due to immigration, and also to economic and employment growth. As a result, AL clubs prospered with respect to admissions and revenues especially from their home games being played at ballparks in the Baltimore, Cleveland, Detroit, and Washington areas.

Third, the AL had an exciting four-team pennant race in 1902 while the Pittsburgh Pirates won an NL title that season by more than 27 games. As such, in that year the AL's total attendance exceeded the NL's by one-half million while on average, the AL clubs that were located in Boston, Chicago, St. Louis, and Philadelphia outdrew their NL rivals by nearly 40 percent. And fourth, the AL was a relatively well-financed organization with visionary leaders who agreed and persevered to maintain the league's identity, control its franchises' rights, and retain the ownership of player contracts. In short, it became apparent from a business perspective that the two leagues should compromise and settle their differences, and to operate interdependently with regard to their respective franchises, schedules, and other baseball-related matters.

AL TEAMS

During the 1901 MLB season, eight AL clubs had existed in different urban places (see Table 1.1). A ranking of these teams' places from most to least populated—as denoted in parentheses was reported for 1900 by the U.S. Bureau of the Census and in other sources as follows: Chicago (2), Philadelphia (3), Boston (5), Baltimore (6), Cleveland (7), Detroit (13), Milwaukee (14), and Washington (15). In comparison, NL teams also existed in such urban places as Chicago, Philadelphia, and Boston in 1901, and furthermore, that year they played home and away regular season games at ballparks in Brooklyn (1), New York (1), St. Louis (4), Cincinnati (10), and Pittsburgh (11). Evidently, places ranked in the top 20, such as San Francisco (9), New Orleans (12), Newark (16), Jersey City (17), Louisville (18), Minneapolis (19), and Providence (20), were considered by baseball officials to be inferior or unattractive sites because of being underpopulated, inferior business centers, or geographically remote as sports markets for current or future MLB teams.[4]

Accordingly, a majority of the eight AL teams located in urban places in 1901 had originally formed as professional baseball organizations during the mid–1890s and therefore they had performed in games within their home ballparks in small or small to midsized markets while they were members of the WL. That is, such urban places as Sioux City, Grand Rapids, and Indianapolis each initially hosted a team in the WL that later evolved into, respectively, the AL's Chicago White Sox, Cleveland Indians, and Philadelphia Athletics. Besides clubs in the former three places, some other WL teams had to abandon such second-tier populated cities during the mid-to-late 1890s

*Table 1.1 Major League Baseball American League Teams
and Baseball Seasons, 1901–2008*

Teams	Seasons
Baltimore Orioles I→New York	1901–1902
Baltimore Orioles II	1954–2008
Boston Americans/Red Sox	1901–1907/1908–2008
California/Anaheim/Los Angeles Angels	1966–1996/1997–2004/2005–2008
Chicago White Stockings/White Sox	1901–1903/1904–2008
Cleveland Blues/Broncos/Naps/Indians	1901/1902/1903–1909/1910–2008
Detroit Tigers	1901–2008
Kansas City Athletics→Oakland	1955–1967
Kansas City Royals	1969–2008
Los Angeles/California Angels→Anaheim	1961–1964/1965
Milwaukee Brewers I→St. Louis	1901–1901
Milwaukee Brewers II	1970–1997
Minnesota Twins	1961–2008
New York Highlanders/Yankees	1903–1912/1913–2008
Oakland Athletics	1968–2008
Philadelphia Athletics→Kansas City	1901–1954
St. Louis Browns→Baltimore	1902–1953
Seattle Mariners	1977–2008
Seattle Pilots→Milwaukee	1969–1969
Tampa Bay Devil Rays/Rays	1998–2007/2008
Texas Rangers	1972–2008
Toronto Blue Jays	1977–2008
Washington Senators I→Minnesota	1901–1960
Washington Senators II→Texas	1961–1971

Note: Teams and Seasons are self-explanatory. A slash (/) simply indicates a change in a team's nickname and an arrow (→) denotes a relocation of a team. Any teams that moved from one city in a metropolitan area to another are listed on separate lines. The Seattle Pilots folded after the 1969 season, then moved to Milwaukee in 1970 and were renamed the Milwaukee Brewers. In 2005, the Anaheim Angels team was renamed the Los Angeles Angels of Anaheim. And in 1998, the Milwaukee Brewers II transferred from the AL to NL.

Source: James Quirk and Rodney D. Fort, *Pay Dirt: The Business of Professional Team Sports* (Princeton, NJ: Princeton University Press, 1992), 399–409; *Official Major League Baseball Fact Book 2005 Edition* (St. Louis, MO: The Sporting News, 2005); "Teams," at http://www.mlb.com cited 12 September 2008.

as Buffalo in New York, Columbus in Ohio, and St. Paul in Minnesota. In short, several cities in small metropolitan areas that had hosted minor league baseball teams before 1900 were unable to provide enough support to retain them after a few seasons.

Based on these population rankings, it is not surprising that the AL's small-market Milwaukee Brewers had to relocate after the 1901 season as did the mid-sized-market Baltimore Orioles at the completion of the 1902 MLB season. Indeed, each club had finished in eighth place and more than 30 games behind the AL champion in these years. So after the Brewers moved to the St. Louis area and then the Orioles to New York City, there were no movements of teams in the AL until 1954 or any expansions by the league until 1961.

Despite the presence of the Federal League in 1914 and 1915, a stable or equilibrium environment prevailed within professional baseball for more than 50 years. In part, that condition existed in MLB because owners of the eight NL clubs had earlier located their franchises in some large cities of the east and midwest, because the areas in America's west were underdeveloped as baseball markets until the late 1950s when Los Angeles and San Francisco each hosted a new NL team, and since the population boom in regions of the U.S. south, southeast, and southwest did not occur until the early to-mid-1960s.

Of further significance, between the early 1900s and 1960s, the MLB teams located in relatively midsized cities like Cincinnati, Cleveland, and Pittsburgh frequently attracted more and increasingly passionate baseball fans to their home games by being occasionally competitive in various regular seasons and during some of the league's postseasons. In fact, the AL Indians' teams were especially popular in Cleveland when they won pennants and the World Series in 1920 and 1948, and another pennant in 1954. Similarly, the NL Reds in Cincinnati and Pirates in Pittsburgh had each succeeded to become champions during several MLB seasons before the early 1960s.

There are other important and relevant factors, however, that explain why the number of teams did not increase within the AL (and NL) until the early 1960s. First, expansion of a league (and also team relocation) in MLB had required unanimous approval by the group of existing franchise owners. As a result, during the early to mid–1900s baseball teams tended to earn above-average revenues and profits as monopolists or oligopolists while playing at their home sites, and especially those franchises that were located in such populated markets as New York, Chicago and Philadelphia. In 1952, however, MLB changed its rules whereby expansions (and also team relocations) were permitted if approved by a majority of the franchise owners in its league. This new policy, in turn, encouraged the initiation of team movements that originated with the NL Braves relocating from Boston to Milwaukee in 1953, and also the implementation of expansions by the AL and NL in the early and late 1960s.[5]

Second, the two World Wars, the Korean Conflict, and the Great Depression during the twentieth century had each created fear, risk, and uncertainty among American investors and commercial organizations and some sports entrepreneurs and officials. For sure, these and other major events had a negative impact on the development and growth of organized baseball in the U.S. In other words, they increased business risk and also reduced the incentives for MLB to approve the entry of additional franchises and expand the number of new teams within existing markets, or in other urban areas of the nation.

Third, except for being challenged after 1900 by the establishment of the Federal League in 1914 and 1915, MLB was not confronted by any other prominent rival baseball leagues until the late 1950s to early 1960s. Thus, MLB operated with eight teams in each league for decades despite the superior success at winning championships as performed by the AL Detroit Tigers, New York Yankees and Philadelphia Athletics, and such dominant and popular NL teams as the Brooklyn Dodgers, New York Giants and St. Louis Cardinals.

Fourth, the ballparks of MLB clubs in urban communities and neighborhoods were apparently adequate in providing amenities that satisfied groups of baseball officials, players and fans. Therefore, the conditions and conveniences of these facilities did not create enough competition among baseball's franchisees within the AL and NL for them to seek additional revenues from their operations and venues besides the money they received from advertising, ticket sales and concessions, and from partnerships, sponsors, and local radio stations. In fact, the regional and national television broadcast of teams' games in regular seasons and postseasons was not a significant revenue source that affected professional baseball until after the 1960s.

Fifth, another issue that may have discouraged expansion by MLB across America before the early 1960s was the growing popularity of clubs in the pre–1950 National Football League (NFL), Basketball Association of America and National Basketball League, and after 1950, the increasing interest of sport fans in many teams of the National Basketball Association (NBA) and ultimately the National Hockey League (NHL). That is, some midsized and large urban areas were the home sites of entrenched and well-organized professional football, basketball, and ice hockey organizations whose fans had little or no experience with—or attachment to—the games played by clubs in big league baseball. Thus from a business perspective, it was costly, risky, and very difficult for any MLB team to invade territories where other professional sports clubs had already established a fan base.

Sixth, expansion is a decision that always involves the benefits, costs, and operations of one or more teams in each league of MLB. As such, causing internal disputes to determine which league to expand, and then where to locate any new team or teams, were each potential problems and threats that challenged baseball's commissioners and also the existing AL and NL franchise owners. Since the Chicago, New York, and Philadelphia areas had each hosted at least two MLB clubs through the early to mid–1950s, it was not feasible or realistic to place a baseball expansion team into one or more of these cities. Thus, the allocation of eight teams in the same areas but within each league of MLB prevailed from 1903 to 1960 inclusive.

In the next three sections, I highlight and then discuss the key aspects of Chapter 1. Indeed, there is an analysis of baseball markets in conjunction with the establishment, development, and success of seven AL expansion teams. Besides the memorable histories of these various sports organizations, there are two tables of data that reveal some population characteristics for each of the respective metropolitan areas and one table about their performances. That is, these sections include background information and interesting and unique facts about when and why these seven sports teams originated in their given markets, and how successful they played in one or more baseball seasons.[6]

AL EXPANSION MARKETS

Los Angeles (1961)

Since 1940, there had been conversations, rumors, and expectations among baseball executives regarding the eventual placement of an AL team within or very near the Los Angeles Area (LAA). The league, for example, denied a request by the owner of the Browns to move his team from the St. Louis area to the LAA in 1940. But one year later, MLB approved such a relocation of the club. However, the bombing of Pearl Harbor in Hawaii by Japan prevented that movement in 1941. Then during the 1950s, some AL officials again reconsidered a transfer of the Browns to the LAA before it was decided to relocate the team and have it play at home in the Baltimore area.

Meanwhile, others in MLB had discussed temporarily moving the AL Athletics from Philadelphia to Kansas City, and then a few years later permanently to the LAA. In any event, when the NL Dodgers and Giants left the New York area for, respectively, Los Angeles and San Francisco to play in 1958, and the Continental League (CL) announced plans in the late 1950s to organize and place some of their teams in cities on the West Coast of America, MLB decided sometime in 1959 or 1960 to put a new AL team in Los Angeles and another in the nation's capital city.

As denoted in Tables 1.2 and 1.3, the LAA ranked second in population among U.S. areas during the early 1960s and also experienced above-average growth. Furthermore, it had hosted four other professional sports teams including the competitive NFL Rams and popular NBA Lakers. Nevertheless, it was the potential competition from clubs in the CL and a decision by the NL to locate new teams in Houston and New York City in 1962 that were, in part, each factors for the AL to approve an expansion into the LAA and compete for baseball fans there against the successful and popular NL Dodgers.

A syndicate headed by the former celebrity, cowboy actor, and movie star Gene Autry purchased the rights for an expansion franchise from the AL in 1960 and 1961 for a fee of $2.1 million. Besides that group, a Hall of Fame player named Hank Greenberg and his partner, Bill Veeck—who was a maverick, promoter, and a former owner of the AL St. Louis Browns—and also

Table 1.2 American League Expansion Areas
Expansion Years and Characteristics of Teams Markets, 1961–1998

Metropolitan Area	Year	Population Rank	Population Growth	Teams MLB	Teams Other
Los Angeles	1961	2	16	2	3
Washington, D.C.	1961	7	38	1	1
Kansas City	1969	25	14	1	1
Seattle	1969	19	28	1	1
Seattle	1977	23	12	1	2
Toronto	1977	1	14	1	2
Tampa Bay	1998	21	9	1	2

Note: Metropolitan Area is the Standard Metropolitan Statistical Area (SMSA) of teams in their expansion year. Each SMSA's rank in population is listed in column three, while its approximate growth rate in column four is stated as a percent. The Greater Toronto Area (or Toronto) ranked first in population among all areas in Canada in 1977. The column titled MLB is the total number of Major League Baseball clubs in an SMSA during the expansion year. The column labeled Other includes the number of professional basketball, football, ice hockey, and soccer teams located in a metropolitan area during the expansion year.

Source: See various editions of The World Almanac and Book of Facts, Statistical Abstract of the United States, Survey of Current Business and Census of the Population, and Frank P. Jozsa, Jr., and John J. Guthrie, Jr., Relocating Teams and Expanding Leagues in Professional Sports: How the Major Leagues Respond to Market Conditions (Westport, CT: Quorum Books, 1999).

Table 1.3 American League Teams
Population Rank of Their Areas in Expansion Year, 1961–1998

Area	1961	1969	1977	1998
Anaheim	–	20	18	17
Baltimore	12	13	14	19
Boston	7	8	10	10
Chicago	3	3	3	3
Cleveland	11	14	19	23
Dallas-Fort Worth	–	–	8	5
Detroit	5	5	5	9
Kansas City	21	25	29	26
Los Angeles	2	–	–	–
Milwaukee	–	–	28	–
Minnesota	14	14	15	16
New York	1	1	1	1
Oakland	–	6	6	12
Seattle	–	19	23	15
Tampa Bay	–	–	–	21
Toronto	–	–	1	1
Washington	7	7	–	–

Note: The numbers in bold are the population rankings of the areas of expansion teams based on the closest census in years. Since United States census of areas' populations are performed in ten-year intervals, the population ranks of teams' areas for 1961, 1969, 1977, and 1998 were reported from, respectively, the censuses conducted in 1960, 1970, 1980 and 2000. The 1998 rank (17) of Anaheim is based on the population of Orange County since Anaheim was not listed as a metropolitan area in the late 1990s. The population of the Greater Toronto Area (or Toronto) was ranked first in 1980 and 2000 among all areas in Canada. A small dash (–) means that an AL team did not exist in that area during the expansion year.

Source: See various editions of The World Almanac and Book of Facts; Official Major League Baseball Fact Book 2005 Edition; and "Historical Metropolitan Populations of the United States," at http://www.peakbagger.com cited 13 September 2008.

Chicago insurance executive and owner of the Oakland Athletics Charlie Finley had bid for an AL franchise. But for various reasons, they each failed in their efforts. That was because Greenberg and Veeck's offer was opposed by Dodgers owner Walter O'Malley, who did not want to compete with Veeck for sports fans in the LAA, while a conflict of interest occurred since Finley had previously acquired majority control of the AL Athletics in Oakland.

As a rich and well known entrepreneur in the entertainment and media business, Autry owned and controlled Golden West Broadcasters—which included radio and television enterprises that were based in the city of Los Angeles. Also, he was a current or former minority stockholder in a Pacific Coast League (PCL) baseball team named the Hollywood Stars, and his wealth exceeded an estimated $300 million. In short, Autry and his group possessed the ambition, money, and power to outbid other groups and become the initial owners of the AL's expansion team in the LAA.

One of the first tasks for Autry's syndicate was to decide on a name for their new team. Since the Spanish words *Los Angeles* translate into English as *The Angels*, Autry paid Walter O'Malley approximately $300,000 for the right to use Angels as a nickname for his team because the Dodgers owner had owned a former PCL team in the city that was named the Los Angeles Angels. When this transaction was completed, the Los Angeles Angels was officially established as an expansion team to play in the AL.

To open its first season, the club played its home games in 1961 at Wrigley Field in South Los Angeles, which was the local ballpark of the PCL's Angels. Then one year later, the MLB Angels moved to play their home games in Dodger Stadium, a baseball facility referred to as Chavez Ravine. At that ballpark, however, the AL Angels was a tenant of the NL Dodgers and thus, the former club was unable to generate a distinct, large, and independent fan base. Furthermore, O'Malley imposed severe lease conditions on the Angels while playing its home games in Dodger Stadium. So in the mid–1960s, Autry attempted to negotiate with city officials in Long Beach for the construction of a new, taxpayer-funded baseball stadium. When these talks failed, Autry successfully concluded an agreement for a new stadium to be built in Anaheim, a suburban city of Los Angeles within Orange County.

As a result, in 1966 Autry's syndicate transferred their franchise—now named the California Angels—to Anaheim and remained as franchise owners for 31 consecutive seasons. Then, when the Disney Corporation bought the team from Autry and his associates in early 1997, the club's title was changed to Anaheim Angels. That name reflected, in part, Disney's headquarters and its amusement business in Orange County of southern California.

During the early 2000s, Disney had other important business interests to manage and operate, and so the company sold its MLB franchise to Mexican billionaire Arte Moreno. In turn, he planned to publicize and exploit the state's largest media market by renaming his team from Anaheim Angels to the Los Angeles Angels of Anaheim. Despite protests from local baseball fans and a lengthy lawsuit filed by the City of Anaheim, the name of Moreno's team has remained the same since 2005.

Washington, D.C. (1961)

Between 1901 and 1960 inclusive, the Washington Senators won just three AL pennants and, in 1924, a World's Series. As such, the Senators' dismal performances and low attendances at its dilapidated ballpark in D.C. convinced owner Clark Griffith to vacate the nation's capital after the 1960 MLB season and move his team to the Minneapolis area in Minnesota. Meanwhile, Congress had held open hearings and inferred or even threatened lifting MLB's antitrust exemption if the league did not amend its policy and increase the number of its franchises above 16. Consequently, after several meetings during the late 1950s to early 1960s, the league conceded to political pressure to avoid public relations problems and approved the entry of new AL clubs within the Los Angeles and Washington, D.C., areas.

Because it ranked seventh in population and experienced a very high growth rate during the 1950s, the Washington area was an appealing site for the AL to place a new team that also would be nicknamed the Senators. For sure, MLB foresaw such economic benefits in Washington as the Senators being an intraleague rival for the nearby Baltimore Orioles and successfully competing for local sports fans with the NFL Redskins but with no local NBA or NHL clubs. Furthermore, other than the cities of Newark, Houston and Buffalo, there were one or more AL or NL clubs located in the largest and in midsized populated areas of the U.S. Even though the Senators would likely perform poorly in its league and struggle financially for a few years, potential profits from expansion and the political pressure from Congress after the relocation of the former Senators team to Minneapolis in 1960 had each compelled MLB to choose Washington, D.C., as a prime location for an AL expansion team.

In turn, it was a powerful and savvy group led by Richard Quesada—an administrator in the Federal Aviation Administration—that had purchased the right to a franchise from MLB for $2.1 million. Although Quesada knew very little about how to operate a professional sports team, he had political connections in the D.C. area and raised the amount of capital necessary to bid for and acquire an AL expansion franchise, but ultimately, he played only a minor role in the organization as an owner. In fact, Quesada sold his interest in the team to another investor during the early 1960s. Anyway, the Senators played one season in Griffith Stadium and then in the mid–to late 1960s, performed at home in $20 million D.C. Stadium, which was later renamed Robert F. Kennedy Memorial Stadium.

In retrospect, Washington was not an optimal area to host the Senators ball club during the 1960s. To clarify, the original Senators teams floundered there because they finished at or near the bottom in most AL seasons, drew more than a million in attendance to their home games in only one year (1946), remained a distant second in popularity and inferior to the hometown NFL Redskins, and otherwise earned a reputation for a famous saying. That quote is, "Washington—first in war, first in peace, and last in the American League." Indeed, longtime owner Clark Griffith failed to invest enough resources and his family's money into the team; that, in part, caused the Washington Senators to lose the majority of their games except when the club won AL pennants in 1924–1925 and 1933, and a World's Series in 1924.

For organized baseball officials to expect a new team and its organization to be successful in the short run after its predecessor had a history of poor performances, below-average home attendances for decades and debilitating financial problems was being overly optimistic. In short, for 11 seasons the expansion Senators franchise could not or did not exploit its potential value by realizing the business, demographic, economic, and social advantages of being located in the nation's capital.

Kansas City (1969)

After his team finished no higher than sixth place in 13 AL seasons while playing at home in the Kansas City area, owner Charlie Finley moved the Athletics to Oakland, California, following the 1967 MLB season. In turn, Finley's decision was severely criticized by Missouri senator Stuart Symington of Missouri and publicized in the media from late 1967 through 1968. As a result, Symington demanded that MLB authorize and put a team in his state to replace the former Athletics. Even so and as denoted in Tables 1.2 and 1.3, the Kansas City area then ranked twenty-fifth in population during the late 1960s, had experienced mediocre economic and population growth, and hosted a popular American Football League (AFL) team nicknamed the Chiefs. In contrast to the superior qualities of the Los Angeles area and the population growth of Washington as a city in 1961, Kansas City appeared to be less than an optimal place for a MLB club from a demographic and business perspective.

In the end, Symington's influence, power, and prestige as a U.S. senator had intimidated MLB and its officials. Therefore in 1969, he persuaded the league to locate one of its two AL expansion teams in Kansas City rather than within a larger metropolitan area such as Phoenix, Arizona; Tampa-St. Petersburg, Florida; or Denver, Colorado. MLB's decision was made, in part, because wealthy businessman Ewing Kaufman was a resident of Kansas City. As such, he had the wherewithal and enough money to pay MLB a fee of

$5.5 million for the right to own an expansion franchise. Besides the involvement of Symington and contribution of Kaufman, the Athletics' former ballpark, Municipal Stadium, was available in Kansas City to play the new team's 81 home games in each regular season.

Given the city's ownership of a 46-year-old, 35,500-seat stadium that met MLB standards, one of Kaufman's first important decisions was to nickname his team in order to generate enthusiasm and excite baseball fans in the area. Since the popular American Royal Livestock Show had been performed in Kansas City for approximately 70 years, Kaufman decided to name his club the Kansas City Royals. Through the 2008 season, the Royals had won seven West Division titles and two AL pennants, and in 1985, a World Series.

In sum, why did MLB select the Kansas City area to be a site for an AL expansion team in 1969? These factors include this area being the home to a former AL team for 13 years; Senator Symington's implicit threat to challenge baseball's antitrust exemption in the federal courts; the availability of a well-known big league stadium in the city; baseball's confidence, respect, and trust in Ewing Kaufman as a franchise owner; and to complete the league's organizational plans of expanding the AL and NL by two teams each in 1969.

Seattle (1969)

For several years, the Seattle area in Washington State had been directly involved in some way with professional team sports. It was home, for example, to a minor league baseball team named the Seattle Rainiers of the PCL. Furthermore, the area contained an NBA expansion club named the Seattle SuperSonics, and also was previously considered as a potential relocation site for the AL Cleveland Indians. Finally, during the late 1960s, Seattle was the third most populated area on the West Coast after Los Angeles and San Francisco.

Besides these few but significant facts, an impressive ownership group had formed in Seattle to campaign for and promote professional baseball, raise millions of dollars as financial capital, and to seriously bid for an existing or expansion AL team. Indeed the group's leaders were Dewey Soriano, a former president of the PCL, and William Daley, who had owned the Cleveland Indians from 1956 to 1966. Meanwhile in 1968, King County voters approved the issuance of a municipal bond to fund the construction of a new baseball stadium in the area, which years later, would become the ballpark for the expansion Seattle Mariners. Based on these factors and other reasons, MLB choose Seattle as one of two cities to host an AL expansion team that adopted Pilots as its nickname.

As noted in Tables 1.2 and 1.3, during the late 1960s the Seattle area ranked nineteenth in population, realized above-average growth in size, and contained a population nearly equal to Minneapolis, which was the home of the AL Minnesota Twins. Unfortunately, however, the Pilots began their inaugural season in 1969 to play at home in 31-year-old, 18,000-seat Sick's Stadium. There were several huge and unique problems associated with this facility. As a ballpark of the minor league Rainiers, it was too small in capacity and had become obsolete by the mid to late 1960s. For example, there were many delays and troubles for local contractors to increase Sick's Stadium's capacity by 30,000 seats before the 1969 MLB season had started. Although many of these seats had been installed by June of that year, most of them had obstructed views for spectators. Also, the ballpark's scoreboard did not operate on opening day and the water pressure fell in the building's toilets and faucets after a few or more innings of the Pilots' home games. Because of these issues and an extremely inferior team, the Pilots' attendances at home in the 1969 season frustrated and did not meet the expectations of its owners. This predicament, in turn, caused the club to struggle and not perform competitively against its AL rivals.

Despite the area's rank and above-average growth in population, it was a colossal mistake for MLB to approve an AL expansion team to play in Seattle during the late 1960s. Sick's Stadium needed major renovations that opponents of the project and thousands of local taxpayers did not and would not support. Furthermore, the team experienced immediate financial problems because for three years it had to forego its share of revenues from baseball's national television contract, and, the team agreed to provide the other AL owners 2 percent of its gate receipts that were collected from home games. After a payment of $5.3 million to MLB for its expansion fee, and poor attendance and accumulating losses during the 1969 season, the Pilots gradually depleted their cash account and dollars of reserves from a bank loan. As a result, the value of the franchise plummeted to less than $15 million before 1970.

In hindsight and given the failure of the Pilots, baseball officials should have unanimously selected the Milwaukee area as an expansion site for an AL team to perform in 1969. Besides hosting the Milwaukee Braves for 13 seasons, that city was represented by an enthusiastic, knowledgeable, and wealthy business group headed by automobile dealer Alan "Bud" Selig. Based on the popularity of 15-year-old County Stadium and a local baseball fan base that consisted of tens of thousands, and the contributions of profitable corporate sponsors such as the beer industry, the Milwaukee area had the demographics, economic power, and infrastructure to successfully host a new AL franchise in organized baseball. For the reasons state before, MLB had preferred and selected the Seattle area for an expansion team rather than Milwaukee, and that proved to be a flawed decision.

Seattle (1977)

When the Pilots had been bankrupted after the 1969 MLB season, a syndicate controlled by 35-year-old Bud Selig purchased the team from MLB in 1970 for about $11 million and subsequently moved it to Milwaukee where it performed as the Milwaukee Brewers in the AL's West Division. As a result of that deal, the City of Seattle, King County, and Washington State sued baseball's AL for a breach of contract. At the trial, league officials agreed to place an expansion team in Seattle if the prosecution dropped its lawsuit. After about a year of intense negotiations, the AL authorized the placement of a new club in the Seattle area, which meant that the lawsuit was void.

As denoted in Table 1.3, between 1969 and 1977 the Seattle area's population had decreased in rank from nineteenth to twenty-third as did the rankings of AL clubs in Baltimore, Boston, Cleveland, Kansas City, and Minneapolis. Even so, in 1974 the NFL Seahawks had joined the NBA Super-Sonics as another professional sports team based in Seattle of King County. Consequently, the decisions made by the owners of these teams suggest this area in the northwest section of Washington State had appealed to professional sports leagues as a prime site for at least one of their franchises. So in 1976, Hollywood actor Danny Kaye—as the spokesperson and principal member of a syndicate—paid a fee of $6.2 million to MLB for the right to own and operate an AL expansion team and locate it in the Seattle area. Thus, Kaye and his colleagues nicknamed their new club Mariners to start the 1977 MLB season and have it compete in the AL's West Division.

There are two interesting features about the origins of Kaye's expansion team. First, the Mariners was chosen as a nickname to reflect the prominence of marine culture in the Seattle area. Second, from 1977 to 1998, the club played its home games in a multipurpose $67 million, 59,500-seat stadium named the Kingdome. This facility was baseball's largest ballpark until being replaced in July 1999 by Safeco Field, a $517 million, 46,600-seat ballpark with a retractable roof. As mentioned earlier for the expansion Seattle Pilots, the construction of the Kingdome experienced delays during the late 1960s and early 1970s, in part, because of lawsuits filed by groups who opposed the use of taxpayer money to finance it. Although these legal disputes continued in the courts, the Mariners played their home games—and so did the NFL Seahawks for awhile—in the Kingdome.

In short, Seattle was a reasonably attractive and viable place to host a baseball expansion team as of the mid-to-late 1970s. Indeed, it was Seattle's new ballpark and productive economy, and the area's above-average population growth and strong job market that convinced the AL to choose a group that represented Seattle and not areas in Denver, Phoenix, or Tampa Bay-St. Petersburg to host the AL's thirteenth team.

Toronto (1977)

Prior to the late 1970s, a few owners of baseball clubs considered the Greater Toronto Area (GTA) to be a prime site for their MLB team. In fact, the NL San Francisco Giants were interested in relocating there until businessman Bob Lurie purchased the franchise in 1976 and then committed to maintain its location in that West Coast city. Nonetheless, the Giants' intentions became news in the media and created such excitement that the City of Toronto decided to renovate Exhibition Stadium—the home of the Canadian Football League (CFL) Argonauts—in order to accommodate games played by teams in professional baseball.

To add a seventh team to the AL's East Division and thus align it with the league's West Division during the mid–1970s, baseball officials evaluated the GTA and other areas as potential sites. Subsequently, for a fee of $7 million, the AL awarded an expansion franchise to a group of sports investors that consisted of Canada's Labatt's Breweries, businessman Howard Webster, and the Canadian Imperial Bank of Commerce. Later, a "name the team" contest was held in Toronto and Labatt's Blue became one choice selected by the area's baseball fans. Ironically, Labatt's Blue was also the name of a top beer brand of Labatt's Breweries who, in part,

Country musician and popular film actor Gene Autry headed a syndicate that purchased an American League expansion franchise for $2.1 million in 1960, and named it the Los Angeles Angels. In 1966, Autry moved his team from Los Angeles to suburban Anaheim and then renamed the club the California Angels. Two years after selling a controlling interest of the franchise to the Walt Disney Company, 91-year-old Autry died. [National Baseball Hall of Fame Library, Cooperstown, N.Y.]

hoped the team's name would be shortened to Blues and accordingly provide free advertising for a popular product of the company. Within a few years, however, a majority of Toronto's baseball fans identified the expansion team as the Jays. As a result, the club's official and public nickname evolved into being the Blue Jays.

During the mid to late 1970s, the GTA had a large and expanding population and an economy that experienced job growth, consisted of households with higher incomes, and contained local industries whose prosperity had significantly increased. Since the Montreal Expos had become moderately popular for about eight years in Canada as an expansion team in the NL East Division, MLB decided to expand and approve a new team within the GTA rather than in a metropolitan area of the U.S. In contrast, some optional areas in the U.S. for a new MLB team during the late 1970s likely included Den-

As an expansion team in the American League's West Division, the Seattle Pilots finished 33 games behind the leading Minnesota Twins and sixth in baseball's 1969 season. Due to low attendances at home games played in Sick's Stadium and also financial problems, the Pilots went bankrupt in 1970. As a result, a syndicate led by current Baseball commissioner Bud Selig bought the team for approximately $11 million and moved it to Wisconsin to perform as the Milwaukee Brewers. [National Baseball Hall of Fame Library, Cooperstown, N.Y.]

ver, Colorado; Miami, Florida; and Washington, D.C. Although each of these areas had midsized or midsized-to-large populations, they also contained popular professional sports teams such as the NFL Broncos and NBA Nuggets in Denver, NFL Dolphins in Miami, and NFL Redskins and NBA Bullets in Washington. Apparently and perhaps realistically, MLB thought that the presence of the NHL Maple Leafs and CFL Argonauts in Toronto would not significantly threaten the business opportunities and potential success of a new baseball club in that area.

Tampa Bay (1998)

Since the 1980s, several civic and business leaders and some prominent newspaper reporters in Tampa Bay had attempted to lure an MLB team to their area because the city is located on the midwestern coast of Florida. To be sure, this area is a destination for tourists and also the home site of the NFL Buccaneers and NHL Lightning; it contains a large number of retirees and thousands of senior citizens; and it hosts various entertainment activities and events each month. Furthermore, for decades, some MLB clubs have spent their preseason in the area by conducting spring training camps and playing exhibition baseball games within or near Tampa Bay and St. Petersburg.

During 1990, the Florida Suncoast Dome—now named Tropicana Field—was built for baseball games in St. Petersburg, a city located only a few miles south of Tampa Bay. Sometime in 1992, there was speculation that San Francisco Giants owner Bob Lurie had attempted to sell his NL club to investors in Tampa Bay, who would then move their team from San Francisco to play its home games at the Suncoast Dome in St. Petersburg. Three years after that deal failed, MLB decided to expand again into a metropolitan area of Florida and subsequent to the expansion of the Marlins into Miami in 1993. Thus in 1995, the league awarded an AL expansion franchise to a group of investors from Tampa Bay that was headed by businessman Vincent J. Naimoli.

Soon after MLB's announcement of expansion was publicized to—and welcomed by—sports fans across Florida and the southeast, owner Naimoli and his organization nicknamed their team the Tampa Bay Devil Rays and then sold the naming rights to the Rays' stadium in St. Petersburg to an orange juice and soft drink company in the private sector named Tropicana Products. To prepare the ballpark for opening day of the 1998 MLB season, an expenditure of $70 million in taxpayer money was used to renovate the building and also increase its seat capacity to 45,000.

Based on such factors as population growth, steady increases in per capita and household income, and ideal weather conditions, MLB made a prudent business decision in 1995 to permit a new AL team to locate in the Tampa Bay-St. Petersburg area. During that year, Phoenix, Arizona, was also granted an expansion team by MLB. As these expansions occurred, the data reveal that in the mid–1990s Washington, D.C.; Riverside, California; and Portland, Oregon, were the only U.S. metropolitan areas ranked among the top 25 in population without being a home to an MLB club. In short, this fact suggests that the AL (and NL) may decide to consider future expansion sites in less populated areas of the U.S. where minor league baseball is popular such as Indianapolis in central Indiana, San Antonio in southeast Texas, Nashville in northwest Tennessee, and Columbus in central Ohio.

The next portion of this chapter—but before a final section and the summary and notes—discusses the performances of the seven AL expansion teams. To denote how competitive these teams have played, the statistics that I selected as measurements are their number of AL division titles and pennants, and victories in World Series, and also their average winning percentage and home attendance. In part, this data provides some interesting information about the quality and rank of these expansion teams while they had existed in specific markets. Furthermore, the statistics reveal their success or failure during seasons and postseasons against other MLB clubs while they had competed as members of the AL.

AL Expansion Teams Performances

To indicate how the AL's seven expansion clubs have performed since their initial season, Tables 1.4 and A.1.1 were prepared. The latter table, which appears in the Appendix, denotes the number of seasons, and the average win-loss percent and home attendance of each team. In total, the two tables expose these teams' previous on-the-field performances, and indirectly, their entertainment appeal and value as sports enterprises to baseball fans in their hometowns and areas.[7]

Established in 1977, the Blue Jays are the AL's most successful expansion franchise based on these performances. While located in Canada's largest metropolitan area for 32 years, the team has won about 50 percent of its regular season games and averaged more than two million in home attendances per year; it has earned five East Division titles, and in 1992–1993, consecutive AL pennants and two World Series. To achieve these impressive results especially during the early 1990s, the club's manager was Cito Gaston and its greatest players included hitters Joe Carter, Dave Winfield and Roberto Alomar, and pitchers Jack Morris, Dave Stieb and Pat Hentgen.

In contrast to the NL Montreal Expos, who struggled to win games and play before sellout crowds for years after their expansion in 1969, the Blue Jays' average attendance at Toronto's Exhibition Stadium substantially improved after 1982. Indeed, the number increased from 15,750 per game in 1982 at Exhibition Stadium to 50,500 in 1994 at the Skydome. After 1994, however, the Blue Jays' attendance per game tended to decline until 2002. But since then, attendance has risen to approximately 30,000 spectators at each game in the 50,500-seat Rogers Centre. Nevertheless, it is unlikely that the club will ever surpass its peak of 4.1 million fans who had enthusiastically attended home games at the Skydome in 1993.

Although the AL's East Division is regarded as the most competitive in MLB, the Blue Jays organization has prospered while located in the GTA. When the Boston Red Sox and New York Yankees visit Toronto to play the Blue Jays at home, there is occasionally a sellout of tickets or total capacity crowd to watch each of them compete at the Rogers Centre. Consequently, the GTA's population and population growth, and Toronto's household and per capital incomes, are high enough to generate excess revenues for the Blue Jays, who perform against their rivals in the AL. Indeed, if the Blue Jays win the East Division again or become a wild card and therefore qualify for the AL playoffs, baseball in Toronto will become increasingly popular although second in demand to professional ice hockey and the hometown NHL Maple Leafs. Simply put, ice hockey has been and always will be the best type of sport entertainment for athletes, fans, and businesses in the Toronto area.

While located for 48 years within or near the second largest media market and metropolitan area in the U.S., Angels teams have won the AL West

Table 1.4 American League Expansion Teams
Number of Seasons and Postseason Results, 1961–2008

| | | | Postseason Results | | |
Team	Year	Seasons	Divisions	Pennants	World Series
Los Angeles/Anaheim Angels	1961	48	7	1	1
Washington Senators	1961	11	0	0	0
Kansas City Royals	1969	40	7	2	1
Seattle Pilots	1969	1	0	0	0
Seattle Mariners	1977	32	3	0	0
Toronto Blue Jays	1977	32	5	2	2
Tampa Bay Devil Rays	1998	11	1	1	0

Note: Team is self-explanatory. Year is a team's first season in the American League. The Angels' 48 seasons include the team's performances while located in Los Angeles and Anaheim. The Pilots played one season in Seattle and then the franchise bankrupted. Postseason Results include these teams' number of division titles in the AL, and their number of pennants and World Series they have won since their expansion year.

Source: The World Almanac and Book of Facts 2006 (New York, NY: World Almanac Books, 2006), 901; "World Series History," at http://www.baseball-almanac.com cited 8 September 2008; "Teams," at http://www.baseball-reference.com cited 9 September 2008.

Division about every seven seasons in MLB. Moreover, since 2003, the club has won four division titles and in 2002 a pennant and World Series. Furthermore, the Angels' home attendances have exceeded three million each season from 2003 to 2008, and these numbers ranked it second among the 13 others in the league. This success occurred during the early 2000s because of manager Mike Scioscia's leadership and achievements of such sluggers as Vladimir Guerrero, Troy Glaus and Garret Anderson, and the team's excellent defense.

With respect to the Angels' pre–2000 performances, the franchise struggled while playing at Wrigley Field in 1961 and at Dodger Stadium during 1962 to 1965. Then in 1966, the Angels shifted operations to Anaheim, California, and played their home games at Anaheim Stadium. As a result, the team's attendances at games have gradually increased despite being located in a city with a much smaller population and media exposure than Los Angeles. In fact, more than two million fans cheered at Anaheim Stadium while the Angels won their first West Division championship in 1979.

In comparison to historical performances of the other six AL expansion teams, the Angels have the highest number of playoff appearances, and are second to the Blue Jays in average winning percentage and home attendance. If the team's popularity and success continues during seasons of the early 2000s, owner Arte Moreno will be expected to increase the salaries of his players. If so, then I predict that the franchise will increase its cash flows, revenues, and also profits from sponsors, ticket sales at home games, and local television contracts. Furthermore, because of economic problems and other reasons, some of the Angels' West Division rivals have failed to improve competitively and therefore have not won more of their regular season games on average since the late 1990s to early 2000s.

Being an expansion team in the late 1960s, but inferior to the Blue Jays and Angels in performance and success, there is the 40-year-old Kansas City Royals. Through 2008, this club on average had won approximately 48 percent of its regular season games and also two AL pennants and one World Series in seven playoff appearances. The Royals' six West Division titles occurred during 1976 to 1985 when Whitey Herzog, Jim Frey, and Dick Howser had each managed various Royals teams that included such great players as George Brett, Hal McRae, and Willie Wilson.

Relative to the other one-half dozen AL expansion teams, the Royals' best years in home attendance were the late 1970s to early 1980s at Royals Stadium. That is, during that era the club ranked second or third in the league when about 26,000 fans attended a majority of its home games. Since 1993, however, the Royals teams have ranked between tenth and fourteenth each season in attendance per game among the 14 AL clubs. And likewise, they failed to qualify for any playoffs of the league. These performances occurred, in part, because Kauffman Stadium will be MLB's fifth oldest ballpark in 2009; Kansas City is a relatively small and financially mediocre metropolitan area; and the team maintains a below-average payroll for its players each season. Thus, the Royals will struggle as a franchise to increase their total home attendance above 1.5 million per season and win an AL Central Division title by defeating in single games and series the large-market Chicago White Sox and Detroit Tigers, and the competitive Cleveland Indians and Minnesota Twins.

Even though the Royals have not been very successful at winning championships since the mid–1980s, a significant portion of the baseball fans in the Kansas City area are passionate and care about their home team. Given its long term lease at Kauffman Stadium and the commitment of the franchise's owners, the Royals will not relocate to another city before 2015. Indeed, the millions in revenues from MLB's national television contract and the money earned from trading its elite players to the Yankees and other AL clubs will provide enough cash flows to keep the Royals playing at home in Kansas City for several or more years. In short, the team has not been an inferior organization during 40 years of operations despite its area being ranked in population only ahead of Milwaukee's in MLB, and also being located in America's twenty-sixth most populated market in 1998.

Based on its performances, the Seattle Mariners is the AL's fourth most successful expansion franchise. Relative to its six peers, the 32-year-old club has won approximately 47 percent of its regular-season games and three West Division titles, and appeared in four of the league's playoffs. These baseball seasons were in 1995, 1997, 2000 and 2001. In fact, the Mariners finished runner-up to the New York Yankees for the AL pennant in 2000–2001. For sure, the team excelled in one or both of these years because of former manager Lou Piniella's strategies and the power hitting of batters Edgar Martinez, Alex Rodriguez and Ichiro Suzuki, and such consistent pitchers as Freddie Garcia and Jamie Moyer.

Since 1996, the Mariners' home-game attendances at the Kingdome—and then in 47,500-seat Safeco Field from 1999 to 2008—have been in the top half of the AL's 14 teams. Specifically, these numbers exceeded three million spectators in 1997 and again in each of the 2001 to 2003 MLB seasons. Nevertheless, the team's attendances have tended to decline in recent years, that is, from 43,700 spectators each game in 2002 to 29,400 in 2008. One reason for this change is the club's weak performances against rivals in the AL West Division, and also the increase in popularity of the NFL Seahawks. Meanwhile, in 2008 the NBA SuperSonics moved from Seattle to Oklahoma City because the club failed in negotiations with the city to replace Key Arena, which is its home court at the Seattle Center. As a result of this relocation, the sports fans in King County may shift their allegiance, passion, and support to the Mariners.

Although Seattle is a midsized area of more than three million, the Mariners have generally been outperformed in attendance by the West Division Angels and also Oakland Athletics—whose area ranked twelfth in population during the late 1990s. Besides these differences in population, the Angels and Athletics have higher lifetime winning percentages than the Mariners, and each of them have also won several West Division titles, and a few pennants and at least one World Series. Unless the Mariners improve in performance by significantly expanding the payroll of their players, the club will continue to struggle and increase attendances in games played at Safeco Field, and thus, will be unable to qualify for the playoffs and win its first AL pennant and a World Series.

Because of its mediocre home attendances per game at Tropicana Field and winning only one East Division title, the Tampa Bay Rays (renamed Rays from Devil Rays in 2008) is the league's fifth most successful expansion team. Established in 1998, the club did not win more than 70 games in a season, or finish higher than fourth place in its division, until ten years later. Since it is located in baseball's sixth smallest area, the Rays franchise has failed to lure sports fans away from the popular NFL Buccaneers and NHL Lightning, and has not been able to attract enough of the area's population of senior citizens to its games at Tropicana Field. Despite an outstanding performance in 2008, the team's home attendance averaged only 22,300 per game which ranked it twenty-sixth among the 30 clubs in MLB.

If the Rays continue to win at least 50 percent or more of games played during regular seasons and thus attract bigger crowds to the team's ballpark in St. Petersburg, then professional baseball in the Tampa Bay area will become increasingly popular and generate more cash flows and revenues for the franchise. If this improvement occurs for consecutive or more seasons after 2008, then the Rays' owners may increase the club's payroll, trade for free agents and use more talented and productive players, and upgrade their team to better compete against the elite Red Sox and Yankees, and rival Blue Jays and Orioles. Otherwise, the Rays will not place much higher than fourth or fifth for years in the AL's East Division.

After being approved by MLB, the Washington Senators joined the AL as an expansion team in 1961. That baseball season, the team won 37 percent of its regular season games with total attendance at home of approximately 597,500. This number amounted to 7,400 per game, which was the lowest attendance among 18 MLB franchises. During the club's 11 years in Washington, the team played above .500 only in 1969 and averaged 664,000 in attendance per season, or about 8,300 spectators for each game played in Griffith, and later, D.C. Stadium.

With respect to that Washington team's athletes, the Senators best' ballplayer was Frank Howard. He led the AL in home runs in 1968 and 1970, and in total bases during 1968–1969 and 1971. Other than Howard's performances, the club had no pitchers who won 20 or more games in a single season or a Cy Young Award, or became the league's Most Valuable Player or Rookie of the Year. Interestingly, a highlight of the franchise was the appointment of former Red Sox outfielder Ted Williams to manage the Senators in 1969–1971. Although the club had finished tenth the previous season, in 1969 it improved to 86–76 and finished fourth in the AL's East Division following the Orioles, Tigers and Red Sox but ahead of the Yankees and Indians.

During the 1960s, apparently local sport fans in the Washington area preferred to attend games and support the NFL Redskins or travel to Baltimore and root for the AL Orioles. Indeed, the Senators were an inferior club that never improved their image or reputation in the AL after losing 100 or more games each MLB season between 1961 and 1964. After businessman Bob Short purchased the team in 1969 for $9.4 million, he moved it to Arlington, Texas, and renamed it the Texas Rangers.

As denoted in Tables 1.4 and A.1.1, the Seattle Pilots were the AL's greatest disappointment as an expansion team. After winning their first game in the 1969 season and then the home opener three days later, the Pilots were defeated by their opponents in all but five games that month and unfortunately, the club never played with confidence or to be successful. Other than stolen base leader Tommy Harper, the team had no players that led the AL in any hitting or pitching category at the end of the 1969 MLB season.

It is unlikely that the Seattle Pilots would have been competitive and won more league games if the club was located in another area. Although conditions at Sick's Stadium undoubtedly contributed to the team's poor attendance while playing games at home in Seattle, the former California

Angels executive and general manager Marvin Milkes, and a previous coach of the champion St. Louis Cardinals and the Pilots' manager Joe Schultz were each unable to organize and prepare the club to compete against such rivals in the AL West Division as the Minnesota Twins and Oakland Athletics. In the end, a federal referee declared the expansion franchise bankrupt on April 1, 1970. As such, this decision paved the way for the team to abandon Seattle early that year and then relocate to Wisconsin and perform as the Milwaukee Brewers.

MLB MARKETS, AL EXPANSION YEARS

When the most attractive baseball markets to locate one or more AL expansion teams had been evaluated and approved by league officials during the early and late 1960s, and in the mid to late 1970s and 1990s, some metropolitan areas in the U.S. already contained MLB teams while others were or were not the home of minor-league baseball clubs or had been the host of professional clubs in other team sports. Besides whether another professional sports franchise or franchises had existed within these markets, such variables as the area's total population and population growth were also important factors for owners of AL expansion teams to consider in determining an urban place to play a schedule of home games during each MLB season. To be sure, the owners of incumbent (or non-expansion) MLB franchises located in other large, midsized, and small baseball markets had an economic and financial interest in where a new team in either league played its regular season schedule of local and away games.

Based on these criteria and knowledge about the areas actually selected as locations for each expansion year that began in MLB during the early 1960s, the following is an analysis of metropolitan areas within the U.S. and Canada that were or were not potential or realistic sites as baseball markets for one or more new AL teams during four years of expansion. If necessary, any data presented in Tables 1.1–1.4 of this chapter and A.1.1–A.1.2 of the Appendix—including the areas' population ranks (listed in parentheses) and each team's attendances and performances—will be used to describe and measure the quality and appeal of these places as sports markets.

1961

During the late 1950s to early 1960s, the AL approved the entry of expansion teams into the metropolitan areas of Los Angeles (2) and Washington, D.C. (7). In retrospect, these two cities were very to moderately attractive markets to league officials even though the NL Dodgers played their home games at a ballpark in Los Angeles (LA), while in 1960, the Senators' owner, Clark Griffith, had decided to abandon Washington and move his attendance-poor, second-division ball team to a city in the midwest, that is, Minneapolis in central Minnesota.

For various reasons, the league did not consider or had rejected the placement of any AL expansion teams into midsized markets where no MLB franchise had existed in 1961. These included such populated areas as Newark, New Jersey (13); Buffalo in northwestern New York (16); and Patterson, New Jersey (19). Meanwhile, some lower-ranked metropolitan areas such as Dallas-Fort Worth (22), Seattle (20), San Diego (23), and Atlanta (24) were each not considered to be viable baseball markets by MLB because of their small to midsized populations and their being located, respectively and for some remotely, in the U.S. southwest, west and south.[8]

Other demographic and also economic facts, and indeed political factors, affected the league's and franchise owners' decisions about evaluating and choosing LA and Washington as AL expansion sites in 1961. First, baseball officials had committed to expand the NL in 1962 and put new teams within the metropolitan areas of New York (1), and Houston (15). That, of course, occurred as planned when the NL Mets and Astros began their initial MLB seasons in 1962. Consequently, the owners of the two AL expansion teams needed to locate their clubs in different places than New York and Houston. Second, the AL realized the prosperity and success of Walter O'Malley's Dodgers in LA during the late 1950s, and also feared a threat by baseball teams in the recently-organized Continental League to invade cities on the U.S. West Coast. Thus, baseball officials compromised with O'Malley by paying him $350,000 for rights into his territory and also agreeing that the expansion LA Angels must play their home games in the city-owned but inferior Wrigley Field, a facility previously owned by O'Malley. He had purchased the ballpark from Chicago Cubs owner Phil Wrigley in 1957, and, one year later, transferred it to Los Angeles in exchange for other property.

Third, in 1960 AL team owners happily accepted a bid by General Elwood "Pete" Quesada for a new Washington franchise that would extend the Senators' treasured name in a dilapidated downtown ballpark named Griffith Stadium. To convince these baseball officials of his commitment, Quesada pledged to spend enough money to assemble and play a competitive AL club in Washington. In turn, there were no groups that represented other places in the U.S. or Canada that had seriously offered bids in the early 1960s for the rights to an AL expansion team. And fourth, the LA and Washington areas had each experienced strong growth in population, contained thousands of households with above-average to high incomes, and ranked well above average among MLB teams as media and television markets.

For why the Angels moved to Anaheim after their teams played five MLB seasons in LA and the Senators to Arlington, Texas, after 11 years in Washington was, in part, because of problems in convincing local governments and taxpayers to build and finance the construction of a new ballpark or the renovation of an existing stadium, and also with fan dissatisfaction from the inept performances of their teams, and due to various ownership issues such as O'Malley's control of Dodger Stadium. Anyway, despite the Angels' and Senators' brief tenures in, respectively, LA and Washington, these places had the demographics and infrastructures that played little to no role in the relocation of the Angels to Anaheim in 1966 and the Senators to Arlington in 1971. In other words, the AL was prudent from a business perspective when it approved the entry of two expansion teams, and then had them play home games at ballparks in the LA and Washington, D.C., areas before 1962.

1969

While MLB prospered throughout the mid to late 1960s, the AL accepted bids from various investors to purchase the rights for two expansion teams. After it approved the two most distinguished, impressive, and well-organized bids, the league then permitted the entry of new baseball franchises into the Kansas City (25) and Seattle (19) areas to play in MLB's season of 1969. That year, the reported populations of the Kansas City and Seattle markets were, respectively, 1.2 million and 1.4 million.[9]

According to *The World Almanac and Book of Facts*, larger populations had existed in such non–MLB areas as Nassau-Suffolk (9) at 2.5 million, Dallas-Fort Worth (12) at 2.3 million, and Newark (15) at 2.1 million. An AL team, moreover, did not occupy the huge sports market in Los Angeles, or in Toronto, Canada. Furthermore, league officials could or would not agree to approve more expansions during the late 1960s, and thus, put new teams in lower-ranked populated places than Kansas City and Seattle such as in the future MLB areas of Miami (26), Denver (27), and Phoenix (35). In contrast to the AL's strategy, the NL also expanded in 1969 and the owners of the league's two new teams chose to locate their franchises within the Montreal, Canada, and San Diego markets.

Besides Missouri senator Stuart Symington's threat that MLB would lose its antitrust exemption if the league did not place a new team somewhere in his state, and also the AL's need to avoid legal action based on Milwaukee's suit against the NL in 1965, Kansas City had some distinct qualities and commercial benefits as a metropolitan area for an AL expansion team. Listed in no specific order, first, this area in Missouri hosted the AL Athletics for 13 MLB seasons (1955 through 1967); second, a group of wealthy businessmen headed by Marion Laboratories president Ewing Kauffman had enough capital, and commitment and local support from civic leaders in Kansas City to purchase the rights for an AL expansion franchise and locate it in the area; and third, several thousands of die-hard baseball fans lived in Kansas City and became enraged in 1967–1968 at Athletics owner Charley

Finley when he moved his team to the Oakland area (6) on the West Coast. Consequently, a unique but appealing and sympathetic sports environment for professional baseball existed within the Kansas City area during the mid to late 1960s.

In comparison to the AL expansions in such areas as LA, Washington, D.C., and Kansas City, Seattle had fewer advantages, assets, and opportunities to be an aggressive, productive, and profitable market for a new MLB team during the late 1960s. Indeed, the Milwaukee area had been identified, promoted, and viewed by baseball officials as a viable expansion site for an AL or NL team after the Braves left there in 1966 to play its home games in 51,000-seat, $18 million Atlanta-Fulton County Stadium in Georgia. But when Chicago White Sox owner Arthur Allyn sold his rights in the club to his brother John during the late 1960s, John because the franchise's new president and announced that no more exhibition or regular season games would be played by the Sox in Milwaukee. Therefore, John had renewed his team's commitment to remain in the Chicago area.

Based, in part, on that decision and the pursuit of former or new baseball markets by MLB officials, the AL decided that the city's economic growth from industrial development and the area's midsized population and other demographics were sufficient for Seattle to host an expansion team. So in 1968, the league approved the entry of another team besides the Royals in Kansas City. Interestingly, the former franchise cost its owners only about $5 million. Nonetheless, as a result of inferior players, deplorable conditions at Sick's Stadium and mismanagement, the Seattle Pilots had dismal home-game attendances because it finished sixth in the AL's regular season in 1969. About six months later, the club received a loan of $650,000 from the AL to defray its operating expenses and debts while in spring training. After the Pilots franchise declared bankruptcy in early 1970, the league approved its movement to Milwaukee. In short, the AL had overestimated the Seattle area as an attractive place for a professional baseball team, and thus, the league made a grave mistake in 1968 to expand and approve an entry of a new club into that city.

1977

The AL consisted of 12 teams in 1976. Some of them were located in such large populated areas as New York (1), Chicago (3) and Detroit (5), some in midsized areas such as Boston (10), Baltimore (14) and Minneapolis (15), and others in relatively small areas such as Cleveland (19), Milwaukee (28) and Kansas City (29). Meanwhile, a dozen NL clubs were scattered among various places in North America including the league's expansions of 1962 into Houston and New York City, and of 1969 into Montreal, Canada, and San Diego.

When sports leagues in professional basketball, football, and ice hockey added a number of new teams in various areas across America during the late 1960s and early to mid–1970s, AL officials became aggressive, anxious, and increasingly confident that some sports markets in the U.S. and Canada could support one or more of its baseball teams. Furthermore, an MLB franchise did not exist in such U.S. areas as Denver (22), Miami (21), Phoenix (26), Tampa Bay-St. Petersburg (24), and Washington (7) in the mid–1970s.

Although the latter five areas had each lacked an MLB team or teams, the AL decided that Seattle (23) and the Greater Toronto Area (1) would be the best locations for new expansion franchises. Between 1970 and 1977, Seattle's population grew from approximately 1.4 million to more than 1.5 million, its area became the headquarters of domestic and international high-growth technology companies, and household incomes in the area increased faster than the national average. Besides, a small but vocal group of baseball fans in Seattle and within the region were very eager to support a new team that would be nicknamed the Mariners, and to attend its home games in the Kingdome.[10]

Unfortunately, within a few years the original owners of Seattle's expansion franchise, including movie star Danny Kaye—who had paid approximately $6 million for it in 1977—blundered and caused public relations problems when they reclassified seats at the Kingdome and raised ticket prices at the ballpark for regular season games, initially refused to invest enough money in the club and make it more competitive in the AL's West Division, and tended to hire a number of inexperienced and unproductive field and general managers. Consequently, the franchise floundered such that California real estate developer George Argyros purchased 80 percent of the Mariners for a reported $10.4 million in 1981, and two years later, he acquired the remaining 20 percent of it.

Since the early 1970s, Toronto's government officials had campaigned for an MLB franchise. In representing the nation's most populated and wealthy area, this group emphasized to baseball dignitaries in New York why Toronto was a prime location to place an expansion club. Although the area's sports fans had adored and supported the NHL Maple Leafs for decades, it was evident that an MLB expansion team could be successful in Toronto based on the demographics and economics of the area and the incomes of households. This prediction proved to be accurate as 1.7 million fans attended the Blue Jays' home games in 1977 despite the team's 54–107 record in the AL West Division and even following its last-place finishes in the 1977 through 1981 MLB seasons. Nevertheless, after 1981 the Blue Jays continued to draw fans at home games and improve enough to win consecutive pennants and World Series in 1992 and 1993.

1998

In the mid–1990s, the three most populated U.S. areas without an MLB club were Washington (7) at 4.5 million, Riverside-San Bernardino-Ontario (13) at 2.9 million, and Tampa-St. Petersburg-Clearwater (21) at 2.2 million. Since two previous Senators baseball teams had struggled to win games while based in Washington during 71 years of the twentieth century, and because Riverside-San Bernardino-Ontario area is in a region near Orange County and Los Angeles, for these and other reasons Tampa Bay-St. Petersburg appeared to be an attractive place for an AL expansion team in 1998.

Internally, Tampa's metropolitan area had a growing population, continued to receive increasing inflows of money and resources as an upscale retirement community, and experienced warm to hot temperatures in various spring, summer, and fall months of each year. Also, a relatively new and modern ballpark had been built in St. Petersburg. So rather than locate an expansion team in larger communities on either of the U.S. coasts or in a city of Canada, AL officials approved the entry of an expansion team into the Tampa Bay area. After purchasing the rights to own and operate his new franchise, owner Vincent J. Naimoli nicknamed it the Tampa Bay Devil Rays.[11]

Until recently, the Rays struggled to win games against rivals in the AL's East Division and its home attendances have continued to lag behind the majority of other clubs in the league. However, because of good pitching, timely hitting, and a smart field manager, the Rays won the East Division and an AL pennant in 2008. Nevertheless, from 1998 to 2007 the club was very inferior in playing regular season games, becoming a major disappointment to sports fans in its marketplace and an embarrassment to baseball officials who had admitted it into the league.

SUMMARY

For 60 consecutive years, the AL consisted of eight teams in several differently populated baseball markets. Then between 1960 and 1999, the league expanded by 75 percent or a total of seven franchises. After the Milwaukee Brewers transferred from the AL to NL after the 1997 season and also the entry of Tampa Bay in 1998, there have been five clubs each in the league's East and Central Divisions, and four in its West Division.[12]

With respect to the AL's four years of expansion, two of the tables in this chapter denote that on average the metropolitan areas of six AL expansion teams (excluding the Toronto Blue Jays) ranked approximately sixteenth in population within the U.S. and they experienced a growth rate in population of about 20 percent. Furthermore, the areas contained one or two MLB clubs and one, two, or three other professional sports teams.

Given the results reported for MLB's regular seasons and postseasons, another table reveals that the two most—and then least—successful AL expansion teams in their performances have been, respectively, the Toronto Blue Jays and Los Angeles/Anaheim Angels, and then least, the Seattle Pilots and Washington Senators. The group of seven AL expansion clubs played a total of 175 seasons from 1961 to 2008, had qualified for and won 23 AL division titles, six pennants, and four World Series.

From a business perspective, four or 57 percent of the AL expansion teams have each succeeded as sports enterprises in their local markets for more than 30 MLB seasons. Also, two or 28 percent of the AL expansion teams failed in their original markets while another one may or may not attract enough fans and sponsors from its area, or earn sufficient revenues to continue operating at its current home ballpark after the early 2000s. In sum, the decisions by MLB to expand the AL from eight to 14 franchises after 1960 benefited some local baseball fans and commercial organizations in their markets but most likely did not improve the economies of the areas or communities in which these teams had performed from the spring to fall of each year.

Based on the research that I performed for Chapter 1, the next AL expansion year will be sometime after 2015. The likely place for a new franchise is a midsized to large populated area in the U.S. without an MLB team such as Riverside-San Bernardino-Ontario, California, or Portland, Oregon. Alternatively, an expansion team may be awarded to an investor or syndicate that will put it in a foreign city, or in an American metropolitan area where minor league baseball is popular, such as Columbus, Ohio, or Indianapolis, Indiana. For more about this topic, see Chapter 5.

2

National League Expansion

During the late 1850s, a baseball organization that was named the National Association of Base Ball Players (NABBP) had formed at a convention in New York City. As such, it consisted of 16 clubs composed of clerks, lawyers, and merchants. Although the NABBP was established as an amateur baseball organization, some teams in it had supposedly compensated their players while others on teams most likely received special privileges from local politicians, businesses, and wealthy people in their communities. Throughout the late 1860s, the NABBP included more than six professional baseball teams and those included the Brooklyn Atlantics, Chicago Excelsiors, and Cincinnati Red Stockings.[1]

In early 1970, it was exposed in the media and reported that several amateur baseball teams were secretly, and in some cases openly, rewarding their players with salaries, shares of gate money, and appointments to jobs. Besides conflicts within the NABBP about these payments of money and other benefits—which caused the best ballplayers to frequently move to those teams that paid the highest amounts—some differences also existed among clubs about whether they should or should not remain as amateurs. As a result of this confusion, some teams withdrew from the NABBP in 1871 and then organized the National Association of Professional Base Ball Players, or simply known as the National Association (NA). When this transformation occurred, the NABBP dissolved and a few of its teams became entities in state and regional baseball groups.

NATIONAL ASSOCIATION

Before its first season in 1871, the NA adopted a number of rules. These involved its membership—that is, charging a $10 franchise fee—and furthermore, the scheduling of games against rivals and how to determine a champion each year. Meanwhile, a majority of the league's clubs established their ticket prices at approximately 50 cents each, and also for regular season games, they jointly decided to hire umpires who would not be paid for their work. Originally, the NA's roster of nine teams represented various urban places in the United States (U.S.). The population rank of each place among the top 100 of them in 1870 (as denoted in parentheses) included New York (1), Philadelphia (2), Chicago (5), Boston (7), Washington (12), Cleveland (15), Troy (28), and Fort Wayne (83). Interestingly, the only place that hosted two of the league's teams in 1871 was in northeast Illinois where the Chicago Forest Citys and Chicago White Stockings each played home games.[2]

Between 1871 and the NA's final season in 1875, several different teams had joined the league (see Table A.2.1 in the Appendix). More specifically, the NA increased by five expansion clubs in 1872, four in 1873, one in 1874, and five in 1875. In fact, some of the league's new teams were scattered among cities in the east and midwest, and also based at home in such high-ranked populated places as Brooklyn (3), St. Louis (4) and Baltimore (6), in mid-sized-ranked markets such as Washington (12) and New Haven (25), and in low-ranked areas such as Hartford (34), and Elizabeth City (64). Alternatively, the NA had none of its expansion clubs located and playing their games in such populated places as Cincinnati (8), New Orleans (9), San Francisco (10), Buffalo (11), Newark (13), and Louisville (14).

Of the total 15 expansion clubs in the NA, zero of them played the entire five seasons, one or 7 percent had existed four seasons, two or 13 percent competed three years and another two or 13 percent for two years, and 10 or 67 percent played one season. Thus a large majority of expansion franchises had folded after playing less than two or three seasons in the league, in part, because they were located in midsized to small baseball markets, experienced below-average attendances at home and performed poorly, and also because of the league's liberal and easy admission standards for the entry of any new clubs. So while the NA had varied in size from a low of eight teams in 1874 to a high of 13 in 1875 due to contraction, expansion, and clubs being replaced, the only three urban places that franchises successfully existed during a total of five NA seasons were in Boston, New York and Philadelphia.

Despite being America's first major, national, and professional baseball organization, and thus performing at a reasonably high and competitive level of play in the sport, the NA folded after completing its fifth season in 1875. In retrospect, there were four important factors that contributed to the league's failure. First, the Boston Red Stockings overwhelmingly dominated the NA. As denoted in Table A.2.1, the only other competitive teams in the league were the New York Mutuals and Philadelphia Athletics. As a result, many baseball fans that lived in places had little to no incentive to attend the local games of their hometown clubs, especially those that existed and played in midsized and small markets. Second, some franchises in the NA had their home ballparks in cities that could not financially afford the sport of professional baseball. This dilemma, for example, included such clubs as the Elizabeth Resolutes, Keokuk Westerns, and Middletown Mansfields.

Third, the NA did not have a central authority and group of business leaders, or even a home office. Unfortunately, this lack of organization meant that some crucial decisions had to be deferred until the annual meeting of the league's franchise owners. Besides these delays, any amateur or professional baseball club in America could join the NA by simply paying admission dues of $10. Two additional problems were that most of the league's existing teams had created their regular season schedules and also chose any combination of opponents they preferred to play in home games. Consequently, a few clubs decided to withdraw or were purged from the NA within a season, particularly after they had played their rivals in games at home but then refused to travel to avoid paying expenses on road trips.

Fourth, other difficulties existed within the league such as the dissension, mistrust, and suspicion among a team's players because of large differences in their salaries; scandals caused by gambling and the fixing of games between baseball officials and criminals and crooks in a community; lack of policies, regulations, and rules to detect, penalize, and eliminate the misbehavior within and between the NA's member clubs; teams that raided others in the league to sign their rivals' best ballplayers; and the poor attendance and performance of inferior franchises at games in their home ballparks.

In short, the NA appeared to be a well-intentioned but disorganized, unethical, and unstable baseball organization that failed after five years because the league and its clubs had little or no accountability to their fans and local communities, and also because it lacked a practical managerial structure. Therefore, the NA was administratively, emotionally, and financially unable to cope with and solve its internal problems and to control its operations.

Given the sport's competitiveness and popularity within areas of the U.S. during the early to mid–1870s, the NAPBBP tried but failed to establish itself in communities, to become an attractive investment to sponsors within the sports industry, and to succeed in an unfamiliar business environment and expand in a cyclical national economy. In fact, there were no other major leagues in professional team sports that existed within America from 1871 to 1875, so many of the NA's clubs played their games in small, urban sports markets and as a result, they did not successfully establish a fan base among populations at those locations.

Meanwhile, the majority of the NA's franchise owners had no experience with how to operate a professional baseball franchise. Thus their clubs performed before tiny and unenthusiastic crowds at both home and away games. In short, although the NAPBBP remained in power as a national baseball organization for five years, the league was challenged and then overcome by various business, economic, and operational problems that doomed its ability to continue after 1875 as a sports enterprise.

More than a dozen different ball clubs had played in the NA during its final season. In turn, most of these teams struggled at least financially within their home markets, and therefore, the majority of them had neither opportunity nor support to enter into and play games within another national or prominent professional baseball league. So in late 1875, such inferior clubs as the Brooklyn Atlantics, New Haven Elm Citys, and Washington Nationals either disbanded or played a few seasons in a minor, independent baseball league. Nonetheless, an attempt to reorganize and revive the NA in March and April of 1876 flopped when only a few officials representing baseball organizations from three states had appeared at a meeting in Philadelphia. When that meeting concluded without plans to further discuss the league's reemergence, the NA became an extinct organization.

In the end, six former NA teams that had the most potential to prosper and succeed for one or more seasons decided to join the recently-organized National League (NL) in early 1876 and so did the independent and midsized-market Red Stockings from Cincinnati and Grays from Louisville. Consequently, the NL emerged and opened its first season in April 1876 and then performed as a league with these eight franchises competing against each other.

NL TEAMS

The visionary leader and original founder of the NL was businessman William A. Hulbert. Early in life, he had prospered as a coal dealer, grocery wholesaler, and a member of Chicago's Board of Trade. In his role as president of the Chicago White Stockings, Hulbert sincerely believed that the NA had become a defective, troubled, and wild and unruly baseball organization within five years. According to Hulbert, that happened because of the inflated salaries of numerous ballplayers who had rotated from one NA team to another during various seasons, problems with gambling scandals and excessive alcohol consumption, and the competitive imbalances that existed among the league's teams because of their different, uncoordinated, and incomplete scheduling of regular season games.[3]

So in early 1876, Hulbert arranged a meeting at the Grand Central Hotel in New York and invited the representatives of four former NA clubs that had their headquarters and home ballparks in various areas of the eastern U.S. At that meeting—which also included officials from midwestern baseball teams located in Cincinnati, Louisville and St. Louis—this group of eight baseball entrepreneurs fully discussed and then adopted a constitution. Furthermore, they replaced the words Association and Players in the NA's title with, respectively, League and Clubs. As such, these leaders' new sports organization became officially known as the National League of Professional Base Ball Clubs.

Besides an increase in the organization's franchise fee from $10 to $100 and implementing new policies to limit the number of its members, and to establish a fair and well-balanced schedule of games and compensate umpires for their work, the NL's constitution also included the following two tenets with respect to the composition and location of its group of teams. First, any city with a population under 75,000 could not be represented by a team in the NL except if approved by a unanimous vote of the league's members. Second, each team's territory must be equally respected since no more than one club would be allowed to exist in a single city. As such, the former rule eliminated the possibility of any club being located in a very small or tiny city, while the latter tenet prevented more than one ballclub in the league from being based in the same market area as another one. Finally, the constitution contained specific reforms and penalties about cheating, drinking and gambling, and moreover, the document provided a procedure to elect a board of directors and its president. In total, these were the primary guidelines, regulations, and standards that identified the operation, performance, and structure of the NL regarding its opening season in 1876.

In short, Hulbert and his group of seven other officials envisioned a compact, permanent, and well-balanced baseball organization of eight teams, that is, four each located in areas of the east and also in the midwest. To effectively operate a baseball league that is controlled by owners and not players—which had inversely prevailed during the early 1870s within the NA—this group of men committed their teams to a complete schedule of regular-season games and naming a champion. Moreover, they agreed that games with any independent or outside baseball teams must be avoided to the greatest extent possible. Based on the type of sports organization that Hulbert and his colleagues formed and had provided a management structure for, the promoters and owners of teams were the individuals that created and would control this nation's first major league in professional baseball.

When it started its first season in 1876, the NL consisted of eight clubs that were each located in eight different urban places (see Table 2.1). Since this chapter focuses, in part, on these specific urban places as baseball markets of the original group of teams and later on the cities of other NL franchises, the ranks in population (as denoted in parentheses) of the areas of the first eight during the mid to late 1870s were New York (1), Philadelphia (2), Chicago (4), Boston (5), St. Louis (6), Cincinnati (8), Louisville (16), and Hartford (43). Therefore, because of demographic, economic, or sport-specific reasons, NL clubs did not exist then in such large to midsized urban places as Brooklyn (3), Baltimore (7), San Francisco (9), New Orleans (10), Cleveland (11), Pittsburgh (12), and Milwaukee (19).[4]

As listed alphabetically in column one of Table 2.1, there were a total of 31 NL teams that played a full or partial schedule of games during one or more seasons between 1876 and 1900 inclusive. However, because of several factors such as below-average and even dismal performances, small numbers of spectators at the ballparks of teams' home games, debts and other financial issues, and also some franchise owners' mismanagement, a large majority of the 31 clubs had problems and thus they could not or would not continue to operate as enterprises for many baseball seasons. So after a few years, they-withdrew from—or were eliminated by—the league and dissolved. Indeed, the only NL teams that played each season from 1876 through 1900 were the Boston Red Stockings (renamed Beaneaters in 1883), and Chicago White Stockings (renamed Colts in 1890 and then Orphans in 1898). As indicated in the next section of this chapter, almost all clubs that had entered the NL after 1876 and before 1901 were there as a result of league expansions.

Table 2.1 Big League Baseball
National League Teams and Their Seasons, 1876–2008

Teams	Seasons
Pre–1901	
Baltimore Orioles	1892–1899
Boston Red Stockings/Beaneaters	1876–1882/1883–1900+
Brooklyn Bridegrooms/Superbas	1890–1898/1899–1900+
Buffalo Bisons	1879–1885
Chicago White Stockings/Colts/Orphans	1876–1889/1890–1897/1898–1900+
Cincinnati Red Stockings	1876–1880
Cincinnati Reds	1890–1900+
Cleveland Blues→St. Louis	1879–1884
Cleveland Spiders	1889–1899
Detroit Wolverines	1881–1888
Hartford Dark Blues	1876–1877
Indianapolis Blues	1878–1878
Indianapolis Hoosiers	1887–1889
Kansas City Cowboys	1886–1886
Louisville Colonels	1892–1899
Louisville Grays	1876–1877
Milwaukee Grays	1878–1878
New York Gothams/Giants	1883–1884/1885–1900+
New York Mutuals	1876–1876
Philadelphia Athletics	1876–1876
Philadelphia Quakers/Phillies	1883–1889/1890–1900+
Pittsburgh Alleghenys/Pirates	1887–1890/1891–1900+
Providence Grays	1878–1885
St. Louis Brown Stockings	1876–1877
St. Louis Browns/Perfectos/Cardinals	1892–1898/1899/1900+
St. Louis Maroons	1885–1886
Syracuse Stars	1879–1879
Troy Trojans	1879–1882
Washington Nationals	1886–1889
Washington Senators	1892–1899
Worcester Ruby Legs	1880–1882
Post-1900	
Arizona Diamondbacks	1998–2008

Teams	Seasons
Atlanta Braves	1966–2008
Boston Beaneaters/Doves/	
Pilgrims/Braves→Milwaukee	1901–06/1907–08/1909–11/1912–52
Brooklyn Superbas/Dodgers→Los Angeles	1901–1910/1911–1957
Chicago Orphans/Cubs	1901–1902/1903–2008
Cincinnati Reds	1901–2008
Colorado Rockies	1993–2008
Florida Marlins	1993–2008
Houston Colt .45s/Astros	1962–1963/1964–2008
Los Angeles Dodgers	1958–2008
Milwaukee Braves→Atlanta	1953–1965
Milwaukee Brewers	1998–2008
Montreal Expos→Washington	1969–2004
New York Giants→San Francisco	1901–1957
New York Mets	1962–2008
Philadelphia Phillies	1901–2008
Pittsburgh Pirates	1901–2008
St. Louis Cardinals	1901–2008
San Diego Padres	1969–2008
San Francisco Giants	1958–2008
Washington Nationals	2005–2008

Note: Teams and Seasons are self-explanatory. A slash (/) indicates a change in a team's nickname. The Brooklyn Bridegrooms, for example, was renamed the Brooklyn Superbas in 1899. An arrow (→) denotes the relocation of a team. The Cleveland Blues moved to St. Louis in 1885 and was renamed the St. Louis Maroons. Any teams that moved from one area to another are listed on a separate line in the table. The 1900+ means a team's name continued after 1900 and it is listed in Post-1900. In 1998, the Milwaukee Brewers transferred from the AL to NL.

Source: "Teams," at http://www.baseball-reference.com cited 9 September 2008; "Teams," at http://www.mlb.com cited 12 September 2008; James Quirk and Rodney D. Fort, Pay Dirt: The Business of Professional Team Sports (Princeton, NJ: Princeton University Press, 1992), 378–383, 391–399; Official Major League Baseball Fact Book 2005 Edition (St. Louis: The Sporting News, 2005).

In contrast to baseball teams of the late 1800s, a total of 21 various NL clubs existed and competed in regular season games between 1901 and 2008 as reflected in Table 2.1. In fact, when Major League Baseball (MLB) formed in 1901, the NL had consisted of eight clubs in a total of seven different urban places. Based on statistics from the Bureau of the Census in 1900, the rank in population (given as a number in parentheses) of each team's market was estimated and reported as follows: Brooklyn and New York (1), Chicago (2), Philadelphia (3), St. Louis (4), Boston (5), Cincinnati (10), and Pittsburgh (11).

Meanwhile in the American League (AL), three of its eight clubs in 1901 played at home in relatively lower-ranked places like Detroit (13), Milwaukee (14), and Washington (15). Consequently, the baseball markets in Boston, Chicago, New York, and Philadelphia were each overcrowded with two or three MLB clubs from the early 1900s until some teams began to relocate to other areas in the mid–1950s, which was then followed by expansion during the early and late 1960s.

In the next section of this chapter, I will discuss expansion of teams in the NL within two distinct time periods. That is, while these clubs had performed in the early NL or from 1876 to 1900, and then since MLB was established in 1901. For this topic, there is considerably more data about baseball teams and other specific information about expansion of the NL in the second period than during the late 1800s. This, in turn, means that the history of expansion and its consequences is more complete with details about the origin, business, and performance of new NL teams during 1901 to 2008 than in 1876 to 1900.

NL EXPANSION MARKETS

Pre-1901

After the NL completed its first season in 1876, the New York Mutuals and Philadelphia Athletics were expelled by the league for not traveling to play such teams in the midwest as the Cincinnati Red Stockings and Louisville Grays. Then in late 1877, the NL dropped teams which were located in Hartford and St. Louis. That occurred, for example, when some of their ballplayers had fixed games, and also because the Dark Blues in Hartford and Brown Stockings in St. Louis were unable to establish a fan base in their respective market and they each had problems with attendances and gate receipts at their home ballparks.[5]

Then the Louisville Grays resigned from the league in early 1878 when its owner could not assemble a competitive roster of players. As a result, three new clubs joined the NL after its second but before the third season. These were the Blues in Indianapolis (24), Grays in Milwaukee (19), and another team nicknamed the Grays in Providence (20). As such, the NL approved the entry of clubs in less populated markets than Louisville and St. Louis, but larger in size than Hartford. So within two years after it was organized, the league had decreased from eight to six members.

As denoted in Tables 2.2 and 2.3, the markets for baseball in Indianapolis, Milwaukee, and Providence during the late 1870s were relatively small in relation to the population of areas of NL teams located at home in Boston, Chicago and Cincinnati, and especially in comparison to some large cities on the East Coast. It seems, therefore, that NL president William Hulbert wanted to maintain the league's balance geographically and likewise its movement westward by admitting one club on the East Coast and two others from areas in the midwest. Furthermore, there were likely higher economic and operating costs for any baseball franchises that played at home within America's biggest cities and also, teams from New York and Philadelphia had each been banished from the NL in 1876 for refusing to travel and compete

Table 2.2 National League Expansion Areas
Expansion Years and Characteristics of Team Markets,
1878–1889, 1962–1998

Market Area	Year	Population Rank	Population Growth	Teams MLB	Teams Other
Pre-1901					
Indianapolis	1878	24	5.6	1	0
Milwaukee	1878	19	6.2	1	0
Providence	1878	20	5.3	1	0
Buffalo	1879	13	3.2	1	0
Cleveland	1879	11	7.4	1	0
Syracuse	1879	32	1.8	1	0
Troy	1879	29	2.1	1	0
Worcester	1880	28	4.1	1	0
Detroit	1881	18	7.6	1	0
New York	1883	1	2.5	2	0
Philadelphia	1883	2	2.3	2	0
Kansas City	1886	24	14.0	1	0
Washington	1886	14	5.6	1	0
Indianapolis	1887	27	4.0	1	0
Cleveland	1889	10	6.3	1	0
Post-1900					
Houston	1962	17	5.9	1	1
New York	1962	1	1.0	2	5
Montreal	1969	2	2	1	2
San Diego	1969	23	3.1	1	2
Denver	1993	24	3.0	1	2
Miami	1993	11	2.3	1	2
Phoenix	1998	14	4.5	1	3

Note: Market Area is an urban place or as renamed later, a Standard Metropolitan Statistical Area (SMSA) of the teams in their expansion year. Year is each team's expansion year. The 1880 and 1890 population ranks of urban places were used to estimate, respectively, the ranks for Years 1878–1883 and 1886–1889. The 1960, 1970, 1990 and 2000 population ranks of cities were used to estimate, respectively, the ranks for Years 1962, 1969, 1993 and 1998. The annual growth rate in each area's population was determined during 1870–1880, 1880–1890, 1960–1970 and 1990–2000 for the nearest expansion years. MLB is the total number of Major League Baseball clubs (including AL teams or those from alternative professional baseball leagues) in a market area during the expansion year. Other includes the number of professional basketball, football, ice hockey, and soccer teams located in these market areas during the expansion year. In 1969, Montreal's population ranked second to Toronto's in Canada.

Source: Official Major League Baseball Fact Book 2005 Edition; Frank P. Jozsa, Jr., and John J. Guthrie, Jr., Relocating Teams and Expanding Leagues in Professional Sports: How the Major Leagues Respond to Market Conditions (Westport, CT: Quorum, 1999); James Quirk and Rodney D. Fort, Pay Dirt, 378–478; The World Almanac and Book of Facts (New York: World Almanac Books, 1930–2007).

Table 2.3 National League Teams
Population Rank of Teams Areas in Expansion Year, 1878–1998

1878	1879	1880	1881	1883	1886	1887	1889	1962	1969	1993	1998
4	4	4	4	1	1	1	1	1	1	1	1
5	5	5	5	2	2	2	2	2	2	2	2
8	8	8	11	4	3	3	3	3	2	2	2
19	11	11	13	5	5	6	6	4	3	3	3
20	13	13	18	11	6	13	10	6	4	4	4
24	20	20	20	13	14	14	13	8	6	5	5
	29	28	28	18	15	15	14	9	9	10	10
	32	29	29	20	24	27	27	16	10	11	11
								17	13	12	12
								18	20	15	14
									21	17	17
									23	19	18
										23	20
										24	22
											24
											35

Note: The numbers in bold are the population rankings of the areas of expansion teams based on the closest census in years. Indianapolis, for example, ranked twenty-fourth in population in 1878 according to the census in 1880. In 1969, Montreal was an expansion market and its area's population ranked second in Canada. The other area ranked second in population that year was Los Angeles. The ranks of these two areas are also listed in NL expansion years of 1993 and 1998.

Source: "Population of the 100 Largest Urban Areas: 1870–1900," at http://www.census.gov cited 15 September 2008; "Historical Metropolitan Populations of the United States," at http://www. peakbagger.com, accessed 13 September 2008; The World Almanac and Book of Facts, 1930–2007; *Official Major League Baseball Fact Book 2005 Edition*; Frank P. Jozsa, Jr., and John J. Guthrie, Jr., *Relocating Teams and Expanding Leagues in Professional Sports*, 1999.

against clubs in the midwest. Anyway, the Indianapolis Blues and Milwaukee Grays each folded after one season, and in 1885, so did the Providence Grays.

The next group of expansions in baseball occurred in 1879 when the NL admitted new franchises placed in Cleveland (11), Buffalo (13), Troy (29), and Syracuse (32). As it happened one year earlier for Indianapolis and Milwaukee, these four expansion clubs were based in cities west of Boston and Providence. Also, three of them existed in midsized areas within the northwest region of New York State. Apparently in 1879, NL officials were not eager or required to add any new clubs from large populated cities on the East Coast and west of Columbus, Ohio.

The NL's decision to expand was, in part, a mistake since the Syracuse Stars faced bankruptcy in mid–September of 1879 and thus were forced to resign from the league. Then the Cleveland Blues moved to St. Louis in 1885, and one year later, a group of investors purchased the Buffalo Bisons but due to financial problems decided to cancel the franchise before the 1886 season had opened. Finally, after four years in operation, the mediocre Troy Trojans failed to continue playing its regular-season schedule of games, and thus in 1882 had to withdraw as a franchise from the NL.

To replace the Stars of Syracuse, the NL added a new team from Worcester (28) in 1880. Then after removing the Cincinnati Red Stockings for not compensating its ballplayers and committing other rules violations in 1880–1881, the league proceeded to admit an expansion club from Detroit (18), which was then a midsized-populated urban place. Despite eliminating some of its franchises during the 1880s, the NL continued to operate its seasons with eight members. However, the latter two expansion teams struggled to win games and make enough money from gate receipts to pay their expenses. As a result, the franchises of the Worcester Ruby Legs and Detroit Wolverines were each cancelled by the league, respectively, after the 1892 and 1898 seasons.

To operate nationally as an elite baseball organization with eight franchises in 1883, the NL replaced the teams in Troy and Worchester with clubs stationed at sites in New York (1) and Philadelphia (2). This decision was made by the NL even though in 1876, teams located in New York and Philadelphia had been expelled from the league for breaking rules about refusing to travel and playing away games. So seven years later, the NL had decided to reenter teams into the two most populated and lucrative sports markets in America. As a result of these expansions in 1883, that year there were NL clubs in four urban places on the East Coast and another four based in areas from the city of Buffalo west to Chicago.

With respect to each of these newest expansion teams, the New York Gothams—who after being renamed Giants in 1885—had financial problems and so in five years the club was forced to borrow money and resell some shares of its franchise. But in 1891, the Giants' owner, John Day, successfully merged his organization with a New York club that competed in the Players League. Meanwhile, the Philadelphia Quakers (renamed Phillies in 1890) has continued to perform as a member of the NL since 1883. As such, it has been a competitive and consistent MLB franchise for more than a century of regular seasons, pennants, and World Series.

Seven years after joining the NL, the Providence Grays was sold to the owner of the Boston Beaneaters for $6,600 who then acquired two of the Grays' best pitchers, Hoss Radbourne and Con Daily. For similar reasons, in 1886 Detroit Wolverines owner Fred Sterns decided to purchase the Buffalo Bisons for $7,000. The demise of the Grays and Bisons after the 1895 season, therefore, resulted in groups from Kansas City (24) and Washington (14) to request baseball charters so that their clubs could be admitted into the NL and compete. However, after the former team finished in seventh place with only 30 wins, the NL bought the Kansas City Cowboys for $6,000 in 1887 and cancelled the franchise. Likewise, the expansion Washington Nationals had performed very poorly for four seasons in the league by finishing in seventh or eighth each year. So after the 1889 season concluded, the owner of the Nationals cancelled his franchise.

During the mid to late 1880s, some business investors from Indianapolis (27) purchased the NL's St. Louis Maroons franchise. Then as baseball owners, in early 1887 they entered an expansion team named the Indianapolis Hoosiers into the league. After it had performed at or near the bottom of the NL for three dismal seasons and also before small home crowds, the Hoosiers was terminated as a franchise in late 1889. Furthermore in that season, the league expanded by adding a club from Cleveland (10). Named the Cleveland Spiders, the team played for 11 seasons and never won a NL pennant. After the 1899 season, the league downsized from 12 to eight franchises. Besides the Spiders being cancelled, other clubs that were eliminated by the NL included the Baltimore Orioles, Louisville Colonels, and Washington Senators. In short, the NL removed two of its former expansion franchises and the Orioles and Colonels, which were two teams that had transferred to the league from its merger with the American Association in 1892.

To review baseball history from 1876 to 1900 within the NL, there were 15 expansion teams located in 13 different urban places, with two each in Cleveland and Indianapolis. Seven or 47 percent of them occurred in the 1870s while eight or 53 percent happened in the 1880s. Furthermore, the population of these teams' areas ranged in rank from first (New York) to thirty-second (Syracuse), and their average annual growth rate varied between a low of 1.8 percent in Syracuse to a high of 14 percent in Kansas City. Except for NL franchises located in Indianapolis, Kansas City, Milwaukee and Syracuse, the other 11 of them competed for more than one season in the league.

Besides an area's population and its growth rate, the other factors that affected the longevity of these expansion clubs were whether they had earned a profit or loss each season, their win-loss records and any championships won, quantity of fans in the market, attendance at home games, and the interaction and respect between each team's owners and players, and people in the local community. Because NL president William Hulbert sought to maintain a disciplined and well-balanced league, he preferred that some of its teams be located in the east and others in the midwest, rather than all of them being concentrated in large markets on the East Coast. Thus, an area's geographic location became increasingly important to the league regarding the distribution of expansion franchises and also existing teams.

Post-1900

Based on the population of their U.S. Standard Metropolitan Statistical Area (SMSA) as compiled by the Bureau of the Census, the rank (in parentheses) of each NL team's core market in 1960 included Chicago (2), Los Angeles (3), Philadelphia (4), San Francisco (6), Pittsburgh (8), St. Louis (9), Milwaukee (17), and Cincinnati (18). Besides in the Chicago area, AL teams also existed then in the SMSAs of New York (1), Detroit (5), Boston (7), Washington (10), Cleveland (11), Baltimore (12), and Kansas City (22). Thus, the six most populated U.S. areas without MLB clubs in 1960—and their respective ranks—were listed in an edition of *The World Almanac and Book of Facts* as Newark (13) and Paterson (19) in New Jersey, Minneapolis (14), Houston (15), Dallas (20), and Seattle (21). Given this distribution and rank of SMSA populations of all big league teams in 1960, two years later the NL had expanded in size, and during the next 37 years, the league periodically invaded various sports markets across America and one in Canada. And except for New York in 1962, the other six expansions of the league occurred in different urban places than those in 1878 to 1889.

HOUSTON.   Since when the Texas League formed in 1888 until a minor league team nicknamed the Houston Buffaloes (or Buffs) moved to the American Association in 1959, that area in Texas had been involved in some way with organized baseball. For example, the city's Buffalo Stadium—when built in 1928—was considered by many experts in the sport to be the finest stadium in the U.S. minor leagues. Nevertheless, during the mid–to late 1950s, a few of Houston's most prominent business leaders, investors and politicians joined forces, and then as a group, made a concerted effort to lure a big league team into the area even though MLB officials showed little interest.

To accomplish their goal of locating a franchise in the area, a few people organized and jointly led a regional campaign to promote it within southeast Texas. In turn, that effort resulted in the formation of a Houston Sports Association (HSA) in 1957. Initially, the three individuals most responsible for this organization included public relations expert George Kirksey, who in 1952 had tried to convince St. Louis Cardinals owner Fred Saigh into selling his franchise to a Houston-based group, and also banker William A. Kirkland and Craig Cullinan, the son of a wealthy oil baron.[6]

After several exploratory meetings with major league franchise owners, these promoters from Houston were told to secure the necessary funds to build a new baseball stadium in the area. To achieve that goal, in 1958 Harris County voters approved a $20 million bond issue for the construction of a new ballpark. So because of meetings with current franchise owners and a decision to provide financing, it appeared to the HSA that the city would be awarded a new MLB team or the transfer of an existing one within one to three years. After the entry of a MLB team did not occur in 1959–1960, entrepreneurs in the HSA became frustrated. Therefore, they joined with promoters in other non-major league cities to organize another major baseball organization, and title it as the Continental League.

Then during early 1960, a rich oil and real estate magnate named R.E.

"Bob" Smith and former Houston mayor and Harris County judge Roy Hofheinz began to play an increasingly important role in the operations of the HSA and ultimately, these men gained control of it. Being close-knit business partners, Smith owned a large amount of financial resources while Hofheinz knew a great deal about public land use and the construction and maintenance of municipal facilities. Meanwhile, in mid–to late 1960, Congress discussed baseball's exemption from the U.S. antitrust laws but then failed by four votes to pass the Kefauver bill, which stipulated that MLB be subject to these laws.

Being alarmed by competition from other ball clubs in a Continental League and also from a narrow defeat of Senate Bill 3483 in Congress, an expansion committee within MLB met and agreed to admit two new clubs each into the NL (and also the AL) no later than 1961–1962. As such, any cities that were targeted by the Continental League as markets would be preferred locations for expansion teams in MLB. And, one of these places was Houston while the others included the Los Angeles, New York, and Washington, D.C., areas. Consequently, during the 1960 World Series that was played between the Pittsburgh Pirates and New York Yankees, and after existing team owners had evaluated all bids that were submitted by individuals or syndicates, the NL awarded expansion franchises to ownership groups from Houston and New York City. As a result of MLB's decision to expand in size during 1961–1962, the Continental League eventually dissolved.

In early 1961, the HSA purchased the minor-league Buffs franchise and then soon thereafter, this group gained control of Houston's expansion team that later would be nicknamed the Colt .45s. Among the leaders of the Colt .45s were general manager and veteran baseball executive Gabe Paul, and field manager Harry Craft, who had coached the Buffs during its final season in the Texas League. As such, Houston's expansion team was assigned to compete against its rivals in the NL until 1969, when it became a member of the league's West Division

After playing three NL seasons in hastily-constructed, 32,600-seat Colt Stadium and then being renamed the Houston Astros in 1964, the club moved one year later to the 54,300-seat Astrodome, a spectacular air conditioned domed stadium built in Houston. Financed with public money, this ballpark was completed largely because Judge Hofheinz successfully sold a concept of it to the local community and also, he had bragged about the grandeur, image, and prestige of the facility to owners of other NL franchises. Despite numerous promotions and marketing efforts, within ten years the Astros' debts exceeded $30 million and for financial reasons, Hofheinz had to declare bankruptcy. As a result, such creditors as the Ford Motor Credit Corporation and General Electric seized control of Hofheinz's assets, and these included the Astros franchise. In 1979, a syndicate headed by John McMullen purchased Houston's MLB team and the Astrodome's lease from creditors for $19 million.

From a demographic and also financial perspective, the NL's decision to expand into the Houston area in 1962 appeared then to be a smart and worthwhile strategy. The area's population of 1.4 million ranked seventeenth in the U.S., and the city's economy had experienced above-average economic growth. Nevertheless, these reasons for expansion into Houston and elsewhere during the early 1960s appeared to be secondary since the threat of a rival baseball league, and congressional hearings on the sport's antitrust exemption, had been the primary factors that influenced MLB's decision.

NEW YORK.   Before the departure in early 1958 of the Dodgers to Los Angeles and the Giants to San Francisco, 1882 was the last year an NL team had not been based in the New York area. This scenario caused the city's mayor, Robert Wagner, to appoint a small committee of prominent people to investigate the possibility of persuading an existing NL team to relocate into the area. Indeed, this group tried but failed in its attempts to attract the league's Philadelphia Phillies, Pittsburgh Pirates, and Cincinnati Reds. Then in 1959, committee member and attorney William Shea and baseball veteran Branch Rickey organized an eight-team Continental League that included at least one of its franchises to be placed in New York. In part, formation of this new league and the U.S. government's scrutiny of baseball's exemption from the country's antitrust laws compelled the NL to unanimously pass a resolution to award an expansion team to a syndicate which would locate it somewhere within an area that included New York City.[7]

To bid for and ensure the entry and location of an NL expansion team into the city, the New York Metropolitan Baseball Club, Inc., was created sometime in late 1959 to early 1960. This syndicate, which consisted of principal owner Joan Whitney Payson, former New York Giants director and Wall Street broker M. Donald Grant and a few other wealthy investors, developed plans and consolidated its resources to successfully purchase a new franchise from MLB in 1960 for $1.8 million. To manage the business operations of the new club, Grant hired former New York Yankees general manager George Weiss to be its first president.

For many decades, the New York SMSA had ranked first in population and its economy included the nation's largest financial companies and several international commercial and investment banks. Therefore, the area's baseball fans and its businesses and politicians could and would enthusiastically support another MLB franchise besides the AL's powerful and high-valued Yankees. So soon after Payson and her group became owners of a new NL franchise, they identified and nicknamed it the Mets. This nickname, in turn, was preferred by these owners to such other potential titles as the Avengers, Burros, Jets, Meadowlarks, Skyliners, and Skyscrapers. In fact, a former team named the New York Metropolitans had played in baseball's American Association from 1883 to 1887.

Even though the New York State Assembly had voted in early 1961 for a bond to fund a new ballpark in Flushing Meadows for the Mets, the decision was too late. Thus, the club had to play its first two seasons of regular-season games after expansion before a total of 1.9 million spectators in the 55,000-seat Polo Grounds. Then in 1964, the Mets moved its home games to 56,700-seat Shea Stadium and the team's attendance immediately increased to an average of 1.8 million per year. During its early years in the league, the Mets' teams were managed by a gnarled, bowlegged legend with a great personality named Casey Stengel. Besides his 50 years of experience in the game, Stengel had coached the New York Yankees to seven World Series championships between 1949 and 1960 inclusive.

In the end, it was challenges from teams in a newly-established Continental League and threats from Congress to eliminate organized baseball's exemption from the antitrust laws that essentially affected MLB's decision to expand into the New York area during the early 1960s. However, another crucial factor in placing an expansion team in New York and then effectively getting it organized and prepared for the 1962 MLB season was the political leadership of Mayor Robert Wagner and the power and wealth of Joan Payson and Donald Grant, and also the baseball experience of President George Weiss and later, the team's manager, Casey Stengel. Without their interest in and dedication to the city as a sports metropolis, New York may not have received a NL team for years after 1962. In the next major section of this chapter, the performances of the NL's Astros, Mets, and other new teams since their expansion year are presented in tables and then discussed.

MONTREAL. Throughout the 1940s and 1950s, a popular Brooklyn Dodgers minor-league baseball team named the Montreal Royals had performed as a member of the International League. Such great Hall of Fame ballplayers and former Dodgers as infielder Jackie Robinson, outfielder Duke Snider, and catcher Roy Campanella each played for the Royals, which in at least one season, had attracted more than 600,000 to its home games and also earned a profit that exceeded $300,000. After the Dodgers moved from Brooklyn to Los Angeles in early 1958, the Royals in Montreal had to terminate its affiliation with the Dodgers.

The attempt to bring an MLB club to Montreal began in the early to mid–1960s. That effort was, in part, led by Canadian Gerry Snyder, who then served as a member of Montreal's City Council from the district of Snowdon. During his 26-year tenure in government, Snyder chaired the city's executive committee, became the mayor's liaison to people in the community who spoke English, and also, he contributed much of his time to bring the 1976 Summer Olympic Games and Formula One Grand Prix of Canada to sites in Montreal. So in late 1967, Snyder presented a bid to an expansion committee of MLB for a new team to be placed in Canada's second most populated metropolitan area. In complete support of Snyder's bid from the NL was the Los Angeles Dodgers' owner, Walter O'Malley. That year, he was the chairman of baseball's expansion committee and for nearly two decades his team had an affiliation with the minor-league Montreal Royals. Consequently, five months after Snyder's bid, NL president Warren Giles announced that Montreal was awarded a franchise to play in the league's East Division as of the 1969 MLB season.

Three months after making this important announcement, the NL demanded a payment of $1.1 million—or about 10 percent of its franchise initiation fee—from the new team's group of investors. Furthermore, the league required that the expansion franchise's ownership be well-organized and structured, and for the syndicate to locate an adequate ballpark in the Montreal area for the club's regular-season home games in 1969 and possibly thereafter. Within weeks, the league's demands became a significant issue when multimillionaire Jean Luis Levesque of Montreal withdrew his support of, and participation in, the baseball project. To replace Levesque, Gerry Snyder then convinced Seagram Ltd. stockholder and wealthy businessman Charles Bronfman to guarantee and provide an amount of Canadian or U.S. dollars to purchase this expansion franchise from the NL. As a result of Snyder's efforts, Bronfman consented and then bought a majority interest in the club, and thus, Bronfman became the baseball project's chairman of its board of directors.

The next task for the ownership group was to choose an appropriate, clever, and marketable nickname for their new expansion team in Montreal. Since a club in Kansas City named the Royals already existed in the AL's West Division, the new owners held a name-the-team contest in Montreal. After they evaluated such nicknames as the "Nationals" and "Voyageurs," the owners selected "Expos" because that word had an advantage of being pronounced the same whether in French or English. Moreover, the 1967 World's Fair or alternatively, Expo 67, was a huge success while it occurred in the Montreal area.

Another crucial obstacle to overcome about the new baseball franchise in Montreal concerned the construction of a large and suitable ballpark that met MLB's standards regarding its architecture, capacity, location, safety, and other features. Delorimier Downs, as the former home of the Montreal Royals, was rejected for being too small even for temporary use while a local facility named the Autostade required more than 10,000 seats, a dome, and other expensive renovations that discouraged city officials from using it as a home ballpark for the Expos. Then during the mid-summer of 1968, NL president Giles and MLB commissioner Bowie Kuhn traveled to northwest Montreal to attend a local amateur baseball game played at 2,000-seat Jarry Park. After he was recognized and enthusiastically cheered by fans while at the game, Giles approved Jarry Park as a temporary site for the home games of the Expos. However, the city had less than one year to adequately renovate it.

For approximately $4 million (Canadian) and within four months, the park's capacity was expanded by adding 26,000 makeshift seats and 5,000 parking spaces. That, of course, delighted the team's ownership group, local sports fans, Giles and Kuhn, and other baseball officials. Meanwhile, the Expos had hired veteran baseball executive John McHale to operate the franchise and then he employed former Philadelphia Phillies coach Gene Mauch as the club's first field manager. After a fall expansion draft in 1968 to acquire players and complete the renovation of Jarry Park, the Expos played its first game in New York's Shea Stadium on the opening day of the 1969 MLB season against the Mets and won 11–10. Then on April 14, 1969, the Expos defeated the St. Louis Cardinals 8–7 before 29,180 spectators at Jarry Park and also broadcast to the millions of Canadians who had watched the game on television or listened to it on the radio. The Expos continued to play their home games in refurbished Jarry Park until 1977, which was the year when 46,000-seat Olympic Stadium opened for the team in Montreal.

Based on these facts and other information discussed thus far in this section, it was certainly a huge risk for the NL to approve the Montreal area as a site for an expansion franchise during the late 1960s. Ice hockey had always been Canada's national pastime while American baseball ranked as an inferior team sport among that nation's athletes, communities and fans. More specifically, before 1969 the minor-league Montreal Royals terminated its affiliation with the Dodgers; at least one major Canadian investor had withdrawn his support of the new expansion franchise as a baseball project; three ballparks within Montreal did not meet MLB's requirements; and many sports events in Canada were broadcast on television and the radio in French and not English. Despite these and other issues, the Expos had played its games at home in Montreal for 36 big-league seasons but nevertheless failed to win a NL pennant or compete in a World Series. After 2004, the club was sold to a new group of investors and then moved to Washington, D.C., by its existing owners.

SAN DIEGO. Since the mid–to late 1930s, a minor-league baseball team nicknamed the San Diego Padres had performed in the Pacific Coast League (PCL) of sunny California. Being identified in name to Catholic missionaries within the region, the club had won several PCL championships. Then in the mid–1950s, prominent businessman C. Arnholdt Smith—whose interests included banking, tuna fishing, real estate, and an airline—purchased the Padres and moved his club from Lane Field in San Diego to the city's beautiful Westgate Park. Meanwhile in the 1960s, voters in the area approved a multimillion-dollar bond issue to build 50,000-seat San Diego Stadium in which the PCL Padres and NFL Chargers would play their home games.[8]

When MLB initially announced that the NL would increase by two new teams in 1969, Smith organized a syndicate to bid for the rights to own one of the league's expansion franchises. Besides Smith, a former Brooklyn and Los Angeles Dodgers executive named Emil J. "Buzzie" Bavasi also led a campaign to bring MLB to San Diego. Basically, Bavasi reminded and then convinced baseball club owners that the metropolitan area's population of 1.4 million would support an MLB team. Furthermore, he said to the group that (a) the city's location on the West Coast had ideal weather conditions and a wonderful climate, (b) San Diego had been a great sports city and baseball site for decades, and (c) a local ballpark contained enough capacity to host big league games.

As a further incentive to obtain a franchise from the NL and have it succeed, Smith agreed to borrow enough money to pay a fee of $12.5 million to the league. Moreover, he persuaded the City of San Diego to establish an association that would advertise and promote the team within the metropolitan area. Thus, it was Smith who provided financial support and also possessed the power to get city officials involved in the project for a new expansion team, while Bavasi had contributed his experience, knowledge, and skill from being involved for more than 25 years in professional baseball operations. During May 1968, a NL expansion franchise was unanimously awarded to Smith and his syndicate.

For a few years, the Padres struggled financially and to compete against the Los Angeles Dodgers for southern California's baseball fans, and also to earn an identity and recognition among MLB franchise owners as being a viable major league enterprise. Furthermore, the Padres did not receive a share of the league's television revenues until 1972 while it tried to lure San Diegans from their other sports activities like fishing, golf and tennis. Besides the team's cash flow, marketing and operational problems, and its mediocre attendance at home games in San Diego Stadium, Smith was indicted for tax evasion in 1973. That year, a group of investors offered to purchase the Padres franchise and move it to Washington, D.C., for the 1974 MLB season. But Smith refused to deal with them and instead, he sold his team for $12 million to McDonald's co-founder Ray Kroc, who committed to keep it located in the San Diego area.

As denoted in Tables 2.2 and 2.3 of this chapter, San Diego ranked twenty-third in population among all U.S. areas during the late 1960s. Moreover, it was a prime market both commercially and demographically because of sustainable economic growth and development. Thousands of people in the area participated in recreational activities and likewise attended sports events. Although businesses in the community did not originally and overwhelmingly support a big league franchise, eventually many of their employees would attend some home games, become baseball fans, and thus, support the Padres' teams each season.

In the end, it was visionaries such as C. Arnholdt Smith and Buzzie Bavasi who combined their experience, financial capital, prestige and power to bring an expansion team into the San Diego area. Although the club has been sold and resold since former owner Ray Kroc's death in 1984, the Padres through 2008 has won five West Division titles and two NL pennants, but not a World Series during its 40-year history. In fact, there are more details about the Padres' performances in the next section of Chapter 2.

DENVER.   Between 1990 and 1992, the population of Denver and its per capita income increased, respectively, by approximately 6 and 9 percent, whereas in 1990, the area ranked twenty-fourth in total population. In professional sports, the former Super Bowl champion NFL Broncos has played its home games in the city since 1970 and as of 1976, so have the competitive NBA Nuggets and NHL Rockies. Likewise, each of them has been popular and well-respected professional teams that perform each season in games at their respective stadiums before relatively midsized to large groups of fans. Thus, through the early 1990s, the Denver metropolitan area had experienced a multiyear history of hosting elite sports franchises.

During the early to mid–1980s, a number of talented Pittsburgh Pirates players had used illegal drugs, including steroids, and then after their court trials, they were given a one-year suspension from the game by MLB commissioner Peter V. Ueberroth. Soon after those suspensions but before a public-private syndicate had purchased Pittsburgh's club for $22 million from John Galbreath and Warner Communications in 1985, some rumors circulated within baseball's community that the Pirates might move its operations from Pittsburgh to Denver. Although that relocation did not occur, a Colorado Baseball Commission based in Denver succeeded later in getting the city's voters to approve a .1 percent sales tax in order to finance a new baseball stadium that would qualify as a big league ballpark and in turn attract an MLB team to the metropolitan area.

Sometime in 1990, Colorado governor Roy Romer organized an advisory committee to recruit an ownership group who would then prepare and submit a bid to MLB for an expansion franchise. The group selected by the committee was composed of various Denver executives from such local and regional businesses as the Phar-Mor drugstore chain, Hensel Phelps Construction, and the Rocky Mountain News. After presenting their bid before the existing owners of NL teams during the summer of 1991, the then-current group of baseball owners approved Denver as a site for a new team to play beginning in the 1993 MLB season. For an expansion fee paid to the league of $95 million, the Colorado Rockies signed a lease to perform its home games at Mile High Stadium as planned in 1993–1994, or until the construction of the club's new ballpark, Coors Field, was completed in the Denver area.

Before the Rockies had played its first MLB game, an accounting and embezzlement scandal occurred in 1992 at Phar-Mor. As a result, two prominent members of the Rockies' ownership group resigned from the team's organization and then sold their shares of the franchise to some other investors. The individuals who resigned were Ohio beverage distributor John Antonucci and Phar-Mor's chief executive officer, Michael I. Monus. Because of their decision to abandon the Rockies, trucking company executive Jerry McMorris replaced them. Thus he became the head of the new franchise's ownership group and also the spokesperson of the team's management. Unfortunately, McMorris' trucking business failed in 1999 and furthermore, he had disagreements and serious disputes with other members of the franchise's syndicate. So in 2005, McMorris' interest in the club was purchased by others in the group. Three years later, businessmen Charlie and Dick Monfort gained control of the Rockies.

Despite a number of ownership problems during several years since 1993, baseball's Rockies has been as popular in Denver as the NFL Broncos, NBA Nuggets and NHL Rockies. To be sure, this MLB club set attendance records at home games in 1993 and again in 1995 through 1998, and also has gradually established a large fan base in the area. In retrospect, MLB made a prudent and wise decision in approving an expansion team for the Denver area in 1991. Although the franchise has experienced some troubles because of problems among its previous owners, the executive management and current leaders of the team's operations seem to have stabilized the Rockies and improved its opportunities to be a profitable business enterprise and successful entertainment company.

The next major task, of course, is for the NL Rockies to win a West Division title, another league pennant, and its first World Series. To accomplish that goal, the club needs to defeat the Los Angeles Dodgers, San Diego Padres, and San Francisco Giants in games at their ballparks and also to win more games played at Coors Field. In the next section of this chapter, there will be more information about performances of the Colorado Rockies and six other NL expansion teams.

MIAMI.   During early 1990, Blockbuster Entertainment Corporation's chief executive officer H. Wayne Huizenga spent an estimated $30 million when he purchased 15 percent of the NFL Dolphins and 50 percent of this professional football team's home facility, that is, 75,000-seat Joe Robbie Stadium. Also, Huizenga announced to the media that he wanted to acquire, invest in, and own an MLB franchise and then locate it in the Miami area. Meanwhile, MLB had stated its goal of increasing the NL from 12 to 14 clubs for the 1993 season. A major concern of Huizenga's, however, was to convince the league of his experience and expertise, and that the best place to locate a new baseball team was in Miami rather than at another site in the Orlando or Tampa Bay areas.

After successfully presenting a bid to a committee of MLB team owners, for a fee of $95 million the NL then awarded Huizenga an expansion franchise that would be based in Miami. That decision meant that $100 million Joe Robbie Stadium—later renamed Pro Player Park, Pro Player Stadium, and now Dolphin Stadium—had to be converted from being a building for football games to a multipurpose facility. Since the Dolphins' founder Joe

Robbie anticipated that a professional baseball team would eventually find a home based in Miami, he ensured that his stadium had an extremely wide field to accommodate future baseball games. As a result, some seats in Joe Robbie Stadium were placed more than 800 feet from home plate while seats in the upper deck of the facility had locations far away from the ball field. Consequently, Huizenga renovated the stadium by reducing its capacity for baseball games from 67,000 to approximately 44,000 and then later to about 36,000. Anyway, within three years after naming his baseball team the Florida Marlins, Huizenga had purchased the remaining 85 percent of the Dolphins and the other 50 percent of Joe Robbie Stadium.

Another issue that affected Huizenga and his new team was the excessively hot and humid summers in south Florida. Indeed, these conditions made it very uncomfortable or even unbearable for most spectators who attended the Marlins' games during afternoons of weekdays and weekends. To solve this particular problem, Huizenga received a waiver from MLB and the Entertainment Sports Programming Network (ESPN) that allowed his team to play some of its home games during Sunday evenings. Years before the Marlins requested and received its waiver, the Texas Rangers had obtained a similar agreement from big league baseball regarding a portion of its weekend games at Ameriquest Field in Arlington.

To conclude this section of Chapter 2, the seventh and final NL expansion franchise—and a discussion of its local and regional markets for professional baseball—is discussed next. Then, this is followed by reviewing the performances of this team and the Marlins, and also the other five NL clubs that had been established before them.

PHOENIX. Since the 1940s, the Phoenix area has tremendously increased its population and also served as a spring training site for various MLB teams. Because of those advantages, an attempt to host a big league club in the area occurred during the late 1980s when the owners of an AAA minor-league team and an affiliate of the San Francisco Giants named the Phoenix Firebirds asked the NFL Cardinals' owner, Bill Bidwill, to share a proposed 70,000-seat domed stadium in the city. That request failed after Bidwill signed a lease with Arizona State University to use Sun Devil Stadium as a home football field when his Cardinals had moved from St. Louis to Phoenix in 1988.

Then in 1993 the majority owner of the NBA Suns, Jerry Colangelo, announced to the media that he had assembled a group named Arizona Baseball, Inc., that would apply for an MLB expansion franchise. After two years of work on a comprehensive and detailed proposal, the group submitted its bid to the league in early 1995. In turn, the bid received enthusiastic support from Chicago White Sox and Chicago Bulls owner Jerry Reinsdorf and from the acting baseball commissioner, Bud Selig. In part, the bid impressed them because Colangelo and Reinsdorf were good friends, but also because it

Left: When baseball's troubled National Association folded in 1875, businessman and Chicago White Stockings president William Hulbert met with officials from seven other teams at the Grand Central Hotel in New York City. At that meeting, Hulbert led this group to establish the National League of Professional Baseball Clubs. In the organization's first season, the Chicago White Stockings won a pennant. During 1877 to 1882, Hulbert served as president of the league. [National Baseball Hall of Fame Library, Cooperstown, N.Y.] *Right:* Between 1951 and 1968, Buzzie Bavasi was the general manager of the Brooklyn and then Los Angeles Dodgers. When the National League decided to expand in 1968→1969, he resigned from the Dodgers and became part owner and president of the newly-formed San Diego Padres. Later, Gene Autry hired Bavasi to be vice president and general manager of the California Angels. Two years after the Angels won a West Division title in 1982, Bavasi retired from baseball. [National Baseball Hall of Fame Library, Cooperstown, N.Y.]

included plans for the construction of a retractable roof stadium to be nicknamed Bank One Ballpark.

After MLB evaluated this and other offers, Colangelo's group was awarded a new franchise for the 1998 season. As a result, this decision required that these investors had to pay an entry fee of $130 million to MLB. Initially, the expansion team was assigned to the AL's West Division. However, for business, demographic and sport-specific reasons, Colangelo insisted his team play in the NL West Division. First, Phoenix was located near San Diego and not too far away from Denver and Los Angeles; second, similar demographic characteristics existed between the fast-growing economies and populations of Denver and Phoenix; third, tourists from San Diego had visited areas within southwest Arizona for decades; fourth, a history of relationships had developed between the Firebirds in Phoenix and Giants in San Francisco; and fifth, for years hundreds of baseball games of the Dodgers, Giants, and Padres had been broadcast into the markets of Phoenix and Tucson. In short, these factors convinced MLB officials to place Colangelo's franchise in the NL's West Division.

To identify the new team, Colangelo's ownership group held a name-the-team contest that appeared in early 1995 on a full page of the *Arizona Republic*. For a prize of two lifetime season tickets to the team's home games, the choice of the winning entry was Diamondbacks, which referred to a species of snake that injected large amounts of venom into its victims. Based on that nickname, Colangelo wanted to promote and market the expansion club to a statewide fan base and not limit its appeal to one city or area. So, he decided to call his team the Arizona Diamondbacks and not the Phoenix Diamondbacks. This was a clever strategy since fans in other areas of the state embraced the word Arizona in the team's title rather than the state's largest city and its capital, Phoenix.

Some other plans of the expansion franchise involved the city of Tucson. Being a 90-minute drive

In 1960 businesswoman, heiress, and sports enthusiast Joan Whitney Payson headed a syndicate that purchased an expansion franchise for approximately $2 million from the National League. Named the New York Mets, Payson was active in the club's affairs as its president from 1968 to 1975. Being the first woman to serve as majority owner of a team within a major North American sports league, she was inducted posthumously into the Mets' Hall of Fame in 1981. [National Baseball Hall of Fame Library, Cooperstown, N.Y.]

from Phoenix, Tucson became home of the Diamondbacks' spring training camp; also, the city hosted the Tucson Sidewinders, which was the Diamondbacks' top minor league affiliate. To generate an interest in the franchise from baseball fans in other areas of the southwest besides Phoenix and Tucson, the Diamondbacks signed broadcast deals with radio stations and television networks based in several cities such as Flagstaff and Prescott in Arizona, and Las Vegas in Nevada.

Other innovations of the new team implemented during the mid–1990s and early 2000s included motor coach trips for fans from Tucson to Bank One Ballpark to attend the Diamondbacks' home games, and public appearances by various sports broadcasters, management representatives, and a number of players before midsized and small groups in communities within Arizona. In short, Colangelo's vision was to expand the team's market far beyond the Phoenix area. According to some officials in baseball, he succeeded.

During various years from the early to mid–1960s to the early 2000s, the seven NL expansion franchises highlighted in this section were relatively more popular in their respective markets and also prosperous business investments for MLB and team owners than were their seven counterparts in the AL (see Chapter 1). Indeed, the AL Senators relocated to Minneapolis after existing for 11 years in Washington, D.C., while the Pilots folded in Seattle after one season, and in 1970, the club filed for bankruptcy and then was moved to Milwaukee. Although the Angels relocated from Los Angeles to Anaheim in 1965, the other four AL clubs have each remained at their original sites. In contrast to those franchises in the AL, the seven new clubs in the NL had each struggled in various years since expansion, but for one reason or another, they recovered and thus, each of them has continued to perform at home games during most seasons before millions of baseball fans from within their cities and surrounding regions.

NL EXPANSION TEAMS PERFORMANCES

Pre–1901

Established in 1878 as new teams, the Indianapolis Blues and Milwaukee Grays each performed for one season in the NL and then disbanded (see Table 2.4). The Blues finished fifth in a six-team league while the Grays won 25 of its games and ended the season in sixth place. The only player of these two teams among the league's leaders in hitting and pitching was the Grays' leftfielder Abner Dalrymple. In fact, he had the NL's highest batting average at .354 and also led his team in doubles, runs, and slugging percentage. Also founded in 1878, the Providence Grays had the league's highest winning percentage and the team won NL pennants in 1879 and 1884. Besides these two championships, the Grays also finished its seasons in

second or third in 1878, and again in 1880 through 1883. Providence's greatest players in one or more of these years included pitchers Charles Radbourn, Charlie Sweeney, and Monte Ward. Interestingly, in 1879 an African American baseball player from Brown University in the U.S. named William Edward White played one game for the Providence Grays. After a fourth place finish in the 1985 season, this Rhode Island-based club folded because of being located in a small market and also due to its financial problems. In short, Providence was perhaps the best team that played in the NL at least prior to 1901.

In 1879, four expansion teams joined the NL. The Buffalo Bisons and Cleveland Blues had the best performances of them while the Syracuse Stars and Troy Trojans each played poorly during their few seasons in the league. The former two clubs won more than 45 percent of their games but did not win a NL pennant. Alternatively, the Stars' batting average equaled .227 in

Table 2.4 National League Expansion Teams
Number of Seasons and Performances, Selected Years

Pre-1901	Year	Seasons	Win-Loss	Pennants
Indianapolis Blues	1878	1	40.0	0
Milwaukee Grays	1878	1	25.0	0
Providence Grays	1878	8	60.9	2
Buffalo Bisons	1879	7	48.7	0
Cleveland Blues	1879	6	45.1	0
Syracuse Stars	1879	1	31.4	0
Troy Trojans	1879	4	40.8	0
Worcester Ruby Legs	1880	3	36.2	0
Detroit Wolverines	1881	8	48.6	1
New York Gothams/Giants	1883	18	55.1	2
Philadelphia Quakers/Phillies	1883	18	51.2	0
Kansas City Cowboys	1886	1	24.8	0
Washington Nationals	1886	4	32.4	0
Indianapolis Hoosiers	1887	3	36.8	0
Cleveland Spiders	1889	11	44.5	0

Post-1900	Year		Divisions	Pennants	World Series
Houston Colt .45s/Astros	1962	47	7	1	0
New York Mets	1962	47	4	4	2
Montreal Expos	1969	36	2	0	0
San Diego Padres	1969	40	5	2	0
Colorado Rockies	1993	16	0	1	0
Florida Marlins	1993	16	0	2	2
Arizona Diamondbacks	1998	11	4	1	1

Note: Team is self-explanatory. Year is a team's first season in the National League or its expansion year. The column Seasons is the total number of baseball seasons of each team in the National League during Pre–1901 or Post-1900. Win-Loss is each team's average winning percentage during its history. The initial World's Series between the winner of the American League and National League was played in 1903. Major League Baseball teams did not play in divisions until 1969. Divisions, Pennants, and World Series are each the number of titles won by these teams since their expansion year. The New York Gothams became the Giants in 1885, the Philadelphia Quakers changed its nickname to Phillies in 1890, and the Houston Colt .45s was renamed the Houston Astros in 1964.

Source: The World Almanac and Book of Facts, 1930–2007; "World Series History," at http://www. baseball-reference.com, accessed 8 September 2008; "Teams," at http://www.mlb.com, accessed 12 September 2008.

1879 when the team finished seventh in the league while the Trojans had existed for four seasons and played their home games at three different ballparks in Troy, which is an area located in upstate New York. The Stars did not play a full schedule of games and then disbanded in 1879, and four years later, the New York Gothams replaced the Trojans with some of the latter team's players transferring from Troy to New York.

During the early 1880s, four new clubs became members of the NL. The most prominent of them were the New York Gothams and Philadelphia Quakers. On average, they won more than 53 percent of their games between

1883 and 1900, and then after the Gothams became known as the Giants in 1885, this New York-based club earned NL pennants in 1888 and 1889. But in 1890, the Giants team finished a distant sixth after its best players had moved to the Players League, whose club from New York was also nicknamed the Giants. As a result, the NL Giants' home attendance plummeted in games played at the Polo Grounds and that forced owner John Day to sell a share of his franchise to other investors. The Quakers—later Phillies—meanwhile ended in second place in the NL's 1887 season but in its other 17 years finished between third and tenth inclusive.

The other two NL expansion teams of the early 1880s consisted of the Worcester Ruby Legs and Detroit Wolverines. In three seasons, the Ruby Legs won approximately 36 percent of its games although one of the team's players, John Lee Redmond, had pitched baseball's first perfect game against the Cleveland Blues in 1880. Then in August of that season, the Buffalo Bisons' Pud Galvin threw the league's first no-hit game to defeat the Ruby Legs 1–0. When Worcester's club dropped from the NL in 1882, one year later the Philadelphia Quakers replaced it although the two of them had no interaction or mutual relationship.

Regarding the expansion team in Detroit, the Wolverines won a league pennant in 1887 and then beat the American Association's champion St. Louis Browns 10–5 in a 15-game series. Two years earlier, however, Wolverines owner Frederick Kimball Stearns became reckless and purchased the entire Buffalo Bisons franchise. In turn, that transaction caused the NL to amend its rules and thereby limit any visiting team's maximum share of gate receipts to no more than $125 per game. Unable to sustain his team's payroll from its receipts at home game, Stearns sold his best players to other clubs after the 1888 season.

Between 1886 and 1889 inclusive, the final four expansion clubs entered the NL during the pre–1901 era. First, the Kansas City Cowboys played one season including competitors at home in Association Park. Nevertheless, the team finished more than 58 games behind the first-place Chicago White Stockings. As a result of its poor performance, the Cowboys disbanded in late 1886. Second, the Washington Nationals used six different managers in four NL seasons and compiled a total win-loss record of 163–337. Catcher Connie Mack played for the Nationals and so did a deaf outfielder named Dummy Hoy. After finishing eighth in the NL during 1888–1889, the franchise folded its operation.

Third, the Indianapolis Hoosiers placed eighth and then seventh twice while performing for three consecutive seasons in the league. During these years, the Hoosiers' two best players were Jack Glasscock, who led the NL with 205 hits in 1889, and also that season pitcher Henry Boyle won 21 games. Because of poor attendance at home and low gate receipts, the Hoosiers became the second expansion franchise from Indianapolis to fail in the NL.

Fourth, after two dismal seasons as a team in the American Association, the Cleveland Spiders shifted into the NL in 1889. Although Cleveland never won a pennant in the latter league, the Spiders played well enough to finish second to the Boston Beaneaters in 1892 and then three years later, defeat the NL champion Baltimore Orioles to win a Temple Cup. Even so, after the Spiders' owners had acquired the NL's St. Louis Perfectos in 1899 and also transferred all of the former team's stars from Cleveland to St. Louis, the Spiders club that year won only 20 games and lost 40 of its final 41. In fact during the season of 1899, the other 11 NL teams refused to perform in Cleveland so the Spiders had to play mostly road games, and consequently lost 109 of them.

While competing at home in its local ballpark, Cleveland's attendance per game amounted to 179 fans. Because of its embarrassing performance in 1899, the twelfth-place Spiders was removed from the NL along with teams based in Baltimore, Louisville, and Washington that had finished their season, respectively, in fourth, ninth and eleventh place. In part, the departure of the Spiders, Orioles, Colonels, and Senators led to the end of the NL's monopoly and also the emergence, popularity, and success of the AL, and then in 1901, to the formation of MLB.

To review expansion in the NL between 1876 and 1900 inclusive, the 15 new baseball teams on average had each played about six years and won approximately 41 percent of their regular season games, and in total, earned five pennants. The three most successful of these clubs were the small-market Providence Grays and big-market New York Gothams (renamed Giants) and Philadelphia Quakers (later Phillies). Alternatively, the three most inferior clubs—each located in a low or midsized populated area—included the Kansas City Cowboys, Milwaukee Grays, and Syracuse Stars. On average, these teams played in one NL season and won about 27 percent of their games.

With respect to the other nine NL expansion franchises, their proportion of wins varied from a high of 44.5 percent for the Cleveland Spiders to a low of 32.4 percent for the Washington Nationals. Because of tiny attendances at home games and not enough gate receipts from them, and also due to a lack of financial capital, ownership problems and dilapidated ballparks, it was only the New York Giants and Philadelphia Phillies that continued to exist and perform as teams in the NL after 1900.

Post-1900

The lower portion of Table 2.4 reveals the on-field performances of seven NL expansion teams since their first season in MLB. As such, each baseball league was restructured in 1969 and divided into three divisions—East, Central and West. Therefore these seven teams' performances differed somewhat from those of the 15 NL expansion clubs that had played during the late

1800s when a title consisted of a pennant since no World Series existed then. As they are listed in the table, the following is an overview of the performances of each NL team that had been an expansion franchise after 1901.

Between 1962 and 2008, the Houston Colt .45s (later Astros) made two appearances in the league's playoffs as a wild card, won four Central and three West Division titles, and then a pennant in 2005. Before that year, the club had been defeated in three NL championship series, that is, by the Phillies in 1980, Mets in 1986, and Cardinals in 2004. Houston's greatest players have included such former pitchers as Joe Niekro, Nolan Ryan and Roger Clemens, such hitters as Craig Biggio, Jeff Bagwell and Jose Cruz, and such managers as Bill Virdon, Harry Walker and Larry Dierker. In turn, the club's highest attendances occurred at 40,950-seat Minute Maid Park (previously named Enron Field) in 2000 and 2004 when more than three million spectators enjoyed watching the Astros play games at home during these two seasons.

With respect to its all-time winning percentage among MLB's several expansion teams, the team in Houston ranks second to the Arizona Diamondbacks and slightly ahead of the Kansas City Royals and Toronto Blue Jays. In the end, Houston's place in professional baseball history will be remembered because of such innovations as being the first franchise to play indoor games in the major leagues and also for playing games on Astroturf.

Since 1962, the various New York Mets teams have qualified for two playoffs as a wild card, won four each East Division titles and NL pennants, and a World Series in 1969 and again in 1986. The club's most popular athletes include such great and well known performers as former pitchers Tom Seaver, Dwight Gooden and John Franco, batters Mike Piazza, Darryl Strawberry and Dave Kingman, and managers Dave Johnson, Bobby Valentine and Gil Hodges. While playing its home games in 56,750-seat Shea Stadium, the Mets' attendances exceeded three million each in 1987 and 1988. Among all of MLB's expansion teams, the Mets' winning share of regular season games has been approximately 47 percent, and that share ranks it ninth. During the early 2000s, the Mets significantly increased its payroll by signing talented free agents and experienced veteran players. As a result, the club will continue to challenge the Braves, Marlins, Nationals, and Phillies for an East Division title.

Between 1969 and 2004, the Montreal Expos played its home games in 28,000-seat Jarry Park for eight seasons and then in 46,000-seat Olympic Stadium for 28 years. At games played in the latter ballpark, the club set an attendance record in 1979 with 2.1 million and again in 1980 with 2.2 million, and then in 1982 and 1983 each with more than 2.3 million. Meanwhile, the Expos won an East Division title in 1981 and 1994, but never earned a pennant or World Series.

To remain solvent, the franchise in Montreal needed to repeatedly sell its high-priced and outstanding players to other clubs. Thus, even though it developed very good players in its farm system, the Expos lacked the financial capital and fan support to retain these athletes when their contracts expired, and they had applied for free agency. Anyway, the most memorable Expos included such excellent pitchers as Pedro Martinez, Steve Rogers and Dennis Martinez, hitters as Andre Dawson, Gary Carter and Vladimir Guerrero, and managers as Buck Rogers, Dick Williams, and Frank Robinson.

After MLB acquired the franchise from its owners and the team played some of its home games in Puerto Rico rather than Montreal, the Expos was sold in 2004–2005 to a new ownership group who then moved the club to Washington, D.C. In short, the market in Montreal failed to support the Expos enough for the team to increase its home attendances above 2.3 million per season, win any championships, and prosper there as a baseball enterprise.

While performing in the NL's West Division since 1969, the San Diego Padres may be considered an inferior team in its performances. To be specific, the Padres have won only five West Division titles and also NL pennants in 1984 and 1998. At San Diego's 63,890-seat Jack Murphy Stadium (renamed Qualcomm Stadium) for 35 years and then at 42,000-seat Petco Park for another five, the club's five highest home attendances averaged about 2.5 million per season which puts it in the lower half of all NL teams. Besides not competing more often for a NL pennant or World Series, the Padres clubs have won about 45 percent of their total games. This percentage, in turn, ranks the club thirteenth among all MLB expansion teams and only ahead of the Tampa Bay Rays. The Padres' most impressive players have been pitchers Randy Jones, Trevor Hoffman and Jake Peavy, batters Dave Winfield, Tony Gwynn and Garry Templeton, and such managers as Jack McKeon, Dick Williams, and Bruce Bochy.

In short, San Diego is a team that rarely wins pennants because it exists in a relatively small area where there are few extremely passionate baseball fans but many households and businesses that prefer to support the NFL Chargers or a local baseball team in a minor league. Without a huge increase in its payroll and hiring more talented ballplayers, the Padres will struggle to defeat the Diamondbacks, Dodgers, Giants and Rockies, and win another West Division title.

Established in 1993, the Colorado Rockies qualified for the playoffs as a wild card in 1995, won a division title and NL pennant in 2007, but then lost the World Series that year to the Boston Red Sox in four games. During its 16-year history through 2008, the club's winning proportion of 47 percent places it eighth among MLB's post–1900 expansion franchises. Nevertheless, the NL Rockies are a popular club in the Denver area even though it competes for the expenditures of the area's sports fans with the NFL Broncos, NBA Nuggets, NHL Avalanche, and MLS Rockies. At 76,100-seat Mile High Stadium and now 50,450-seat Coors Field, the team has achieved its five highest attendances. That is, 4.4 million in 1993 and then between 3.3 million and 3.8 million during the mid–to late 1990s. The baseball Rockies' finest players have been Larry Walker, Todd Helton and Dante Bichette, and besides them, such managers as Don Baylor, Clint Hurdle, and Buddy Bell. Unless the NL Rockies' owners invest more resources in their team and also sign to-notch free agents and high-priced veterans to multiyear contracts, the franchise will not likely win another NL title or its first World Series for several MLB seasons.

While playing in the NL East since 1993, the Florida Marlins has never won a division title. Nevertheless, the club qualified as a wild card in 1997 and again in 2003, and then played outstanding baseball during these seasons to win two each NL pennants and World Series. These championships had occurred, in part, because owner H. Wayne Huizenga went on a spending spree and signed several talented but expensive players who excelled in regular- season and postseason games. At 36,300-seat Joe Robbie Stadium (now Dolphins Stadium) in Miami, the Marlins drew 3.1 million fans to its home games in 1993 and also 2.3 million in 1997, but fewer fans in 2003. As a 16-year-old team through 2008, the Marlins defeat other clubs in about 47 percent of their games, which ranks the franchise eleventh among all expansion teams.

During its history, the club's most productive personnel include such men as pitchers Kevin Brown, A.J. Burnett and Brad Penny, hitters Luis Castillo, Jeff Conine and Derek Lee, and managers Jack McKeon, Jim Leyland, and Rene Lachemann. To be more competitive against the large-market Mets and also the Braves, Nationals and Phillies, the Marlins desperately need more revenue streams from its market and ballpark. That is, the facility must be renovated or replaced with a modern building. Currently there are negotiations between the team and city for a new stadium to be funded and then constructed somewhere in the Miami area.[9]

To some experts in the sport, the most successful expansion team in MLB is the Arizona Diamondbacks. In its 11 seasons through 2008, the franchise has earned four West Division titles and in 2001, it won a NL pennant and World Series. Since the Diamondbacks' average about 82 victories each season, this number of wins ranks the club first among all expansion franchises in the AL and NL. The team's attendance at 49,100-seat Bank One Ballpark in Phoenix exceeded, for example, 2.8 million in 2003, 2.9 million in 2000, and three million each in 1998, 1999 and 2002.

For the most part, an important reason for the Diamondback's accomplishments in MLB seasons since 1998 have been the contributions of pitchers Randy Johnson, Byung-Hyun Kim and Greg Swindell, batters Luis Gonzalez, Steve Finley and Tony Womack, and managers Bob Brenly, Buck Showalter and Al Pedrique. Because Johnson is near his retirement age, the Diamondbacks will rely on such ballplayers as pitcher Brandon Webb and slugger Luis Gonzalez to excel in regular season games and defeat its rivals in the NL's West Division, which include the Dodgers, Giants, Padres, and Rockies.

This concludes my discussion of the performances of 22 NL expansion teams from when they began to compete in the league. To complete the core contents of this chapter, the next section presents a concise historical review of baseball markets during the NL's various expansion years of the late 1800s and mid–to late 1900s. The intent of that section, and its relationship to expansion in baseball, is to denote where and to what extent the sport's markets had developed and prospered within urban places and cities of North America. As described before, the rank in population of these various places or cities is contained in parentheses, such as New York (1) and Philadelphia (2).

MAJOR BASEBALL MARKETS, NL EXPANSION YEARS

1870s

For business, demographic and sport-specific reasons, the NL expanded in 1878 and located new teams in midsized urban places such as Indianapolis (24), Milwaukee (19), and Providence (20), and then in 1879 into relatively higher-ranked places such as Buffalo (13) and Cleveland (11), and also into less populated places such as Syracuse (32) and Troy (29). In fact, within a few years after the National Association had failed in 1875, it was NL teams based in New York (1), Philadelphia (2), Hartford (43), Louisville (16), and St. Louis (6) that did not comply with the league's rules, for example, because their players cheated and fixed games, or they lacked enough financial capital within their organizations to continue in operation, experienced ownership problems, or simply could not compete against the professional baseball clubs located in Boston (5), Cincinnati (8), and Chicago (4). As a result, the former five teams either withdrew from the NL or were removed by league officials and then replaced with franchises located in other markets.

Between 1876 and 1879, the entry and exit of several clubs from different urban places suggests that some baseball markets in the U.S. were underdeveloped then, and therefore, unable or unwilling to financially support a NL franchise beyond one to eight years. This means that to exist and continue to perform during and after these four seasons in the league, professional baseball teams needed to attract groups of new fans to their ballparks by being competitive, playing a full schedule of games, and providing sports entertainment within their communities and regions.

In other words, most local markets for baseball were temporary sites and especially vulnerable to scandals, the unethical behavior of managers, owners and players, and to inferior athletes who selfishly played the game for money rather than as teammates. So from 1876 to 1879, the only NL clubs to remain solvent for these four seasons included the Boston Red Stockings, Chicago White Stockings, and Cincinnati Red Stockings. As such, each of these franchises had existed then in baseball's three most stable markets.

1880s

During this ten-year period, eight more expansion teams entered the NL, and except for the Indianapolis Hoosiers and Cleveland Spiders, they each played their home games in different urban places than the clubs that joined the league within the 1870s. Besides the new franchises in Indianapolis (27) and Cleveland (10), the rank in population of the other six baseball markets of the expansion teams were Worcester (28), Detroit (18), New York (1), Philadelphia (2), Kansas City (24), and Washington (14). Concurrently, the rival American Association (AA) was formed in 1882, Union Association (UA) in 1884, and then six years later, the Players League (PL).

During the ten-year, one-year, and again one-year tenures, respectively, of each of these three baseball organizations, a few of their teams played at home sites in areas already occupied by various expansion and other NL teams throughout the 1880s. For example, the AA had at least one club in one or more of its ten seasons based in Boston, New York, Philadelphia, and St. Louis (see Table A.2.1); the UA in Boston, Chicago, and Philadelphia for one season; and the PL for one season in Boston, Chicago, Cleveland, New York, Philadelphia, and Pittsburgh. As a result of invading each other's home markets, only the AA's Baltimore, Cincinnati, Louisville, and Philadelphia franchises existed from 1892 to 1891, whereas the UA folded after its 1884 season and so did the PL following its 1890 season. In short, the 1880s were years when some of the NL's existing teams had to compete for local sports fans with clubs from other professional baseball leagues.

As denoted in Table 2.4, 13 of the NL's pre–1901 expansion teams played from one to 11 years but then ceased to exist and disbanded because of financial difficulties, mergers of professional baseball leagues, poor attendances at their home games and lack of support from local sports fans, loss of players who had transferred from one team to another, and other issues. In short, the New York Gothams (Giants) and Philadelphia Quakers (Phillies) were the only two NL expansion teams that survived the competition, risk, and turmoil within the sport during the late 1800s and continued as clubs in MLB.

1960s

Within this second ten-year period of expansion, two teams each joined the NL in 1962 and 1969. During the former expansion year, it was the Colt .45s in Houston (17) and Mets in New York (1), and in 1969, the new clubs were the Expos in Montreal (2) and Padres in San Diego (23). After a few teams in MLB had successfully moved to other markets during the 1950s, the league's expansion committee decided to approve the entry of new franchises and agreed to them being located in these four cities.

Furthermore the NL had two fewer teams than the AL in 1961 and so to rebalance these organizations one year later, Houston in southeast Texas appeared to be an attractive and open baseball market for a new team while the New York area had more than enough people and also above-average income per capita and positive economic growth. Moreover, New York sport fans would generously support another MLB club after the Dodgers and Giants each left there in 1958 for the West Coast. Lastly, the Continental League had plans to place one of its clubs in Houston and another in New York. In fact, similar but not identical demographic and economic reasons existed for expansion within Montreal of southeast Canada and in the San Diego area of southern California.

Given my research of the sport, the NL's strategies to finally expand by two clubs each during the early and late 1960s were smart and well-timed decisions. That is because professional baseball within the U.S. and in some provinces of Canada had become increasingly popular such that the demand for MLB teams exceeded the supply of them within several major cities. Meanwhile, to maintain their dominance as leagues, the NBA, NFL, and NHL had also experienced competition and challenges from the entry of new leagues into their sport which, in turn, had forced MLB to react and expand in size during the 1960s.

In other words, after the movements of some big league teams throughout the 1950s and the economic growth and development within areas of the U.S. and in provinces of Canada, and also despite decisions by other professional sports leagues to increase the number of their franchises—while for several decades the NL consisted of eight clubs—it was an optimal time for MLB to become more aggressive and permit the entry of new clubs in four different markets. It would be more than 20 years, however, before the NL would expand again.

1990s

During the NL's third ten-year expansion era, two clubs entered the league in 1993 and another one in 1998. With respect to the former year, it had been 24 years since the league had expanded in 1969. With Denver's population greater than 1.6 million and Miami's above four million during the early 1990s, NL officials unanimously agreed that a new baseball team would thrive in eastern Colorado and also another one in southern Florida. Furthermore, between 1990 and 2000, the population of the Denver and Miami areas had each increased by more than 23 percent.

Consequently the economies, fans, and markets of the NFL Broncos, NBA Nuggets, and NHL Avalanche in Denver, and the NFL Dolphins, NBA Heat, and NHL Panthers in Miami had provided average to above-average financial returns for the owners of these sports franchises. As a result, two business syndicates were willing to risk their resources and financial capital, invest in the sport of baseball, and thus finance the operations of professional teams that were then and now nicknamed, respectively, the Colorado Rockies and Florida Marlins.

Similarly, the Phoenix area had hosted NFL, NBA, and NHL clubs before 1998. So because of this market's expanding population—which exceeded three million during the mid-to late 1990s—MLB realized that an opportunity existed in southwest Arizona for another professional sports team to locate there. Since a few minor-league baseball clubs and also some MLB team's spring training camps for decades had sites and played games within or near the city of Phoenix, the NL decided to award a franchise to a group led by Jerry Colangelo and then allow his club to play its home games in that area of Arizona. Fortunately from 1998 to 2008, the Arizona Diamondbacks have performed before capacity or near-capacity crowds in their regular season games held at Bank One Ballpark. In the end, a booming national economy during the late 1990s was an appropriate period for the NL to expand into the Phoenix area and provide professional baseball to sports fans in that community and region.

SUMMARY

Based on readings contained in the literature and other sources in this chapter, the NL added a total of 22 teams in various markets between the late 1870s and second half of the 1990s. Relative to the 15 expansions in the league that occurred before 1901, two clubs survived and remained in their areas while the other 13 folded within 11 seasons. On average these 15 teams each had existed for about six years, and won approximately 42 percent of their regular season games and also a total of five NL pennants. In contrast, the seven expansion teams of the post–1900 period averaged more than 30 years at their respective sites, and through 2008, had won a total of 22 division titles, 11 pennants, and five World Series. In sum, there have been no expansion teams to fail in the NL since the late 1890s.

In contrast to the number of new clubs which have performed for many years in the AL, this chapter indicates that the majority of NL expansion teams—since being established between the early 1960s and late 1990s—have been marginally more competitive, prosperous, and successful in their respective home markets. Simply put, the latter league's expansion franchises in Houston, Montreal, New York, San Diego, Denver, Miami, and Phoenix have made a larger and more profound contribution to the image, popularity, and prestige of MLB during their lifetime of seasons than did the AL expansion clubs within their areas of Kansas City, Los Angeles, Seattle (twice), Tampa Bay, Toronto and Washington.

3

American League
Team Relocation

In American professional team sports, there are a variety of leagues. Each of these leagues, in turn, consists of several franchises that exist as enterprises in cities within small, midsized, large, or very large cities. To operate as professional sports organizations and also as business groups, leagues must establish, implement, and enforce various rules that govern the activities of their member franchises whose primary objective according to economists is to maximize economic profit or minimize loss. Two historical requirements and most significant tasks of each sports league—which is essentially controlled by a commissioner and current franchise owners—are that it must evaluate and approve or reject expansion into existing or new markets, as discussed in Chapters 1 and 2, and also the movements of any of its current teams into familiar other territories, as analyzed in this chapter and Chapter 4.

Because sports markets are different demographically and geographically across the United States (U.S.) and Canada with respect to their location, quality and size, these variations create opportunities but also economic and financial problems for franchises and especially those that exist in small and midsized areas. That is, these enterprises are unlikely to earn enough revenues from their home games and other operations to effectively compete against their rivals and consistently win titles and other championships in any seasons of a league.

As denoted in Chapters 1 and 2 of this book, respectively, since the early 1900s in the American League (AL) of Major League Baseball (MLB) and late 1800s in the National League (NL), some big league teams had to disband after one or more seasons of performances while others withdrew from the AL or NL, or had to merge and consolidate their rosters of players, or they simply transferred to another professional baseball league, renamed themselves, and then played at home in a new or renovated ballpark. In fact, during several years of the twentieth and early twenty-first centuries, similar circumstances, conditions, and events had also affected and determined the success or failure of several clubs in the National Basketball Association

(NBA), National Football League (NFL), National Hockey League (NHL), and Major League Soccer (MLS).[1]

Rather than disband, merge and consolidate, or secede and transfer, another option available for the owners of some inferior, unpopular, or unprofitable teams was for them to request—from other existing owners in a professional baseball league—the right to leave their current headquarters and ballparks within a specific city and relocate to a site in a different urban place or metropolitan area of North America. Although this activity has not occurred very often, relocation is certainly a way that some baseball franchises in the AL and NL have temporarily or permanently recovered financially, and then survived for one or more years as businesses within populated markets which contained a larger and enthusiastic fan base and greater potential to generate revenues. Alternatively, for a number of demographic, economic, and sport-specific reasons, a few baseball franchises in the AL and NL had decided to move to another area but nevertheless, they failed to accomplish their goals in the short or long run and thus eventually folded as enterprises and abandoned the professional sports business.

In this and the next chapter, I will reveal to what extent relocation has occurred during the history of MLB. To support my discussion with various historical facts, each chapter contains a few tables of data which, in part, identify the particular baseball teams that had relocated and also reveal some information about their former and new areas as sports markets. Furthermore, the tables indicate how well they performed in games prior to and after their movement. Finally, I provide the reasons for—and consequences of—their owners' decision to abandon one market for another in a metropolitan area. Besides these matters and topics, the two chapters will also explain why some AL and NL clubs did not move from their original areas whether they were located in small, midsized, large, or very large markets.

In contrast, I decided to not discuss in great detail—or elaborate too much about—some of the theoretical issues that relate to relocation of franchises in professional baseball. These issues are, first, that playing strengths and profits are concentrated in the big-city teams of a professional sports league; second, that franchise moves emerge simply as a device to permit small-city teams to capture short run profits in a new market; and third, that fans in small cities can expect little protection from franchise moves as a result of self-regulation by a typical sports league. According to the research performed by James Quirk and Rodney D. Fort in "An Economic Analysis of Team Movements in Professional Sports," these issues are truths in reality about relocations in MLB based on the data they had collected and reported for the years 1946 to 1972.[2]

Given these general but necessary and important remarks beforehand about what will and will not be covered in different sections, Chapter 3 discusses the relocation of teams in the AL since 1901. The first item, however, is a brief review of a minor league based in the U.S. that existed during the mid–to late 1890s, and essentially how it had evolved into being renamed the AL. Then, the remaining parts of this chapter will focus on team relocations because it is one of the two most relevant topics of interest (besides expansion) for those who read this book.

WESTERN LEAGUE

As mentioned in Chapter 1, a minor-league baseball organization named the Western League (WL) was formed during the late 1870s within the U.S. but then it expired a few years later because of internal corruption and leadership problems. Even so, at a business meeting held in late 1893, Ban Johnson successfully revived the WL and became its president. Johnson, the son of a college professor and as a sportswriter for the Cincinnati *Commercial-Gazette*, was recommended to head the league by his friend and NL Cincinnati Reds manager Charles Comiskey. So in that year, the WL had officially organized with teams from eight different urban places. Originally, the home areas of these eight clubs and their rank in population (stated as numbers in parentheses) then were Detroit (15), Milwaukee (16), Minneapolis (18), Kansas City (24), Indianapolis (27), Toledo (34), Grand Rapids (47), and Sioux City (78). In short, the WL's teams decided to exist and play their games in ballparks that were located in small to midsized markets within seven Midwestern states of the U.S.[3]

Between 1894 and 1900 inclusive, a few owners of franchises in the WL (renamed AL in mid–to late 1899) moved their operations to different urban places. The names of these former clubs and their new homes, population rankings, and relocation years included the following: Sioux City Cornhuskers to St. Paul (23) in 1895, and then to Chicago (2) in 1900; Toledo White Stockings to Columbus (28) in 1896, and then to Buffalo (8) in 1899; Grand Rapids Rustlers to St. Joseph (34) and then Omaha (35) in 1898, and back to Grand Rapids (44) in 1899, and one year later, to Cleveland (7). Meanwhile, the league's Tigers team continued to perform at home in Detroit, and so did the Brewers in Milwaukee, Millers in Minneapolis, Blues in Kansas City, and Indians in Indianapolis. Consequently, three of the WL teams had moved to larger places while the other five remained to play home games in their original cities.

In short, during its multiple years as a minor baseball league, the WL struggled as a commercial organization although it gradually became a competitive threat and challenged the business of teams within the almighty and powerful NL. Indeed it was Johnson who had transformed his circuit into somewhat of a success in the early years of the sport. That is, he recognized, promoted, and supported the decisions of those who umpired WL games, insisted on a dignified, ethical, and righteous atmosphere among the league's member clubs and their respective owners, managers and players, and he provided a way for the WL to be renamed and eventually gain major league status in professional baseball. In fact, Johnson declined an opportunity in late 1899 to merge his league with a new American Association of teams which had met as a group that year in the city of Chicago. Consequently, after these events and the earlier movements of WL teams during the mid–to late 1890s, Johnson's AL opened its initial season in 1900 with clubs playing at home in Buffalo, Chicago, Cleveland, Detroit, Indianapolis, Kansas City, Milwaukee, and Minneapolis.

Before the AL became accepted among more sports officials and had performed as a major baseball league in 1901, several changes occurred among its member clubs. That is, teams in Buffalo, Indianapolis, Kansas City, and Minneapolis either voluntarily withdrew from the league or had been demoted or folded for financial reasons, while franchises based in Baltimore (6), Boston (5), Philadelphia (3), and Washington (15) each received permission from Johnson and his group of owners to join the AL. These changes, of course, led to the formation of MLB in 1901 and then two years later to an agreement that resulted in the NL completely recognizing Johnson's AL as an authentic major league and partner in the sport. Thus, any relocation of clubs in the AL is discussed in the following sections of this chapter as of 1901 and thereafter.

AL TEAM RELOCATIONS

Milwaukee→St. Louis

After four small to midsized market teams dropped out of the WL during the late 1800s and then its successor in early 1901, the AL's eight clubs played their games at home within urban places whose ranks in population ranged from second (Chicago) to fifteenth (Washington). Thus in 1901, the Detroit Tigers and Milwaukee Brewers were the only clubs from the former WL that continued to perform as MLB franchises in the AL. During the season of these two teams in the league, the Tigers finished third and placed second in attendance with more than 259,000 spectators at games played in 8,500-seat Bennett Park in Detroit. Meanwhile, the Brewers ended MLB's year in last place (eighth) and only about 139,000 people attended its home games at 10,000-seat Lloyd Street Grounds in Milwaukee. Because of these dismal results, Brewers' owners Henry and Matthew Killilea decided to sell their franchise sometime in 1901 or 1902 for $50,000 to a syndicate headed by businessman Robert Leed Hedges and his partners Ralph Orthwein and R. Gardner.

Unable to attract and excite enough baseball fans in the Milwaukee area, this syndicate then moved their franchise to St. Louis (4), which besides Chicago was the largest city that allowed ballgames to be played on Sundays (see Table 3.1). After being nicknamed exactly as an NL club that had played in St. Louis during the early to mid–1890s, the Browns played its home games at 30,500-seat Sportsman's Park and thus challenged the NL's St. Louis Cardinals for the support of baseball fans in that eastern Missouri market. In fact, the Browns' home attendance in the 1902 season was approximately 272,300—which ranked it fifth among the eight clubs in the AL—and 20 percent greater than the 226,400 that had attended Cardinals games in 14,500-seat Robison Field. Also, the Browns nearly won a pennant in 1902 by finishing second in the league while the Cardinals ended in sixth and more than 44 games behind the Pittsburgh Pirates.

Even though two MLB franchises had existed then in St. Louis, that area's population of 575,000 was much larger than places without a big league team such as Buffalo at 352,000, San Francisco at 342,000, and New Orleans at 287,000. In any event, for several years after 1902 the Browns had few winning seasons but nonetheless, the club frequently outdrew the NL Cardinals at home games and also attracted more fans than such AL teams as the Cleveland Indians, Detroit Tigers, and Washington Senators.

After evaluating these and other facts, it was a rational business decision for the franchise's new owners to move their operation in 1902 from Mil-

Table 3.1 Major League Baseball
American League Teams That Relocated, by Seasons,
Years and Areas, 1901–2008

Teams	Seasons	Years	Areas From	To
Milwaukee Brewers I	1901–1901	1902	Milwaukee	St. Louis
Baltimore Orioles I	1901–1902	1903	Baltimore	New York
St. Louis Browns	1902–1953	1954	St. Louis	Baltimore
Philadelphia Athletics	1901–1954	1955	Philadelphia	Kansas City
Washington Senators I	1901–1960	1961	Washington	Minneapolis
LA/California Angels	1961–1965	1966	Los Angeles	Anaheim
Kansas City Athletics	1955–1967	1968	Kansas City	Oakland
Seattle Pilots	1969–1969	1970	Seattle	Milwaukee
Washington Senators II	1961–1971	1972	Washington	Arlington

Note: Teams and Seasons of Major League Baseball are self-explanatory. Years are when teams relocated from one area to another and played their first season there. Each Area, in columns four and five, was classified as an urban place during the early 1900s, and later renamed as a Standard Metropolitan Statistical Area (SMSA). LA is Los Angeles.

Source: James Quirk and Rodney D. Fort, *Pay Dirt: The Business of Professional Team Sports* (Princeton, NJ: Princeton University Press, 1992), 399–409; *Official Major League Baseball Fact Book 2005 Edition* (St. Louis, MO: The Sporting News, 2005); "Teams," at http://www.mlb.com, accessed 12 September 2008.

waukee to the St. Louis area. The Brewers had previously struggled to win regular-season games while playing in the minor WL, failed to establish a large fan base there during the mid–to late 1890s, and in 1900–1901, the franchise was not profitable or prosperous as a baseball enterprise in southeastern Wisconsin. In contrast, the St. Louis area ranked fourth in population and contained thousands of people who loved baseball more than they did any other professional and amateur sport. Since in these years the AL was being transformed from a minor to a major league, this initial movement of an AL franchise from a city in the midwest to another place in eastern Missouri resulted in benefits for the league and also for other AL clubs with respect to their attendances, gate receipts, and popularity.[4]

Baltimore→New York

After the completion of its season in 1899, the NL reduced itself in size from 12 to eight teams. One of the clubs to be eliminated by the league in that year was the Baltimore Orioles. As a result, when Ban Johnson reorganized the AL in late 1900, he admitted the Baltimore Orioles, which was then managed by John McGraw and owned—for the most part—by Harry Goldstein, S. Mahon, and Sidney Frank. During the 1901 and 1902 seasons, respectively, the club had finished in fifth and eighth place in the league, and its attendances at Oriole Ballpark in Baltimore averaged 157,500 per season, which was the lowest average among eight AL clubs in these years. Furthermore, Johnson became enraged when McGraw secretly transferred himself as a manager of the Orioles to the same position for the NL New York Giants, and then he raided the Orioles roster to acquire its best players for his Giants team. Consequently, the AL intervened in this affair and assumed partial control of the Orioles' franchise.

It was not a surprise, therefore, that Goldstein and his group of investors offered their club for sale when the 1902 AL season had concluded. Therefore, within a few months, ex-saloonkeeper Frank Farrell and New York gambler Bill Devery headed a syndicate that purchased the Orioles for $18,000 from Goldstein and then appointed coal dealer Joseph Gordon to be a front man. Later, the syndicate installed him as the franchise's first president. Meanwhile, very early in 1903, AL and NL officials met to settle their disputes and attempt to coexist. One outcome of that conference was that the NL agreed to allow an AL team to exist and play at home somewhere in the New York area. So in response to this arrangement, Farrell moved the Orioles from Baltimore to Manhattan within the Big Apple and then renamed his club the New York Highlanders.

Before June of 1903, a rickety and wooden 15,000-seat stadium named Hilltop Park (or formally known as American League Park) had been constructed for $75,000 between 165th and 168th Streets in northern Manhattan, and only a few blocks away from the NL Giants' home ballpark, the Polo Grounds. With respect to games at its new local site in the New York area, the Highlanders franchise had received its nickname due to Hilltop Park's location on one of the island's highest points, and also because of a British military unit referred to as the Gordon Highlanders, which in turn relates to the club's president from 1903 to 1906, that is, Joseph Gordon. For several years the Highlanders team was sometimes called the New York Americans. Finally in 1913, that name was changed to the New York Yankees, who for the next ten years played its home games in the 38,000-seat Polo Grounds as tenants of the NL Giants.

The Highlanders soon became a popular and successful sports team in New York. For example, the club finished second in the AL seasons of 1904, 1906 and 1910. Also, after attracting only 211,000 to its home games in 1903, the club's attendance at Hilltop Park increased to more than 434,000 per season during 1904, 1906 and 1909, and continued to average between 242,000 and 620,000 each year after 1912 while playing at New York's Polo Grounds. Meanwhile in 1914, Colonel Tillinghast Huston and Jacob Ruppert purchased the Highlanders' franchise from Farrell and Devery for $460,000 and then eight years later, Ruppert acquired Huston's 50 percent portion of the team for $1.5 million.

The movement of this franchise from Baltimore to New York was a smart decision by its owners, especially after the Orioles had finished the 1902 season in eighth place. Indeed, there was no way that the club would survive for more than a few years in Baltimore because of its inferior performances within the league and some financial problems, and also due to the small number of passionate baseball fans who lived in that area. Even though the AL and several of its teams had struggled to become prominent baseball organizations during the early 1900s, the New York area was very capable and well-dispersed in size to support another MLB club besides the NL Giants. Interestingly, Ban Johnson's initial suspicion of and reluctance to negotiate with two questionable businessmen and shady characters like Farrell and Devery diminished after these individuals provided enough money to acquire the Orioles and move the club to New York, and then for them to assist in the construction of a new ballpark in Manhattan.

In short, the relocation of a team from Baltimore to New York in 1903 contributed to the AL being recognized as a major organization in the sport. If that move, alternatively, was made to a less-populated and lower-income area such as Buffalo, New Orleans or Newark, it would be decades before the league became as or more popular and prestigious than its counterpart or NL. In the next section of this chapter, I will discuss in more detail the performances of the Orioles, Highlanders and Yankees, and other AL clubs before and after they had relocated from one market in a region to another in a different area.[5]

St. Louis→Baltimore

During its 52 years while entertaining fans at home in St. Louis, the Browns were a very marginal and largely unsuccessful team. After being sold and then resold again between the mid–1910s and the late 1940s, a syndicate headed by Bill Veeck purchased more than 55 percent of the franchise and also the club's stadium in 1951 from the DeWitt brothers for $1.4 million. That year, Veeck's group bought an additional 21 percent of the team for $350,000. While in control of the Browns' franchise, Veeck's primary interest was to force the NL Cardinals to vacate the eastern Missouri area, which in part seemed to be possible since the Cardinals' owner, Fred Saigh, had serious problems with government about his income taxes. However, Veeck's strategy failed when beer mogul August Busch and his subsidiary purchased the Cardinals franchise and replaced Saigh.

Anyway Veeck—who was a very popular man during the mid–to late 1940s while in Cleveland where his promotions attracted a record number of baseball fans—then tried some unique stunts in St. Louis. For example, he hired a three-foot-six-inch midget named Eddie Gaedel to hit in a Browns game against the Detroit Tigers. Furthermore, Veeck occasionally allowed fans in the grandstands to manage his team by them holding up cards during games and signaling to Browns players to bunt, hit, steal a base, or initiate other actions. Specifically these tactics angered MLB's commissioner and other AL team owners, and also failed to attract many spectators to the club's home games in Sportsman's Park.

In 1953, Veeck was reportedly broke while the Browns finished eighth and more than 46 games behind the New York Yankees. When the league twice denied Veeck's bid to relocate his franchise to Baltimore, he sold a majority of it that year for $2.5 million to a syndicate who represented an area of Maryland and also he transferred Sportsman's Park to multimillionaire Busch for $850,000. Later, the NL Cardinals had pledged about $300,000 for the Browns' movement to a city near the East Coast. As a result, a syndicate of new owners from Baltimore including brewer Jerry Hoffberger, attorney Clarence Miles, and Mayor Tommy D'Alesandro moved the team from St. Louis into a recently-renovated 53,750-seat ballpark named Memorial Stadium and changed the franchise's name to the Baltimore Orioles.

During the early 1950s, some officials in baseball had suggested that the Browns would be better off to relocate to Milwaukee because of the city's new ballpark and local efforts to lure a MLB club into this well-populated area in southeast Wisconsin. The league, however, cancelled any type of deal due to Veeck being an owner while the Browns had performed poorly in St. Louis, other AL teams having to play their away games against the Browns in an inferior and dilapidated facility such as Sportsman's Park, and disputes with Veeck about his publicity stunts at home games. Apparently there was no practical or realistic option for Veeck to consider other than selling his club and retiring from baseball as the principal member of an ownership syndicate. Meanwhile the Cardinals continued to play excellent baseball in the NL and thus to prosper as an enterprise in St. Louis during several years of the 1950s and in most decades thereafter.

In the 1950s, the population of the Baltimore area increased from 1.4 million to 1.8 million while in comparison, St. Louis' expanded from 1.7 million to less than 2.2 million. It seemed, therefore, that St. Louis could successfully host only one MLB club during those and other years whereas the AL Senators in Washington failed to attract fans from southern neighborhoods in Baltimore. This situation meant that baseball's Orioles had a larger market to exploit during the mid–to late 1950s than did the Browns in St. Louis within the late 1940s to early 1950s. Moreover, other areas in the U.S. that had a population of one million or more such as Atlanta, Denver, Houston, Miami, San Diego, and Seattle were not developed as baseball towns in those years. Consequently, the league's approval to permit relocation of an existing team out of St. Louis into Baltimore in 1953 was a proper decision and in the long run, it has resulted in relatively more attendances at AL teams' home and away games, and additional profits for all these franchises since the late 1950s to early 2000s.

Philadelphia→Kansas City

During most years between 1901 and the early 1950s, Connie Mack had served in several different positions in the Philadelphia Athletics organization besides being the franchise's majority owner. That is, at one time or another he held such titles as field manager, general manager and president. In other words, Mack kept the club operating—but not necessarily profitable—for more than 50 years. Nevertheless after World War II ended, for personal reasons Mack donated 30 percent of the team to his sons, Connie Jr., Earle and Roy. Then when the senior Mack became too old to devote more time to the franchise and not thoroughly perform his duties, the club became somewhat leaderless as the family argued among each other about who, for example, should be the organization's coaches, executives and players. This was obvious in 1950 when Earle and Roy Mack mortgaged the team's 33,600-seat ballpark named Shibe Park and borrowed enough money to buy out the minority interests of their mother, Connie Jr., and the heirs of original owner Ben Shibe, and also the shares of the McFarland family. But unfortunately, the franchise's concession operator, Sportservice, had to provide funds to the Mack brothers to pay the team's operating expenses and some bank debts.[6]

Throughout the spring and summer of 1954, a few wealthy investors from Dallas, Los Angeles, and Philadelphia expressed a willingness to purchase the Athletics and perhaps its stadium. Besides them, another bidder was a vending machine executive from Chicago named Arnold Johnson whose real estate holdings included Yankee Stadium. In fact, Johnson agreed to be a front man for a syndicate from Kansas City that was formed to purchase the team from the Macks and move it to that metropolitan area in the midwest. When the AL turned down an offer for the Athletics from eight Philadelphia businessmen in late 1953, Johnson and his group became even more enthused and optimistic about owning the franchise and then relocating it to a site in Kansas City.

In November of 1954, Johnson presented his bid to the league's team owners at a meeting in New York. As testimony, he cited the success of the NL Braves' transfer from Boston to Milwaukee and the movement of the former Browns from St. Louis to Baltimore. Moreover, in his remarks, Johnson stated his dedication and commitment to the Kansas City area and also that he would sell his investment in Yankee Stadium. That compromise convinced Detroit Tigers owner Spike Briggs to approve Johnson's bid, which was then passed in a six to two vote by the league. A few days later, 91-year-old Connie Mack signed his name on the back of a stock certificate representing 302 shares that, in turn, transferred ownership of the team to Johnson and his syndicate. Within a few months, Mack's former club had moved to the Kansas City area and became recognized as the Kansas City Athletics.

In the end it was disunity, infighting and mistrust, a lack of mutual interest among family members, and also Connie Mack's inability to keep the team's business in operation after his health had declined that, in total, most likely caused the Athletics to fail as a team in Philadelphia. Moreover the ambition, determination, and persistence of Johnson and his group from Kansas City, and the Athletics' pathetic performances and poor attendances at home games played in Shibe Park, in part, had finally persuaded the AL to approve the relocation of this franchise into a small to midsized area in northwest Missouri. Since other regions in America such as southeast in Atlanta, west in Denver, and southwest in Houston were not yet fully developed or experienced enough as markets to host one or more MLB franchises, Kansas City was an appropriate and sensible location to move the Athletics in 1954.

Besides the influence of these factors, of course, was the Philadelphia area's sports fans. That is, in the majority, they had enthusiastically cheered, supported, and respected performances of the popular NL Phillies and NFL Eagles rather than the AL Athletics. Accordingly, athletes and their parents and thousands of other households located in southeast Pennsylvania willingly purchased tickets to attend Phillies and Eagles home games, and also to watch them on any regional television networks and listen to these teams compete on local radio stations. So although Philadelphia has been an above-average sports market since the 1920s and 1930s, the Athletics teams' could not overcome their increasingly poor image and inferior reputation in that market as a second-division MLB team. Nevertheless, Connie Mack will always be remembered as a legend in the sport for his great leadership and historical contributions to the game during years when baseball had dominated professional sports in the U.S.

Washington→Minneapolis

For most seasons that the original Senators' teams played while based in the nation's capital, Clark Griffith and members of his family had controlled the franchise. From when Griffith became its manager and invested in the team in 1912 and then acquired a 50 percent share of it seven years later, the ballclub was operated primarily as a closed family business until the mid–to late 1950s. During its 60-year history in Washington, the Senators had won three AL pennants and in 1924, a World's Series after defeating the NL New York Giants in seven games. In most other MLB seasons, however, the team did not perform well while its attendances at home games lingered at or near the bottom of the league.

After Clark Griffith died in 1955, his nephew Calvin inherited 50 percent of the franchise from him. Calvin, in turn, was a visionary businessman who, for financial reasons, appeared intent on moving his team to an area in the upper midwest of the U.S. In part, his strategy had been inspired by the Dodgers and Giants relocation from New York to the West Coast in 1958 and also by the plans for future AL and NL expansions into a number of sports markets. In fact, Calvin had spoken to insiders about the potential of big league baseball existing somewhere in Minnesota. He knew that the sport was popular there since Ted Williams had played with the Minneapolis Millers, and for other baseball clubs, as did such Hall-of-Famers as Carl Yastrzemski, Duke Snider, and Willie Mays.

A decision permitting the Senators to leave Washington for Minneapolis occurred in the fall of 1960 at a meeting of the league held in New York's Savoy-Hilton Hotel. At that conference, AL franchise owners expressed a strong interest to compete against the NL for markets within the midwest and also to offset the senior league's expansions into southern California during the late 1950s. In closed-door sessions, Griffith argued before this group of owners that his team could not survive much longer in Washington. And thus, he requested they grant him permission to relocate his franchise to Minneapolis. Although many of them feared an outrage from local politicians and baseball fans in D.C., the AL approved the Senators' movement to another area no later than early 1961. To minimize criticism from the media for their decision, these owners then confirmed that a new franchise would replace the former Senators for the 1961 MLB season. After relocating to the Minneapolis area, the Senators team was renamed Minnesota Twins.

Despite the movement of the NBA Lakers from the Twin Cities to Los Angeles in 1960, Minneapolis became an increasingly popular sports town and metropolis for other professional sports teams. The NFL Vikings, for example, started playing there in 1960 and a few years later, so did the American Basketball Association's Minnesota Pipers and NHL North Stars. Meanwhile the Twins began to play games in 1961 at 45,900-seat Metropolitan Stadium, which was located in the city of Bloomington. Anyway, for that MLB season, the club won only 70 games and finished seventh in the league, but also featured a combination of veterans and a number of competitive and talented young ballplayers who eventually would become stars for the team in future years.

Being the league's fifth relocation since 1901, this transfer of a six-decades-old franchise from one area to another in the early 1960s had occurred for several reasons. First, Clark Griffith's death in 1955 provided an opportunity for his nephew Calvin to abandon Washington and increase the team's profits elsewhere, or alternatively, to reduce its losses in a smaller sports market. Second, such great Senators players as pitcher Walter Johnson and fielders Goose Goslin, Joe Cronin, and Mickey Vernon had retired from the sport, and thus, the loss of these athletes resulted in fewer victories and smaller attendances for the club at home games during the 1950s. Third, AL franchise owners needed to reinvigorate their organization and radically restructure it after the movements of the NL Braves, Dodgers, and Giants during the 1950s and to prepare for the expansions planned to occur in the early 1960s.

Fourth, after the departure of the Senators to Minneapolis in 1961, a new expansion team that played in Washington would excite baseball fans in the area and create some additional revenues for the nine existing teams in the league. And fifth, Minneapolis was expected to be an above-average and popular market for professional teams throughout the 1960s even though the NBA Lakers had left there in 1960. In fact, the Lakers experienced ownership and financial problems during the late 1950s which meant that Los Angeles was a prime market for this troubled NBA team. In short, for 48 years Twins' teams have been moderately competitive, especially at home in Minneapolis, and thereby the franchise has succeeded to continue in business despite the poor performances of its predecessor as an enterprise in most MLB seasons between 1901 and 1960.

Los Angeles→Anaheim

As a five-year-old expansion franchise in Los Angeles, the Angels struggled in games against its opponents in the AL. Meanwhile, the team's attendances at its home ballpark had exceeded a million only in one of these seasons. As such, former singing cowboy and multimillionaire Gene Autry—

who then owned the club—realized in 1964 and 1965 that his investment in the franchise could not reach its highest potential in value as long as the Angels continued to rent and play their home games in Walter O'Malley's Dodger Stadium in Los Angeles. Indeed, while leasing and competing in that facility, Autry's Angels had several problems. To highlight one of them, the various Angels' teams had performed in their games as an inferior option for the area's baseball fans who, in turn, preferred to root for the popular and successful Dodgers. According to Autry, this meant less exposure and revenues for his team and the other AL clubs that played the Angels in regular-season games at Dodger Stadium.[7]

There were two other significant issues that adversely affected the cash flows and profits of the Angels while being tenants in Dodger Stadium during the MLB seasons of 1961 through 1965. First, O'Malley charged the Angels for expenditures of any type even though there were no tangible benefits or rewards associated with these charges. The Angels, for example, paid 50 percent for all supplies and other items used at the ballpark even though the club's attendances each season equaled about one-half to two-thirds of the Dodgers'. Second, any parking lot repairs for labor and material expenses at the stadium had been entirely charged to the Angels. These costs were later rescinded by O'Malley after being informed that Autry's team did not receive any share of the ballpark's parking revenues. Thus, these and other infractions caused the Angels owner to not renew his lease of the stadium with the Dodgers when it had expired in 1965.

Autry's first choice was to immediately move his team to Long Beach where the city would build the club a new stadium. That deal failed, however, because government officials there insisted on renaming the team with a title such as Long Beach Angels. Then, the nearby city of Anaheim created a plan for a modern facility that would be completed and opened before the start of the 1966 MLB season. Although Anaheim was located within Orange County—which was approximately 30 miles from downtown Los Angeles and contained 150,000 people—municipal officials there offered to construct a new 45,000-seat stadium for the Angels. After that offer was accepted by Autry, the Angels signed a 35-year lease for the building followed by three 10-year options of it. When the new ballpark opened in April 1966, more than 31,000 fans bought tickets to attend the Angels' first home game in Anaheim. In fact, that crowd was larger than any of the club's games played in 1965 at Chavez Ravine—which was the name of property occupied by Dodger Stadium in the Los Angeles area.

Anaheim Stadium provided some short-run benefits for the newly-named California Angels. Between 1966 and 1970, for example, the club's average attendance at home games increased to more than one million spectators and in 1967, the team finished fifth in the AL and then third in its division in 1969 and 1970. During these years, such Angels' ballplayers as batting champion Alex Johnson, 20-game-winning pitcher Clyde Wright, infielder Jim Fregosi, outfielder Albie Pearson, and catcher Buck Rogers each became heroes for baseball athletes and fans within the Anaheim area. Given the franchise's situation and mistreatment while playing games in Dodger Stadium during the early 1960s, it was the best decision for Autry to not renew his lease of that facility and then move the Angels from its original site in Los Angeles to a modern ballpark located 30 miles south in Anaheim.

Although the Angels' teams played their home games within a relatively small city especially from the late 1960s to 1970s, there were approximately six to seven million people that lived then within 25 to 35 miles of Anaheim Stadium. Besides population of the area, moving his club such a short distance from Los Angeles in early 1966 required much less of a hassle and cost for Autry than if he had relocated it somewhere else in the west, or to an area within the midwest, or to a place on the East Coast. With respect to the Angels' accomplishments as a business enterprise in MLB, the franchise has likely prospered while in Anaheim and during recent years, it also won an AL pennant and a World Series. In the next major section of this chapter, I will highlight the team's performances since it had moved from the city of Los Angeles in southern California to Anaheim.

Kansas City→Oakland

From 1955 to 1967, the Athletics finished no higher than fifth place in the AL. Furthermore, the club failed to develop a productive farm system while it periodically traded several of its talented players to the New York Yankees and other teams. It was in 1960, however, that owner Arnold Johnson had died and his heirs sold more than 50 percent of their interest in the franchise to insurance executive Charlie Finley for $1.9 million. Within a few months of that year, Finley then acquired the remaining share of the club from Roy Mack's widow for $1.8 million.

During the next seven years in Kansas City, Finley tried a number of unusual but ridiculous promotions to entice more local baseball fans to attend the Athletics home games. Although he took credit for all of them, many of these stunts had been implemented before by Bill Veeck while he owned the Indians in Cleveland or the Browns in St. Louis. Anyway, Finley continued to sell his best ballplayers after each season to primarily the Yankees while his teams struggled to win games against nine other opponents in the league. According to local baseball fans and some reporters in the media, the Athletics owner had deliberately fielded bad teams in order to justify moving his franchise from Kansas City to another area. Meanwhile, the annual attendance at the Athletics home games declined from 1.4 million in 1955 to 963,000 in 1959, and then fell to 726,000 in 1967.

There were other problems associated with Finley's activities, decisions and intentions. That is, he frequently criticized his managers in postgame interviews and publicly denounced players at clubhouse meetings. In turn, they usually ignored or simply rejected these insults from him. Also it became apparent to some people in the Kansas City area that Finley was preparing to move the Athletics because the franchise had reportedly not made a profit since the late 1950s to early 1960s. As a result, season ticket sales to home games gradually declined while baseball fans in the market participated in other events during the summers. To some extent, visiting teams also realized that the Finley's teams were demoralized and not competitive, and thus, the Indians, Tigers, White Sox, and others in the AL defeated the Athletics in single games and weekend series.

After his club had finished tenth and 29 games behind the Red Sox in 1967, Finley requested permission from the AL—and then received it—to move his big-league operation from Kansas City to Oakland, California. Even though voters in Missouri's Jackson County approved a multimillion-dollar bond issue to construct a new baseball stadium there, Finley had already spoken to city officials in several cities including Dallas and Louisville to determine if any of them were interested as a place to host his team. Since the city of Oakland had successfully supported a professional baseball team in the Pacific Coast League before the Giants had moved from New York to San Francisco in 1958, Finley was certain that another MLB team could exist within the Bay Area. So he met with the community's decision-makers in the area and agreed to lease the Oakland Coliseum from them for the 1968 MLB season. To ensure their support, Finley also told these officials he would establish his residence in Oakland and predicted the Athletics (nicknamed the A's) would attract more than one million each season to the club's home games and soon win an AL pennant.

Because of a five-year $5 million radio and television contract in Oakland rather than the $56,000 earned from a media contract in Kansas City, and the low rent to lease the city's Coliseum and share it with the hometown NFL Raiders, and due to a large sports market within the Bay Area that also included the NL San Francisco Giants, Finley made increasing amounts of money from investing in the Athletics. In fact, this occurred while the A's home attendances at games increased to more than 800,000 in 1968 and 900,000 in 1971, and then to one million in 1973. Moreover, the club performed much better in Oakland than Kansas City when it finished second in the league's West Division in 1969 and 1970 and first in 1971 to 1975, and also winning three each AL pennants and World Series in 1972–1974. After refusing two offers in 1977 to sell the A's for, respectively, $10 million and $12 million, Finley sold the franchise in 1980 for $12.7 million to Walter Haas, Jr., and his son Wally, and to son-in-law Roy Eisenhardt.

The potential financial rewards and business opportunities open to Finley from relocating his franchise from Kansas City to Oakland after the 1967 MLB season suggests, in part, that he was unable to negotiate a more attractive deal with city officials from Dallas and Louisville, and also from such places as Denver, Milwaukee, New Orleans, San Diego and Seattle. These were also above-average to superior markets for the Athletics to perform in during 1968. But, Finley had decided that an area in northern California was where his club would be most profitable and likewise successfully compete as a franchise in the AL. Indeed when a representative from the New York Yankees had switched his vote from no to yes on the second ballot during a league meeting in October 1967, the Athletics movement to the West Coast made Finley a wealthier man.

According to some readings in the literature about the relocation I just discussed, Finley—like Veeck and some other owners of MLB franchises—was a shrewd character and ruthless businessman who knew and cared more about the commercial aspects of professional baseball than about the emotions, feelings, and opinions of his managers, players and fans, and sports writers and economists. Although this style of management did not succeed for Finley in Kansas City, as a strategy it improved his club's performances, prosperity, and value in Oakland.

In short, Finley's contribution to the sport and MLB was a unique experience and also worthwhile to remember and study. Yet alternatively, the results of this relocation were not necessarily in the best interest of his team's social impact in the Kansas City and Oakland communities and among some groups who preferred entrepreneurs to be more benevolent. In fact, within the next major section of this chapter I discuss in more detail the performances of Oakland A's teams during their respective seasons in the AL.

Seattle→Milwaukee

As an AL expansion team in the Seattle area, the Pilots failed miserably after playing one season. Besides finishing sixth in the West Division in 1969, the club's attendance at home games in 25,420-seat Sick's Stadium ranked last (twelfth) in the league at less than 678,000. During regular-season games, the Pilots' ballplayers—who were primarily retreads and castoffs from other clubs—wore bizarre caps and uniforms on the field and their opponents scored more than 700 runs to their team's 639.

As a result, the franchise suffered a huge operating loss. So in the fall of 1969, majority stockholder and President William Daley offered to sell the Pilots to the highest bidder. Soon thereafter a private corporation composed of several Milwaukee businessmen, and headed by 35-year-old car dealer Bud Selig, offered $10.8 million for the Pilots, which was approximately $5 million more than the original price of the franchise. But then a syndicate led by James Douglas and Westins Hotel owner Eddie Carlson bid $11.5 million for the club. However, this offer was rejected by the AL because of the group's outstanding financial problems.[8]

During early 1970, the Pilots had to borrow more than $600,000 from the AL to pay the team's debts. Even so, the franchise declared bankruptcy while in spring training and only one week before the scheduled start of MLB's 1970 season. Eager to sell his team in a hurry and without any delays, William Daley sold it for $10.8 million to Selig's group—who within a few weeks—moved their franchise to Milwaukee and renamed it the Milwaukee Brewers. Interestingly, this was only the second time since 1901 that any city in the U.S. had lost a professional team after it had performed for only one season in the big leagues.

Although the NL Braves left Milwaukee for Atlanta in early 1966, it was apparent to some in the sport that this city in southeast Wisconsin had more than enough fans to support a professional baseball team at least for several MLB seasons and perhaps for decades. First, the Braves' annual attendance at County Stadium exceeded one million for five years and two million for another four of them. After some of the club's most productive ballplayers retired or had transferred to another team in the league during the early 1960s, attendance at its home games in Milwaukee still topped 900,000 in 1964 and also 750,000 each in 1962 and 1963.

Second, Selig and his group made a competitive, impressive, and well-financed proposal to the AL for the Pilots. In turn, the league needed to make immediate decisions to approve a sale of the franchise and also the movement of it from Seattle to Milwaukee. Besides, a bid from another syndicate did not meet the league's expectations or requirements regarding the condition of its balance sheet and other financial statements. And third, natural intra-league rivalries between the Brewers and such competitors as the Minnesota Twins and Chicago White Sox could quickly develop and thereby excite baseball fans in each of the three markets, and thus, increase these clubs' home-game attendances and gate receipts when playing each other.

The relocation of this AL franchise from Seattle to a small to midsized city in the upper midwest proved to be an instant success. Within the first three weeks of April 1970, more than 4,000 season tickets were sold to fans in the Milwaukee area along with another 2,000 ticket plans each priced at $150 to $375. When the Brewers had returned from its first road trip in early 1970, in excess of 8,000 people greeted them at the airport while 37,000 attended the club's opening game at home against the Anaheim Angels. Despite being a very mediocre club until the late 1970s—after which it won more games and finished higher in the league's East Division—the Brewers drew more than 900,000 to County Stadium in 1970, and at least one million in 1973 and again in 1975 through 1980 and after 1982. It appears, therefore, that a relocation Seattle to Milwaukee in 1970 greatly improved the operation of the AL from a business viewpoint, and also the league's economic and financial potential.

Given the circumstance and problems of the Pilots during and after the 1969 MLB season, Milwaukee was the most accessible and practical place for the AL to approve and put an existing team in 1970. Such populated sports markets as Denver, Miami, and Phoenix were not mature enough to adequately support a professional franchise, especially in baseball. So it was Selig and his group that should be applauded for spending almost $11 million to purchase a risky but potentially profitable club in 1970 and then locating it somewhere within the Milwaukee area. This investment, in turn, developed through a dozen MLB seasons and then peaked in 1982 when the Brewers won the AL East Division but then lost in seven games to the NL Cardinals in a World Series. In 1998, MLB moved the Brewers from the AL to NL Central Division. For the team's performances before and after it had transferred between these leagues, see the next major section of this chapter.

Washington→Arlington

As an expansion franchise in the AL, the Senators had struggled to win its regular-season games and indeed, never placed higher than fourth in the league's East Division. The team's annual attendances at 27,400-seat Griffith Stadium and 45,000-seat RFK Stadium in Washington varied between 535,000 and 918,000 during a total of 11 seasons, while being sold and resold to different groups of investors. Then in 1969, Democratic National Committee treasurer Robert Short purchased 90 percent of the Senators for approximately $9 million from a syndicate who owned it. As a sports entrepreneur and capitalist, he had acquired the NBA Minneapolis Lakers during the late 1950s and then moved the team to Los Angeles in 1960. Five years later, Short sold the club for $5 million to Jack Kent Cooke.[9]

As another asset in Short's portfolio, the Senators served primarily as a corporate tax shelter that could be depreciated at its full value over five years. Therefore, after the club's terrible performances since becoming an expansion team in 1961 and Short's well-publicized statements of moving it soon to another metropolitan area, baseball fans in Washington became angry, bitter, and disillusioned about the future of their hometown franchise. In fact, during one game, a few fans ran onto the field at RFK Stadium and for that action the umpire forfeited the contest to the visiting New York Yankees. Also, some spectators had held up obscene banners before, during and after home games, and likewise others made derogatory gestures to the Senators' coaches and ballplayers. Thus to keep the franchise in operation, Short became determined to move it soon out of the Washington area.

When the 1970 MLB season concluded, Short tried to sell the Senators for $12 million to a syndicate and also threatened to not renew his lease of the ballpark from the city. The former effort failed, however, because no investors would agree to Short's asking price. Then after a series of secret discussions with Mayor Tom Vandergriff of Arlington, Short announced he would move his franchise to that city in northeast Texas; other AL team owners agreed to the club's relocation by a vote of 10–2. As a condition to relocate within the Dallas-Fort Worth area, the Senators' Short consented to pay six Texas League franchises $40,000 apiece for invading their territory, and he also agreed to host an annual exhibition game against an all-star team from that minor baseball league.

To pay off the majority of his debts in Washington while establishing a market after moving to Arlington, Short received more than $7 million in cash from an arrangement with Vandegriff in exchange for ten years of broadcast rights within the area. That transaction plus Arlington's 10,000-seat Turnpike Stadium were additional reasons for Short's team to perform in the Dallas-Fort Worth sports market. Built in 1965 as the home site of the AA Spurs in the Texas League, this stadium had been constructed according to MLB specifications, existed in a natural bowl, and needed only minor renovations to expand its capacity by thousands of seats.

Consequently, between October 1971 and April of 1972, the ballpark was renamed from Turnpike to Arlington Stadium. Meanwhile, its capacity was increased to 43,500 seats to accommodate MLB's Texas Rangers. As these changes occurred, however, Short sold 90 percent of his interest in the franchise for $10 million to a group of investors headed by businessman Brad Corbett. Although the Rangers finished sixth in the AL West Division in 1972 and 1973, one year later attendance at Arlington Stadium increased to 1.1 million and remained above one million until 1981, and then stabilized between one and two million in 1982 and again in many years thereafter. For more information about the Rangers' attendances and performances while playing in the league's West Division, there is a section later in this chapter that discusses these results.

Given the previous information and table about the relocation sites of nine franchises in the AL since 1901, Table 3.2 denotes the differences in populations and population ranks of the urban places or cities when they were homes of these various clubs first before and then after each movement had occurred. Since I assume that an area's population is a proxy or rough measure of a professional baseball team's central market, what does the following table reveal to the reader, in part, about each of these relocations?

First, based on their populations and population rankings, three or 33 percent of the franchise movements were from small to midsized to midsized to very large places, or referred in future years as between cities. These three changes included the Brewers from Milwaukee to St. Louis (renamed Browns) in 1902, Orioles from Baltimore to New York (renamed Highlanders) in 1903, and Athletics from Kansas City to Oakland (renamed A's) in 1968. Alternatively, the other six or 67 percent of the relocations in the AL took effect from small, midsized, large, or very large markets into those that were either small or midsized. In other words, the greater number of people—and likely population of baseball fans—within their respective new markets appealed and mattered relatively more to the former group of three relocating clubs than it did for the latter six.

Second, there were substantial differences in population between places— or the areas—for a majority of these nine team relocations. In fact, the two most significant variations in percentages between market sizes were each greater than 500 percent. These occurred, respectively, in 1903 when the franchise in Baltimore moved to the New York area, and in 1965 when the Angels relocated from its market in Los Angeles to the city of Anaheim. In contrast, the least differences in percentages between the populations of two areas before and after relocation were in 1954 when a club in St. Louis moved to Baltimore, and in 1970 when the Pilots folded in Seattle and the franchise transferred into the Milwaukee area. In short, these four movements suggest that the relative population of different markets was at least one factor that franchise owners evaluated in selecting another home for their team.

Third, the average rank in the population of areas—prior to and then immediately following each of these nine movements of AL clubs—was

Table 3.2 American League Teams
Population Characteristics of Areas Before and After Relocation,
1901–2008

Years		Areas		Population		Rank	
Before	After	Before	After	Before	After	Before	After
1901	1902	Milwaukee	St. Louis	285	575	14	4
1902	1903	Baltimore	New York	508	3,437	6	1
1953	1954	St. Louis	Baltimore	1,681	1,337	9	12
1954	1955	Philadelphia	Kansas City	3,016	814	4	17
1960	1961	Washington	Minneapolis	2,076	1,482	10	14
1965	1966	Los Angeles	Anaheim	6,755	1,161	2	25
1967	1968	Kansas City	Oakland	1,201	2,942	26	6
1969	1970	Seattle	Milwaukee	1,424	1,403	17	19
1971	1972	Washington	Arlington	2,910	2,377	7	12

Note: Years Before is a team's final season to perform within the pre-move area. Years After is a team's first season to play within the post-move area. Areas Before and After are each self-explanatory. Population is the total population in hundreds of thousands of the teams' home areas in the year before and after their relocation. Similarly, Rank is each of the home areas' rank in population in the year prior to and following relocation. Population and Rank were reported by the U.S. Census Bureau in issues of The World Almanac and Book of Facts. The Oakland area includes San Francisco and Arlington the cities of Dallas and Fort Worth, while Minneapolis includes the city of St. Paul.

Source: "Population of the 100 Largest Urban Places: 1870–1900," at http://www.census.gov, accessed 15 September 2008, and various editions of *The World Almanac and Book of Facts* (New York: World Almanac Books, 1930–2007).

Left: Besides being flamboyant and a promoter of memorable publicity stunts during his career in Major League Baseball, Bill Veeck had owned various franchises. While owning the American League St. Louis Browns, Veeck tried but failed to convince the National League Cardinals to abandon the St. Louis area. After Anheuser-Busch purchased the Cardinals and then Sportsmans Park in 1952–1953, Veeck's group sold the Browns to a syndicate that moved the team to Baltimore. [National Baseball Hall of Fame Library, Cooperstown, N.Y.] *Right:* As a nephew of Washington Senators owner Clark Griffith, Calvin Griffith inherited 50 percent of the club when Clark died in 1955. Dissatisfied with the Senators attendances and performances while in Washington, Calvin moved his team to the Minneapolis–St. Paul metropolitan area in 1961 and changed its name to the Minnesota Twins. In 1984, Griffith sold the Twins for about $35 million to Minneapolis banker Carl Pohlad. [National Baseball Hall of Fame Library, Cooperstown, N.Y.]

approximately tenth for before relocation and then twelfth for after it. That is, the clubs moved on average from moderately more-populated or higher-ranked places to those that were less populated or lower in rank. Since MLB teams located in large and very large markets have economic and political power and also are dominant enough within a league to successfully protect their markets from being invaded by others currently in small to midsized areas, two-thirds of the clubs that are listed in column three of Table 3.2 had moved to smaller cities. Because of strict rules concerning the home territory of MLB franchises, these are results that should be expected. However, there has been a placement of one or more new franchises into some very large markets of baseball due to league expansion.

Fourth, two of the most and least successful moves were, respectively, from Baltimore to New York in 1903 and Los Angeles to Anaheim in 1965, and from Milwaukee to St. Louis in 1902 and Philadelphia to Kansas City in 1955. Indeed, the 106-year-old Yankees has become the most valuable and wealthiest franchise in American professional team sports while the Angels improved and played much better and before larger crowds in Anaheim than it did during the club's five total seasons at Wrigley Field and then Dodger Stadium in Los Angeles. Alternatively, despite the team being located in a much larger market than Milwaukee, the Browns struggled to attract baseball fans in the St. Louis area during most of its 52 MLB seasons there. Similarly, the Athletics failed to win an AL pennant while located in Kansas City or establish itself in the local community there from 1955 to 1967. These circumstances changed for the Athletics, however, when the franchise shifted in 1968 to the Oakland area.

Fifth, between 1901 and 2008 inclusive, an AL team had moved about every 12 years. Since the league was stable geographically with the same eight clubs located in their respective areas from 1903 to 1953, the frequency of relocations in other years was almost one every seven MLB seasons. In short, any more team movements than these nine may have destabilized the league whereas fewer transfers would have caused some franchises to exist for years in inferior

After an unsuccessful attempt to acquire the Philadelphia Athletics from the Mack family in 1954, Charley Finley purchased a controlling interest in the Kansas City Athletics for about $4 million in 1960 when owner Arnold Johnson died. Then in 1967, Finley redeployed his club to northern California and named it the Oakland Athletics. During the early to mid–1970s, the team won five division titles and three each consecutive American League pennants and World Series. [National Baseball Hall of Fame Library, Cooperstown, N.Y.]

markets, incur losses from their operations or even become bankrupt, perform poorly against any rivals, and perhaps disband and exit the AL forever. Thus, a decision to relocate was implemented by the owners of various AL teams when their opportunities to win additional games, attract baseball fans, and earn greater profits had more potential within other markets across areas of the U.S.

The next major section of this chapter focuses on the performances of nine AL clubs after each of them had relocated from one to another place or area. Based on their results, these clubs are listed in Table 3.3 from the most to least successful with respect to their postseasons. The rankings of teams are somewhat distorted, however, since the AL (and NL) did not consist of divisions before 1969 and no World Series occurred in 1904 and 1994, playoffs in 1994. Nonetheless, these performances combined with those in Table A.3.2 of the Appendix indicate which teams won championships within the AL and in MLB, and also how well each of them had competed, on average, in their regular seasons as of five years before they relocated and then during five years after being moved to another area.[10]

PERFORMANCES: AL TEAM RELOCATIONS

New York Highlanders/Yankees

From 1903 to 1912 inclusive, the New York Highlanders won several more games each season and doubled their annual attendance at Hilltop Park in New York than while the club had performed as the Baltimore Orioles in 1901–1902 (see Table A.3.2). Interestingly, the Highlanders had seven different managers as coaches, including such legends as John McGraw and Clark Griffith, and also played an outstanding pitcher named Jack Chesbro who won 41 games in 1904. Then after the franchise's nickname was changed to Yankees in 1913, the team excelled for seasons within several decades.

Besides claiming several titles in the league's East Division and numerous AL pennants, Yankees teams won 26 World Series between 1923 and 2000 for a total of 81 championships. In fact, 15 of the franchise's World Series victories occurred from 1932 to 1958. Some of the all-time great Yankees were field managers Miller Huggins, Joe McCarthy, Casey Stengel and Joe Torre, who each won more than 1,000 games; pitchers Lefty Gomez, Red Ruffing, and Whitey

Table 3.3 American League Franchise Relocations Postseason Results, by Teams and Seasons, 1901–2008

Teams	Seasons	Divisions	Postseason Results Pennants	World Series
New York Highlanders/Yankees	106	16	39	26
Oakland Athletics	41	14	6	4
Baltimore Orioles II	55	8	6	3
Minnesota Twins	48	8	3	2
California/Anaheim/LA Angels	44	7	1	1
Milwaukee Brewers II	28	2	1	0
Texas Rangers	37	4	0	0
St. Louis Browns	52	NA	1	0
Kansas City Athletics	13	NA	0	0

Note: Teams are self-explanatory. The slash (/) indicates a change in a team's nickname. Columns two through five are, respectively, the number of each team's seasons and their division titles, pennants, and World Series won while in the AL. NA means not applicable because MLB established divisions for the AL (and NL) in 1969. LA Angels is the Los Angeles Angels of Anaheim.

Source: Official Major League Baseball Fact Book 2005 Edition and various editions of The World Almanac and Book of Facts, 1930–2007.

Ford; and sluggers Babe Ruth, Joe DiMaggio, and Mickey Mantle. Along with the immense contributions of these coaches and athletes, much of the franchise's success also happened because of the investment, oversight, and vision of such owners as Jacob Ruppert, Del Webb and George Steinbrenner.[11]

From 2001 to 2008, the Yankees did not win a World Series despite an annual payroll that exceeded $175 million to $200 million. Because manager Joe Torre left to coach the Los Angeles Dodgers in 2008, and although aging superstars like Derek Jeter, Alex Rodriguez, and Mariano Rivera have consistently and competently performed during recent seasons, the Yankees may need to trade some of their veterans and other skilled ballplayers in the minor leagues to acquire expensive free agents and perhaps both young and experienced players from other teams to be adequate replacements.

In 2009 and thereafter, the revenues from a brand new $1.5 billion baseball stadium in New York will provide additional financial capital and resources for the Yankees organization to continue its achievements as the most popular, valuable, and winning franchise in MLB history. Other clubs within the AL East Division, however, improved their rosters of players in recent years and furthermore, some of them have performed at or above expectations. Consequently, the Yankees will not only be challenged in the future by the Blue Jays, Orioles and Red Sox, but also tested by the emerging Rays, who surprisingly won a division title and AL pennant in 2008. But if any of these latter four teams are unable or reluctant to expand their payrolls and remain increasingly competitive, then the Yankees will once again dominate them in regular-season games and during the league's playoffs.

Given the occasional improvement in the performances of low-budget teams in each AL division like the Rays, Twins and A's, there is little justification for a significant increase in luxury tax rates on high-payroll clubs, and more revenues from them, above the thresholds previously established in MLB's current collective agreement, which expires in 2011. In my judgment, any subsidies from such very large market teams as the Yankees and Red Sox are sufficient to maintain competitive balance within divisions of the AL. Moreover, these redistributions of revenues may ultimately discourage teams located in big markets from investing increasing amounts of money in contracts for ballplayers and hoard the cash, but encourage clubs in small to mid-sized areas to subsist and not aggressively generate additional funds from their operations and sponsors within their local markets. In part, the policy of reallocating revenues will become a more controversial, sensitive, and unpopular issue in the future among all owners of franchises in MLB.

Oakland Athletics

The 41-year-old Oakland Athletics is the second most successful AL team involved in relocation. Within five years after moving from Kansas City, the club's average winning percentage and attendance at regular-season home games increased especially at 43,662-seat Oakland Alameda County Coliseum—that was later renamed Network Associates Coliseum (see Table A.3.2). Besides 14 West Division titles and six AL pennants, the A's won World Series in 1972 through 1974 and again in 1989. According to a few prominent baseball officials, they contend that the A's three consecutive championships during the early 1970s occurred primarily because owner Charles Finley had the foresight, patience, and wisdom to gradually develop a competitive roster of ballplayers while the franchise had existed earlier in Kansas City. Thus, some of these athletes eventually became superstars for the franchise in Oakland.

During its many seasons while playing in the West Division, the A's most impressive performances occurred in the early 1970s and late 1980s. With respect to the former period, the club had played outstanding in games due to managers Dick Williams and Alvin Dark, and such hitters as Reggie Jackson, Sal Bando and Joe Rudi, and pitchers like Catfish Hunter, Rollie Fingers, and Vida Blue. Then in the 1980s, various A's teams were led by manager Tony La Russa, sluggers Jose Canseco, Mark McGwire and Rickey Henderson, and such hurlers as Dave Stewart, Dennis Eckersley, and Bob Welch. As a result of winning a World Series in 1989 and also finishing runner-up in 1988 and 1990, the franchise established its five highest attendances at home in the 1988 through 1992 seasons of MLB.

In the late 1990s and early 2000s, an A's executive named Billy Beane became a legend for being a clever, smart, and very intense general manager. As such, he created and applied different statistical measures, or sabermetric principles, to accurately determine the skill and value of various ballplayers based on their performances in games on defense or offense. Although most of these athletes did not lead the league or even their team in such all-important categories as hitting, pitching or fielding, it was when they became free agents or had been released that Beane recruited and signed them to modest contracts to play for the A's. Consequently for years, Oakland had one of the lowest payrolls in the AL but nevertheless, won more games than clubs that wasted millions of dollars for much greater talent. In fact, Beane's application of statistics and his decision to hire the best ballplayers at each position on the field and as substitutes for the least cost elevated the role of general manager in other franchises in MLB.

During recent seasons, the Angels have been the most dominant club in the AL West Division. In contrast, the A's share a midsized to large sports market with the NL Giants and also establish an annual payroll that is below average among AL teams and usually less than the Angels and sometimes below payrolls of the Mariners and Rangers. Therefore, to compete for additional championships in the league, it may be necessary for the A's to allocate and spend considerably more money to retain or hire experienced managers and skilled ballplayers. If this franchise's owners cannot or refuse to increase the club's payroll by a reasonable amount, then the A's teams may struggle even more to attract baseball fans to their ballpark in Oakland. If that occurs for years, then the A's will not generate enough revenues to effectively challenge and then defeat the competitive, glamorous, and successful Angels.

Baltimore Orioles II

After Bill Veeck sold the Browns for $2.4 million and also Sportsman's Park for $850,000 in 1953, the new owners decided to move the team from St. Louis to Baltimore and change its nickname to the Orioles. During the Orioles' first five years in Baltimore, the club won relatively more regular-season games than it did in St. Louis and the attendances at 53,371-seat Memorial Stadium in Baltimore increased by almost 200 percent each season (see Table A.3.2). Between 1966 and 1997, the Orioles played well enough to win eight East Division titles, six AL pennants, and a World Series in 1966, 1970, and 1983. Based on these results, the Orioles performed much more competitively before larger groups of hometown fans while Clarence Miles, Jerry Hoffberger, Edward Williams, and Eli Jacobs owned it than when Veeck and his predecessors had operated the franchise.

The men responsible, in part, for the Orioles' accomplishments in many AL seasons included such managers as Hank Bauer, Earl Weaver and Davey Johnson, batters as Brooks Robinson, Frank Robinson and Cal Ripken, and pitchers as Jim Palmer, Dave McNally, and Mike Flanagan. Other notable athletes who had played on various Orioles' teams were sluggers Rafael Palmeiro, Eddie Murray and Boog Powell, and 20-game winners like Mike Cuellar, Mike Torrez, and Steve Stone. In fact, some of these ballplayers had caused the team to establish its highest attendances at 48,190-seat Camden Yards in Baltimore during five years in the 1990s with the number of spectators ranging on average from 3.5 million to 3.7 million each season.

While being located within a midsized area near the East Coast, the Orioles have not won an East Division title since 1997, and an AL pennant and World Series in more than 25 years. With the movement of a NL team from Montreal to Washington in early 2005, a portion of the Orioles' fans in lower Baltimore probably shifted their support to the Nationals in the nation's capital city. Furthermore in recent years, the Yankees and Red Sox have increased their payrolls and to a lesser extent, so did the Blue Jays and Rays. As a result of these changes, an opportunity for the Orioles to win another championship will be extremely difficult. In other words, without a multimillion-dollar growth in its budget for ballplayers and an excellent staff of coaches, this franchise will likely be a mediocre performer in the league's East Division. Thus, it may be several years and perhaps a decade or more before the Orioles are able to challenge the Yankees and other clubs for a title.

Minnesota Twins

The fourth most productive AL team to ever perform from when it was established after relocation is the 48-year-old Minnesota Twins. When long-time owner Clark Griffith died, his nephew Calvin inherited 50 percent of the Washington Senators in 1955. Six years later, Calvin concluded that the future of the franchise was in the Minneapolis area, so he moved it there in early 1961. Despite playing in a smaller market than Washington, D.C., the Twins' average winning proportion for its first five seasons increased to about 53 percent (in contrast to 40 percent as the Senators in 1956 through 1960) and the club's home-game attendances improved at 46,000-seat Metropolitan Stadium by almost 150 percent per year (see Table A.3.2). Consequently, the Twins became a very popular and well-respected team in the Minneapolis-St. Paul area during the early to mid–1970s.

While in Washington for 60 MLB seasons, the Senators won three AL pennants and in 1924 a World's Series after it defeated the NL New York Giants in seven games. In contrast, between 1961 and 2008, different Twins' teams in their postseasons had won four each Central and West Division titles, a league pennant in 1965 and then in 1987 and 1991, two more pennants that were followed by victories in a World Series. To achieve these results during various MLB seasons, the club's most competent managers included Sam Mele, Bill Rigney and Tom Kelly, while its best athletes were hitters Tony Oliva, Rod Carew and Kirby Puckett, and also such pitchers as Jim Kaat, Frank Viola, and Bert Blyleven. Besides the contributions of managers and ballplayers, Carl Pohlad purchased the franchise in 1984 from Calvin Griffith for about $35 million and provided the leadership for it to win pennants and two World Series, and also other titles in the early 2000s.

Similar to the AL Cleveland Indians, Seattle Mariners and Tampa Bay Rays, the Twins are located in a small to midsized area that contains the NFL Vikings, NBA Timberwolves and NHL Wild. Furthermore, the very large market White Sox in Chicago and the big-market Tigers in Detroit each play in the league's Central Division. So although the Twins have been very efficient at winning regular-season games and occasionally being competitive enough to earn a division title or wild card, Pohlad has not increased his club's payroll much each year because the revenues from the 48,678-seat Metrodome are reportedly lackluster and insufficient. For these reasons and other financial opportunities, superstar pitcher Johan Santana abandoned the Twins in late 2007 and joined the NL Mets, where he signed a six-year $137.5 million contract in early 2008. Thus, Pohlad has lobbied politicians in Minneapolis and Minnesota's state government to assist him with financing the construction of a new ballpark somewhere in the Twin Cities area.

For several years, Pohlad had threatened to move his team from Minneapolis to another market. In fact, he considered the movement of it into such sports towns as Charlotte, Columbus, or Portland. Nonetheless, if a new ballpark is not erected—or alternatively is built for the team somewhere in Minneapolis—the respective owners of other AL clubs will be reluctant to approve a relocation of the Twins since that requires a majority vote of the group and their complete support of it. Much more likely to happen, however, is that Pohlad will eventually sell the Twins to a syndicate of investors and then allow these new owners to decide what is best for the club including its optimum place.

California/Anaheim/LA Angels of Anaheim

During the five years after owner Gene Autry had moved his expansion franchise from Los Angeles to Anaheim, the Angels' number of wins each season slightly declined from 76 (pre-relocation) to 74 (post-relocation), while its average attendance at home games increased by approximately 43 percent, that is, from 755,000 at Wrigley Field and Dodger Stadium to 1.1 million at Anaheim Stadium. Then in three seasons of the 1980s and two in the early 2000s, the club enjoyed its five highest home attendances at between 2.6 million to 3.3 million spectators. This improvement occurred, in part, because the Angels' teams became more popular when they won seven West Division titles, and also an AL pennant and World Series in 2002. If trends somehow continue after 2008–2009, the club will likely win more pennants and World Series based on its consistent performances such as four division titles each in 2004–2005 and 2007–2008.

Unlike some rich and well-known teams in the AL like the Red Sox and Yankees, the Angels have employed only a few popular baseball personalities as the club's coaches and players. During various MLB seasons, these personnel have been—or currently include—such field managers as Gene Mauch, Doug Rader and Mike Scioscia, sluggers like Troy Glaus, Garret Anderson and Vladimir Guerrero, and pitchers as Nolan Ryan, Chuck Finley, and Frank Tanana. Interestingly, Ryan led the AL in strikeouts for seven seasons and also pitched four no-hit games while Guerrero has established the franchise's single-season records in runs and total bases. Meanwhile, Scioscia has coached the Angels for eight consecutive years through 2008, and he won a manager-of-the-year award in 2002.

Besides the abilities and accomplishments of these managers and players, Angels teams have succeeded especially in recent MLB seasons because billionaire owner Arte Moreno has invested his resources and millions of dollars into marketing and promoting the team to sports fans throughout the

Los Angeles area. Furthermore, manager Mike Scioscia has taught his ballplayers to concentrate on playing good defense, getting hits with teammates on base, and making the right pitches in games to outperform and defeat any rivals in the league's West Division. If these strategies continue into the early 2010s, then within five years an Angels team will win the franchise's second AL pennant and World Series.

For more than a decade, the performances of the Oakland A's, Seattle Mariners, and Texas Rangers have declined particularly in recent MLB seasons. Since 1991, these three clubs have not won an AL pennant. During each season, they seem to be competitive for nearly 100 games but eventually lose their confidence after being defeated in close games and series to the Angels, and also to each other. As a result, the AL West Division has become less competitive, entertaining, and interesting than the games of teams and their players within the East and Central Divisions of the AL. Unless these circumstances, performances, and results change in the future, the Angels will continue to dominate the West Division in regular seasons and thus be most likely to qualify for the league's playoffs.

Milwaukee Brewers II

Between 1970 and 1997 inclusive, the Milwaukee Brewers played at least one season in the AL's East, Central and West Division. During its first five years after relocating from Seattle, the club's average number of wins increased from 64 (pre-move) to 70 (post-move) and its attendances per season at home games expanded by 27 percent, that is, from 677,000 at Sick's Stadium to 862,000 at County Stadium. While performing in the East Division, the Brewers set all-time attendance highs at County Stadium in 1982–1983 and again in 1989 at 1.9 million to 2.3 million spectators. The former record in attendance occurred, in part, because the team won the second half of the East Division in 1981, but played and lost to the Yankees in a divisional play-off. Then in 1982, a Brewers team defeated the Angels to win the franchise's first and only AL pennant. Yet in October of that year, the club lost in a World Series to the NL St. Louis Cardinals in seven games.

As an AL franchise for 28 years, the Brewers' organization had a number of experienced coaches and outstanding athletes. Among these men in baseball were such field managers as George Bamberger, Buck Rodgers and Tom Trebelhorn, outstanding batters as Robin Yount, Paul Molitor and Cecil Cooper, and good pitchers as Mike Caldwell, Jim Slaton, and Teddy Higuera. In fact, Yount holds two of the club's single-season hitting records while Molitor has four and Cooper three. Other exceptional ballplayers who had excelled for the Brewers during a few seasons in the league included Gordon Thomas in home runs, Tommy Harper in stolen bases, and Greg Vaughn in total bases.

After the 1997 MLB season concluded, the Brewers franchise was transferred into the NL Central Division in order to complete a realignment that put the Rays in the AL East Division, moved the Tigers from the AL East to Central Division, and positioned the Arizona Diamondbacks in the NL West Division. Although the Brewers did not win a division title between 1998 and 2008, the club improved somewhat to place third in 2000 and then eight years later, it performed above expectations and qualified for the NL playoffs by winning 90 games and finishing only seven games behind the Chicago Cubs. Since its transition from the AL to NL, the Brewers' most impressive personnel have included managers Davey Lopes, Ned Yost and Ken Macha, batters Richie Sexson, Geoff Jenkins and Jeromy Burnitz, and pitchers Ben Sheets, Danny Kolb, and C.C. Sabathia.

Within the NL Central Division, the small-market Brewers teams have been challenged each season especially by the Cubs, and also by the Cardinals and Astros. However, if Milwaukee's MLB franchise invests more revenues into its minor-league system and player development programs, and also acquires one or two experienced pitchers, there will be a better opportunity for the Brewers to qualify for the playoffs and eventually win a NL pennant. Because of an increase in demand within the Milwaukee area for the club as happened in 2008, baseball fans in southeast Wisconsin will enthusiastically support the Brewers in its home games played at 41,900-seat Miller Park at least in the short-run and perhaps throughout the 2010s.

Texas Rangers

After moving from Washington, D.C., to Arlington in early 1972, the Texas Rangers' franchise was sold and resold among different syndicates during the 1980s. However, before those transactions occurred, the club won relatively fewer games on average during its first five seasons (1972 through 1976) in comparison to 1967 through 1971 while performing as the Senators in Washington. Even so, Rangers teams have attracted more fans to home games played in 43,521-seat Arlington Stadium than the Senators did at RFK Stadium in the D.C. area (see Table A.3.2). Then, when The Ballpark in Arlington (renamed Ameriquest Field in Arlington) was constructed in 1994, some Rangers clubs established five attendance records at 2.8 million to 2.9 million in each season of 1996 through 1998 and later in 2000–2001.

Besides those facts, various Rangers' teams won four West Division titles in the 1990s. But unfortunately, each of these clubs failed to advance in the AL playoffs when, for example, the 1994 MLB season was cancelled, and also because of their losses in a series of games to the Yankees in 1996, 1998 and 1999. Throughout its history, the Rangers had some good coaches and outstanding ballplayers. Some of them included managers Bobby Valentine and Johnny Oates—who each won more than 500 games—and such single-season leaders as Alex Rodriguez in total bases and home runs, Juan Gonzalez in doubles, runs-batted-in and slugging percentage, and furthermore, as pitchers Ferguson Jenkins in complete games, innings and wins, Rick Heiling in winning percentage, Nolan Ryan in strikeouts, and Francisco Cordero in saves.

One significant event of the franchise occurred during 2000–2001 when owner Tom Hicks negotiated with a players' agent and then signed all-star shortstop Alex Rodriguez to a 10-year, $252 million contract. That deal, in turn, was criticized by many AL team officials and fans because it triggered an increase in the potential salaries of ballplayers that had or would soon become free agents. Although Rodriguez played superior baseball in games for the Rangers, his exorbitant contract meant that Hicks had to cut back salaries and to limit the size of payments to coaches and other athletes on his club. When Hicks decided to trade his all-star shortstop to the highest bidder, the Yankees had enough money to sign Rodriguez and pay off his contract for its remaining years. As a result, Yankees third baseman Rodriguez may win hitting and fielding awards for his performances in regular seasons. Nevertheless, through 2008, the club did not win a World Series with Rodriguez in the lineup.

As discussed in this section before for the Kansas City Athletics, the Rangers teams have not won an AL pennant as of the 2009 MLB season. Indeed, the club rarely played well enough to compete for a West Division title. When any great player such as Mark Teixeira or Kenny Rogers excels for one or more seasons, he will eventually leave the Rangers after becoming a free agent or alternatively, Hicks will trade him to another team in the AL or NL. Based on the team's performances since the late 1990s, the Rangers will continue to flounder as a West Division team during the majority of years and thus, not win enough games each season to consistently qualify for the AL playoffs. Consequently, this may cause sports fans in the Dallas-Fort Worth area to support the NBA Mavericks, NFL Cowboys, NHL Stars, and even MLS' FC Dallas.

St. Louis Browns

After the original Milwaukee Brewers franchise in the AL was sold in 1902 and then moved to eastern Missouri and renamed the St. Louis Browns, the latter team's initial five-year performances substantially changed. That is, the club's average number of wins increased from 48 in Milwaukee to 66 in St. Louis while its attendances at home games improved by almost 150 percent per season at Sportsman's Park (see Table A.3.2). In 1944, a Browns team won an AL pennant but later lost in six games to the cross-town Cardinals in a World Series. Also, during the franchise's 52-year-old history in St. Louis, at least four different investment groups owned it including the

DeWitt brothers, who in 1951, sold a major share of the Browns and Sportsman's Park to Bill Veeck for about $1.8 million.

Between 1902 and 1953 inclusive, the Browns had 20 different coaches and a number of well-known ballplayers. The team's managers—who each won more than 400 games—were Jimmy McAleer and Luke Sewell, while the club's most productive players in hitting included George Sisler, Ken Williams and Vern Stephens, and in pitching were such athletes as Urban Shocker, Rube Waddell, and Ned Garver. Other great players had set single-season records for the Browns. For example, Jack Tobin hit 179 singles in 1921, Heinie Manush batted 20 triples in 1928, Harlond Clift scored 145 runs in 1936, and pitcher Jack Powell threw 36 complete games in 1902.

From 1946 to 1953, the Browns finished no higher than sixth place in the AL standings and worse, won less than 50 percent of their regular-season games each of these years. The team's attendances at Sportsman's Park, meanwhile, averaged about 350,000 per season, which was less than the number of spectators who had attended games of the Philadelphia Athletics at Shibe Park and of the Washington Senators at Griffith Stadium. Unable to compete for baseball fans and share the St. Louis market with the popular NL Cardinals, Veeck's syndicate sold the club in September 1953 to another group of investors. Interestingly in November of that year, the U.S. Supreme Court ruled that baseball was a team sport and not an interstate business, and therefore, it was not subject to the federal antitrust laws.

Kansas City Athletics

After Arnold Johnson had purchased the Philadelphia Athletics and Connie Mack Stadium for about $8 million in 1954, he immediately moved his club to play its home games in Kansas City. During its first five seasons there, the Athletics won nearly 63 games each year as it did previously in Kansas City. As a result, the club became instantly popular in Kansas City and its home-game attendances increased in the short run from 413,000 per season at 33,600-seat Shibe Park in Philadelphia to more than one million at 35,000-seat Municipal Stadium. Despite the team's improvement in attendances at home games, however, Johnson sold his ballpark in 1955 to the city for $650,000 in a leaseback transaction. When Johnson died in 1960, his estate decided to sell the Athletics for approximately $4 million to local businessman Charlie Finley.

While performing for 13 seasons as an AL team based in Kansas City, the franchise finished its first season in sixth place but never ranked higher than seventh in the other 12 years. The team's most respected personnel during this period were managers Lou Boudreau, Hank Bauer and Alvin Dark, hitters Gus Zernial, Norm Siebern and Bob Cerv, and pitchers Bobby Shantz, John Odom, and Orlando Pena. So besides the contributions of a few coaches and several ballplayers, the various Athletics' teams that played in the league between 1955 and 1967 inclusive had not established one season or game record in the history of this franchise, that is, from when the franchise had existed in Philadelphia during 1901 through 1954 to while in Oakland during 1968 to 2008. In other words, the Athletics ranked ninth or last for being the worst-performing club from its first season after relocation to its final year in Kansas City.

This paragraph concludes a review of the performances of nine AL teams that had moved from one area to another sometime between 1901 and 2008. Table 3.3 and also A.3.2 in the Appendix denote how successfully each of the clubs had performed for various MLB seasons. Specifically the former table reveals that the New York Highlanders/Yankees and Kansas City Athletics had won, respectively, the most and fewest championships. In contrast, Table A.3.2 indicates that the Anaheim/LA Angels and Texas Rangers were the only clubs whose average winning percentages actually declined during the five years after they had transferred from another place. Moreover, that table also shows that the average attendance of the nine relocated clubs increased at home after each of them had moved into a new area, especially the Baltimore Orioles II, Kansas City Athletics, and Minneapolis Twins.

Given the information presented in this and previous sections, the next and final major segment of Chapter 3 highlights the identity and quality of cities as markets of AL teams besides those clubs already discussed. Following that portion of this chapter is a brief summary that highlights relocation and then some notes that contain books, readings, and other references in the bibliography.

AL TEAMS MARKETS

East Division

Other than the Orioles in Baltimore and Yankees in New York who are each within this division, the home areas of the Red Sox, Rays, and Blue Jays are, respectively, in Boston, Tampa Bay, and Toronto. The Red Sox franchise has existed for 108 years in its large market and accordingly succeeded to win six division titles, 12 AL pennants, and seven World Series (see Table A.3.3). As a sports enterprise, the club has been prosperous through the years and also very popular among fans who may attend home games of the NBA Celtics, NFL Patriots, NHL Bruins, and MLS Revolution. The Red Sox's attendances at Fenway Park are excellent because the team wins far more games than it loses and has employed some of the most talented players in the league. These athletes have included such superstars as Ted Williams, Manny Ramirez, and Carl Yastrzemski. Because of the club's competitiveness, performances and traditions, the Red Sox will remain in Boston for many years after 2008 and perhaps for several decades.

Until the 2008 MLB season began, the various Rays' teams have struggled to win games and finish higher than fifth place in the East Division. Then surprisingly, the franchise won a division title and AL pennant in 2008 but later was defeated in five games by the NL Philadelphia Phillies in a World Series. Despite this recent accomplishment, the Rays' attendance at 44,500-seat Tropicana Field during the 2008 season was among the lowest in the league. However in 1998, more than 2.5 million fans had attended the team's home games in St. Petersburg but that total gradually declined to 1.2 million in 2004. Apparently the performances of such outstanding players as Carl Crawford, B.J. Lipton, and Scott Kazmir did not motivate sports fans enough for them to watch the Rays compete against the Yankees and other visiting clubs in the AL. Because of apathy among baseball fans in the Tampa Bay area and the team's relatively small payroll, the Rays' performances and business successes after 2008 may not meet expectations of the franchise's owners.

Various Toronto Blue Jays teams have performed for 32 seasons in the league's East Division. For its most significant performances since expansion in 1977, the club won five division titles and in 1992–1993, consecutive AL pennants and also two World Series. During these two successful seasons, Cito Gaston brilliantly managed the club and also coached such great ballplayers as hitters John Olerud, Roberto Alomar and Joe Carter, and winning pitchers as Pat Hentgen, Duane Ward, and Jack Morris. At the 45,100-seat SkyDome in Toronto, the Blue Jays' attendances at home games have frequently exceeded four million spectators per year. So whether the Blue Jays will win another division title and AL pennant depends, in part, on the ability of the Red Sox and Yankees in the East Division, and also on the willingness of the franchise's owner to spend more money and retain star athletes who currently play for the club, and furthermore, to sign expensive free agents to contracts. However, if other AL teams such as the Orioles and Rays significantly upgrade their rosters with better ballplayers, the Blue Jays are likely to finish in third, fourth, or fifth place in its division but continue to perform before relatively large crowds at the SkyDome.

Central Division

The transfer of an AL franchise from Washington, D.C., to Minneapolis in 1971 and the performances of the Minnesota Twins since then were each a topic discussed earlier in this chapter. As a result of that relocation, the Twins' rivals in the Central Division for numerous MLB seasons have primarily been the 108-year-old Chicago White Sox, Cleveland Indians and Detroit Tigers, and the 40-year-old Kansas City Royals.

Since 1901, various White Sox teams have shared the Chicago area as a baseball market with different clubs of the NL Cubs. With respect to the former franchise's performances through 2008, the White Sox played well enough to win five division titles, six AL pennants, and a World Series in 1906, 1917 and 2005. Furthermore, the club's home attendances during the 1990s and early 2000s at 44,000-seat New Comiskey Park (later renamed U.S. Cellular Field) averaged more than 2.5 million per season. These and other results of the White Sox occurred because of great efforts by managers like Fielder Jones, Pants Rowland and Ozzie Guillen, batters Nellie Fox, Eddie Collins and Luke Appling, and pitchers Ed Walsh, Ed Ciotte, and Ted Lyons. More recently, the stars of the team have included sluggers Frank Thomas, Magglio Ordonez and Jermaine Dye, and hurlers Mark Buehrle, Jack McDowell, and Alex Fernandez. Because Chicago is an above-average to excellent market that historically has hosted one or more teams in the majority of professional sports, the White Sox will remain located there indefinitely and compete each season for local baseball fans with the more popular Cubs.

Since 1901, some Cleveland Indians teams won a total of seven Central Division titles, five AL pennants, and a World Series in 1920 and again in 1948. Among the franchise's most productive years were when Lou Boudreau had managed a number of Indians teams during the 1940s, when Al Lopez coached six others in the early to mid–1950s, and when Mike Hargrove led some of Cleveland's best clubs to win 721 regular-season games throughout the 1990s. Rather than the Indians' players being recognized as great hitters, infielders and outfielders, various pitchers had contributed most to the club's different championships. Six of those who excelled for years on the mound have included Bob Feller, Stan Coveleski, Mel Harder, Bob Lemon, Early Wynn, and Sam McDowell. When 43,400-seat Jacobs Field opened in 1994, the franchise established home attendances during some seasons between 3.3 million and 3.5 million spectators. So even though the NFL Browns and NBA Cavaliers play their home games in the Cleveland area, the Indians prosper there and thus, the franchise will not relocate to another sports market within North America.

The Detroit Tigers, meanwhile, had performed much more competitively as a baseball franchise before the 1990s than in the latest 15 to 18 years. In total, the club has won three division titles, 10 AL pennants, and four World Series. Furthermore, the majority of its attendance records were established during the 1980s at 47,000-seat Tiger Stadium with an average of 2.1 million to 2.7 million spectators there at 81 home games in each of four years. Among the club's greatest personnel throughout its history were managers Sparky Anderson, Hugh Jennings and Mayo Smith, batting champions Ty Cobb, Hank Greenberg and Al Kaline, and such winning pitchers as Hal Newhouser, Jack Morris, and Mickey Lolich. In 2006, the Tigers won its most recent AL pennant but then was defeated in five games in a World Series played against the St. Louis Cardinals. Based on the team's longstanding performances and traditions as an enterprise in the AL, the Tigers will not move from the Detroit area for any reason other than the failure and collapse of MLB.

From when it became established and played as an expansion team beginning in 1969, the Kansas City Royals have seemingly struggled to achieve great success. As a club in MLB for 40 years, it has won seven division titles, two AL pennants, and in 1985, a World Series. During the 1970s, field manager Whitey Herzog coached Royals' teams to more than 400 victories and so did Dick Howser in the 1980s. Besides the achievements of Herzog and Howser, the team's most well-known ballplayers had formerly consisted of George Brett, Willie Wilson and Hal McRae, and such outstanding pitchers as Bret Saberhagen, Dan Quisenberry, and Paul Splittoff.

Since the early 1980s, Royals' teams have tended to attract approximately 2.1 million to 2.5 million spectators each season to their home games at 40,800-seat Kauffman Stadium. Being located in a small and inferior sports market, the Royals do not earn enough revenues from gate receipts and any local broadcasting contracts to afford and maintain an above-average payroll for the players on its roster. Consequently, the club has not won a championship since the mid–1980s. Therefore, the Royals may be forced after some MLB season in the future to relocate from its home in Kansas City if a syndicate of investors decide to purchase the franchise and then move it into a new ballpark that exists somewhere in another, and perhaps more populated, U.S. metropolitan area.

West Division

Earlier in this chapter, the accomplishments and performances of the California Angels/Anaheim Angels/Los Angeles Angels of Anaheim, and then the Oakland A's and Texas Rangers were discussed because these teams had been moved from other places to their current sites. As a result, the fourth and final member of this division to be highlighted is the Seattle Mariners. Sadly, this expansion franchise has won only three titles but not any AL pennants through the 2008 MLB season. Field manager Lou Piniella coached the team to more than 800 victories between 1993 and 2002, while batters Ken Griffey Jr., Edgar Martinez and Ichiro Suzuki, and pitchers Randy Johnson, Jamie Moyer, and Mark Langston each had established one or more of the Mariners' records with their outstanding performances.

While playing home games at 47,700-seat Safeco Field, the club's attendance normally exceeds three million spectators each season. But for the franchise to become more competitive and prosperous as a sports business enterprise in the Seattle area, its owners must invest additional resources and capital into the team's minor-league system and other player development programs, and also marginally increase the club's payroll in 2009 and thereafter. If these strategies are not implemented soon, it is doubtful that the Mariners will consistently finish higher than second or third place in the AL West Division.

SUMMARY

Chapter 3 basically analyzed various aspects about—and consequences of—the relocation of nine franchises in the AL. There were six tables of data—including three in the Appendix—that denoted some interesting characteristics of these clubs' areas prior to and following their movements, and also that revealed any differences in their performances within a division and across the league. Finally, the achievements of MLB teams that did not relocate such as the Boston Red Sox in the East Division, Cleveland Indians in the Central Division, and Seattle Mariners in the West Division, are briefly discussed. For the most part, the majority of teams moved to relatively less-populated and lower-ranked cities, played before more fans at home games in ballparks for a few years after their relocation, and also, won a higher percent of regular-season games.

Based on the unique circumstances, events, and problems of these nine franchises at their former locations, it was necessary and potentially profitable for each of them to transfer to—and operate within—another area, and also in the best interest of the AL and MLB. According to the research that I performed for this chapter, the New York Highlanders/Yankees and then Oakland A's have been the two most successful teams subsequent to their movements while the least impressive in performances were the St. Louis Browns and Kansas City Athletics. Moreover, because no movements of clubs have occurred in the league since 1971, this result suggests how critically important, extremely risky, and commercially challenging decisions by MLB to evaluate and approve or reject relocation, and whether or not to implement it, are for investors, officials in franchises, organizations associated with professional baseball, and most of all fans of the sport.

4

National League
Team Relocation

Between 1870 and 1871 and when the American League (AL) and National League (NL) joined to form Major League Baseball (MLB) in 1900 and 1901, a few independent professional baseball organizations existed for one or more years in the United States (U.S.). Besides the NL and AL who, respectively, played their initial seasons in 1876 and 1900, there were such groups as the National Association (1871 to 1875), American Association (1882 to 1891), Union Association (1884), Players League (1890), and Western League (1892 to 1899).

Within the contents of previous chapters, the histories of these leagues were briefly discussed including their expansions, if any, and also the placement of their new baseball teams into occupied or unoccupied urban places. Moreover, Chapter 3 revealed the origins of the eight-year, multi-team Western League (renamed AL in 1899) and furthermore, highlighted the movements of its franchises from and into various sports markets across the U.S.

In contrast to the shift from one location to another of nine AL teams as presented and described in Chapter 3, this chapter identifies—and provides data, facts, and other specific information about—the movements or transfers of clubs in professional baseball's pre–1900 leagues, but more significantly, about the relocation of any franchises within the 133-year-old NL. Indeed, the spatial distribution, location, and movement of teams in four of the early leagues likely affected the longevity, performance, and prosperity of franchises in the NL particularly before 1900 and somewhat of other MLB teams in 1901 and thereafter.

Chapter 4 is organized into four distinct but interconnecting parts. The first and second of them describe, respectively, any relocations or transfers of teams within or between a few of the early or pre–1900 major baseball leagues, and then specifically any movements of clubs in the NL before and after 1900. To establish and clarify these activities or events of leagues, there is at least one table in each part that provides some characteristics, dates, names, and other historical facts that relate to these baseball teams while they were located and playing games during seasons at their pre-move and post-move sites.

After these two sections conclude, the third part of this chapter examines the different performances of NL teams before and after they had relocated and whether they became more or less prosperous and successful in the league. Again, a table there and another one in the Appendix reveal how well these clubs performed during their regular seasons, and if they had qualified for the playoffs in baseball's postseasons. Finally, the fourth part of Chapter 4 focuses on the performances of other teams, or those not previously discussed, who also had played in the league's East, Central, or West Division as of 2008. Moreover, I predict their opportunity and potential for relocation in 2009 or during later decades of the twenty-first century.

Although it had operated in America during years of the nineteenth century, the National Association of Base Ball Players (NABBP) was primarily considered an amateur organization of baseball clubs between the late 1850s and mid-to-late 1860s. Nonetheless in 1869 and 1870, some of the most competitive and popular members of the NABBP were permitted by officials in the organization to declare themselves as professionals and thus, these clubs paid their ballplayers to perform in games. This policy, in turn, created confusion between the NABBP's amateur and professional interests because of ambiguities about how championships would be decided and whether to regulate the conduct of players who continued to transfer between teams in order to earn the highest payment of money from them.

As a result of these differences in interests, most of the prominent professional clubs in the NABBP dropped from the league in 1871 and two years later, the organization disbanded into state and regional baseball groups. Therefore, due to various disputes, instabilities and other conflicts, any relocations or transfers of NABBP teams were not included as topics in forthcoming sections of this chapter.

EARLY BASEBALL LEAGUES

Besides the eight-year-old WL and 25-year-old NL, four other professional baseball leagues had existed during various years in America and before 1900. These groups of teams were the National Association of Professional Base Ball Players or alternatively the National Association (NA), and also the American Association (AA), Union Association (UA), and Players League (PL). The important issue to expose here is whether any teams within these organizations moved from one urban place to another, and whether any of their franchises had transferred between leagues for business, demographic, or sport-specific reasons.[1]

The primary features of the NA—which replaced the NABBP and had existed for five years—were the lack of a centralized administration, the intervention, influence and suspicion of gamblers, and the instability of the league's franchises. As denoted in Table A.2.1 of the Appendix, the majority of NA teams played only a few seasons and then dissolved for financial reasons. Some of them, in fact, had joined the league, competed for one season, but dropped from the NA and then reentered it in a future year. Geographically, NA clubs had been scattered among small, midsized, and large cities such as Baltimore, Boston, and Philadelphia in the east to Fort Wayne, Keokuk, and St. Louis in the midwest.

It was expansion, therefore, and not relocation that primarily determined the number, lifespan, and home places of many teams in the NA. Thus rather than survive even temporarily by moving from one city to another, most clubs either withdrew from the league, disbanded, or ceased operating for a few years and then later rejoined the NA. Finally in 1876, six franchises from the NA and two other independent teams organized into a group and established the NL.

Six years after the NL's opening season in 1876, the AA began to operate with one-half dozen teams located in different urban places. Other ways the AA distinguished itself from the NL is that its teams sold tickets to fans at discount prices and also offered beer and whiskey at their ballparks before, during, and after regular-season games. Interestingly, during its 10-year history, the AA varied in size from six franchises in 1882 to a total of 12 in 1884. Although none of the AA's different clubs had relocated from their original home sites, some changes in composition occurred within the league such as the replacement of the Washington Statesmen by the Richmond Virginians in 1884. Seven years later, the Philadelphia Athletics franchise was replaced by the PL's Philadelphia Quakers and also the Cincinnati Porkers by the Milwaukee Brewers.

Besides these three replacements, eight clubs had shifted from the AA to NL between 1887 and 1891 inclusive. As indicated in the various columns of Table 4.1 and also in Table A.4.1 of the Appendix, the most to least experienced AA franchises that had transferred were, respectively, the Baltimore Orioles, Louisville Colonels, and St. Louis Browns with ten seasons each in the league, and alternatively at five or less years were the Pittsburgh Alleghenys, Cleveland Spiders and Washington Senators. Meanwhile, the AA clubs that had established the highest winning percentages included the St. Louis Browns at 63 percent, Cincinnati Reds at 58 percent, and Brooklyn Bridegrooms at 52 percent. The remaining five teams, however, had each won fewer than 50 percent of their total games, and that especially meant the Spiders and Senators who each lost about seven out of ten of them.

After playing at least eight seasons in the NL, the Orioles, Colonels, Spiders, and Senators were each eliminated by the league. In contrast, the Reds, Pirates, Cardinals, and Superbas continued as NL franchises after 1899 and then one year later, the Spiders (renamed Cleveland Blues) joined the AL. Furthermore in 1901, an Orioles and Senators franchise each entered the AL

Table 4.1 Team Transfers
From American Association to National League, 1882–1891

Teams	Years	Pre-1901 Seasons American Association	National League
Baltimore Orioles	18	1882-1891	1892-1899
Cincinnati Reds	19	1882-1889	1890-1900
Louisville Colonels	18	1882-1891	1892-1899
Pittsburgh Alleghenys/Pirates	19	1882-1886	1887-1900
St. Louis Browns/Perfectos/ Cardinals	19	1882-1891	1892-1900
Brooklyn Bridegrooms/ Superbas	17	1884-1889	1890-1900
Cleveland Spiders	13	1887-1888	1889-1899
Washington Senators	9	1891-1891	1892-1899

Note: *The transfer of some teams occurred, in part, as a result of a merger between the American Association and National League in 1891. A slash (/) indicates a change in a team's nickname. For each team, the Years in column two are the number of combined seasons in columns three and four. Regarding teams' changes in nicknames, the Alleghenys became the Pirates in 1891, Browns became the Perfectos in 1899 and then Cardinals in 1900, and Bridegrooms became the Superbas in 1899.*

Source: *James Quirk and Rodney D. Fort,* Pay Dirt: The Business of Professional Team Sports *(Princeton, NJ: Princeton University Press, 1992); David Pietrusza,* Major Leagues: The Formation, Sometimes Absorption and Mostly Inevitable Demise of 18 Professional Baseball Organizations, 1871 to Present *(Jefferson, NC: McFarland, 1991); "Teams," at http://www.baseball-reference.com, accessed 9 September 2008.*

as expansion clubs. Consequently, the two superior sports markets that hosted AA teams were Cincinnati and St. Louis, while the worst markets included Cleveland and Washington. Thus between 1882 and 1891, there were zero AA franchises that had moved their operations to other places within the U.S. Apparently during these years, professional baseball was a developing sport in America. Therefore, relocation did not exist then as a viable option for teams in this league, or previously, in the NA.

One year after officials in the AA and NL had signed a new national agreement that ensured respect for player contracts under the auspices of a controversial contract system, the UA formed in Pittsburgh with some of its clubs playing at home in ballparks located within small, midsized, large, and very large urban places of the U.S. During the new league's 1884 season, a number of UA teams existed within sports markets that had also hosted AA or NL franchises. These included such urban places as Baltimore, Boston, Chicago, Cincinnati, St. Louis, Philadelphia, Pittsburgh, and Washington. So the other markets that contained only an UA team for part or the entire year were Altoona, Pennsylvania, and Wilmington, Delaware, and the cities of Kansas City, Milwaukee, and St. Paul.

Because of either a poor performance or being located where other professional baseball clubs had played, or based in an inferior sports town, a few teams within the new league were forced to fold or to relocate to another place (see Table A.4.2). With respect to relocation, the Altoona Mountain Citys moved to western Missouri and became the Kansas City Cowboys; the Chicago Browns relocated to western Pennsylvania and was renamed the Pittsburgh Stogies and shortly thereafter the Stogies moved to northern Minnesota and played in games as the St. Paul Saints; then, the Philadelphia Keystones relocated to Delaware to perform as the Wilmington Quicksteps, who later moved to southeast Wisconsin and changed its nickname to Milwaukee Brewers.

Interestingly the 2005 edition of the *Official Major League Baseball Fact Book* lists Chicago-Pittsburgh as a single UA franchise in 1884. As such, the relocation of the Browns from Chicago to Pittsburgh in midseason undoubtedly occurred. But since there is no clear distinction in the baseball literature between the numbers of games won while based in each city, the team's primary name may have actually been Chicago-Pittsburgh.

Although five of the different UA clubs had ultimately won more than 50 percent of their games, including the Milwaukee Brewers at 8–4, the league's organization and structure was flawed, and also, most of its teams' ballplayers did not attract or excite hometown baseball fans especially in such sports markets as Altoona, Kansas City, Philadelphia and Wilmington. Nonetheless, the St. Louis Maroons' Fred Dunlap, Baltimore Monumentals' Bill Sweeney, and the Washington Nationals' Hugh Daily each played outstanding baseball and indeed led the league in one or more hitting or pitching categories. In the end, the UA never established a well-respected identity, image or reputation among fans and the media, and thus, it failed to challenge the AA or NL as an accomplished, competitive, and professional major baseball league.

After various members of the Brotherhood of Professional Base Ball Players left the NL because of a mistrustful and unfair relationship between them and their teams, they organized the PL in 1890. Except for a PL club nicknamed Bisons in Buffalo, the league's other seven franchises located in places where one or more AA or NL teams had played at home in their local ballparks. Despite the presence of other major baseball teams within their markets, such PL clubs as the Boston Reds, Brooklyn Ward Wonders, and Chicago Pirates frequently played before big crowds at games in their home ballparks. Even so, the majority of the new league's franchises were disorganized and underfunded while the owners of them lacked confidence and refused to make any significant investment in ballplayers, managers and staff.

When the PL's New York and Pittsburgh teams combined their operations with, respectively, the NL's New York Giants and Pittsburgh Alleghenys, the new league's investors and franchise owners panicked and tried to seek deals with other clubs in the NL in order to remain solvent. As such, besides the merger of teams in New York and Pittsburgh, the PL Ward Wonders linked with the NL Brooklyn Bridegrooms and the Pirates with the Chicago

Colts. Also, the Cincinnati Reds joined the AA and so did the Philadelphia Quakers when the Philadelphia Athletics team was expelled from the NL in 1890 because it had bankrupted, reorganized, and then lost 22 consecutive games to finish its season.

One of the most famous ballplayers on a team in the PL was 16-year-old Willie McGill, who pitched for the inferior Cleveland Infants. He became the youngest major leaguer to throw a complete game when the Infants defeated the Buffalo Bison in 1890. Other well-known athletes on PL clubs were Boston's Hoss Radbourn and Addison Gumbert, who won a total of 50 games as pitchers, and Chicago's hitter Hugh Duffy and pitcher Mark Baldwin, who became leading players in the league. When the PL folded after the 1890 season, these and other outstanding ballplayers joined clubs in the AA or NL and some of them excelled in these leagues as batters, fielders, or pitchers. As an aside, a committee appointed by MLB commissioner William Eckert ruled in 1968 that the PL was, in fact, a major league in professional baseball.

After 1900, one of the final groups of baseball clubs to organize and seriously challenge some NL and AL teams in several of their home markets was the Federal League (FL). Most sports officials considered the FL to be an outlaw minor league in 1913. But one year later, the FL declared itself a major league of professional baseball. To co-exist with the NL and AL and also succeed in the sport, the FL originally placed some clubs in big cities like Brooklyn and Chicago, in midsized places such as Pittsburgh and St. Louis, and in marginal areas like Buffalo and Kansas City. During each of its two seasons as a major league, the FL had very close pennant races that resulted in a championship for the Indianapolis Hoosiers in 1914 and then for the Chicago Whales in 1915. However, despite winning the league's first pennant race, the Indianapolis franchise experienced attendance and financial problems, and thus in late 1914, it relocated to a city in New Jersey and played there with a new nickname, that is, the Newark Peppers.

To challenge MLB in early 1915 and declare it to be an illegal trust that should be dissolved, the FL filed a lawsuit in a court under the authority of organized baseball's future commissioner Kenesaw Mountain Landis. Rather than review the evidence presented and immediately settle this case, Landis stalled for awhile and encouraged both of these baseball organizations to meet and negotiate with each other to jointly and amicably resolve their dispute. Because of this delay and tactic by Landis, the FL experienced extreme financial difficulties and consequently, it had to disband in December of 1915.

As a result of the new league's demise after two years in operation, some of MLB's franchise owners purchased FL clubs located in Brooklyn, Buffalo, Newark, and Pittsburgh. Furthermore, after receiving permission from MLB, the FL St. Louis Terriers acquired and then merged with the AL St. Louis Browns, and likewise, the Whales merged with the NL Chicago Cubs.

Finally, the FL Kansas City franchise declared bankruptcy and then, the league's team based in Maryland dissolved and sold its ballpark to the owners of the Baltimore Orioles, who continued to play regular-season games in the International League. After these transactions concluded in late 1915, the NL and AL decided to co-exist in America with eight teams each located in their respective home markets until the early 1950s.

So years before and after early 1900, the owners of dubious, failing, and weak franchises in the early baseball leagues—other than the NL—mostly did not move their clubs to different places in the U.S. Instead, some of these teams had transferred to other leagues, some ceased to operate either during or after seasons and then disbanded, and also some were bought out and merged with clubs in another professional baseball league. Evidently the cost, risk, and problem of relocating into new territories by poor-performing and undercapitalized teams was not a common or well-thought-out strategy that franchise owners knew then how to evaluate, plan, and implement.

Without much, if any, current and reliable data to measure and judge the size and quality of markets in other sports towns, these early baseball leagues and the owners of various teams in them lacked information and also the funds to aggressively initiate relocation as a way of maintaining competitive balance and running a baseball enterprise. In contrast, one transfer occurred in the FL when the Hoosiers team in Indianapolis successfully moved to Newark after the league's 1914 season. This happened, of course, several years after the AL Milwaukee Brewers relocated to St. Louis and Baltimore Orioles to New York. Anyway, the Newark team's owner sold his club in 1915 to other investors who were affiliated or associated with MLB.

In the next section of this chapter, I will discuss the relocation of clubs in the NL during its extensive history of more than 130 seasons (see Table 4.2). For details, this and another table reflect something interesting and relevant about these NL teams and their markets before and subsequent to relocation. After this section concludes, the performances of these clubs will denote how successful or poorly they had played in regular-season and post-season home and away games while based at their pre-move and post-move sites. As such, this discussion follows the same format as presented in Chapter 3 for the nine AL teams that had relocated between 1901 and 2008.[2]

NL TEAM RELOCATIONS

Cleveland→St. Louis

In 1878, the NL consisted of six franchises. As such, they played their games at home in six different urban places whose rankings in population (in parentheses) were Chicago (4), Boston (5), Cincinnati (8), Milwaukee (19),

Table 4.2 Big League Baseball National League Teams
That Relocated, by Seasons, Years, and Areas, 1876–2008

Teams	Seasons	Years	From	To
			Areas	
Pre-1901				
Cleveland Blues	1879-1884	1985	Cleveland	St. Louis
Post-1900				
Boston Braves	1912-1952	1953	Boston	Milwaukee
Brooklyn Dodgers	1901-1957	1958	Brooklyn	Los Angeles
New York Giants	1901-1957	1958	New York	San Francisco
Milwaukee Braves	1953-1965	1966	Milwaukee	Atlanta
Montreal Expos	1969-2004	2005	Montreal	Washington

Note: Teams, Seasons, and Areas are self-explanatory. Years is each team's first season after relocation.
Source: James Quirk and Rodney D. Fort, Pay Dirt, 378–383, 391–399, and Frank P. Jozsa, Jr., and John J. Guthrie, Jr., Relocating Teams and Expanding League in Professional Sports: How the Major Leagues Respond to Market Conditions (Westport, CT: Quorum, 1999).

Providence (20), and Indianapolis (24). In turn, the population of these places varied from 500,000 people in Chicago to 75,000 in Indianapolis. To expand the league's size, three new teams gained entry and joined it in 1879, including the Blues in Cleveland (11). Meanwhile, the franchises based in Indianapolis and Milwaukee were dropped from the NL because they each finished at least 17 games behind the Boston Red Stockings. These changes not only increased the number of clubs from six to eight, but also committed them to play complete regular-season schedules and control their debts and other important obligations.

As an expansion team, the Blues finished no higher than third place during its six seasons in the NL and that result, in turn, caused attendance and financial problems for franchise owner C.H. Bulkley. After the Blues finished seventh and 49 games behind the Providence Grays in 1884, Bulkley sold his club for $2,500 to Henry Lucas in early 1985. But when Lucas purchased the Blues, former owner Bulkley had apparently sold the club's ballplayers to the Brooklyn Bridegrooms in the AA. Despite a series of court cases against Bulkley's action, Lucas then moved his team from Cleveland to a midsized sports market in East St. Louis and nicknamed it the St. Louis Maroons.

During the early to mid–1880s, St. Louis ranked sixth in population with a total of 330,000 people and its area's growth rate was 2.8 percent (see Table 4.3). The Browns, a popular team in the AA, had played at a site in St. Louis since 1882 and successfully drew a relatively large number of fans each season to its games at home. Because other NL and AA teams had existed in very large cities like New York and Philadelphia, and other AA clubs played in such populated places as Baltimore, Cincinnati and Pittsburgh, Lucas determined that St. Louis was a big enough city to host another major league baseball club besides the Browns.

Table 4.3 National League Teams Population Characteristics
of Areas Before and After Relocation, 1876–2008

Years		Areas		Population Rank		Growth	
Before	After	Before	After	Before	After	Before	After
Pre-1901							
1884	1885	Cleveland	St. Louis	11	6	6.3	2.8
Post-1900							
1952	1953	Boston	Milwaukee	6	16	3.0	3.0
1957	1958	New York	Los Angeles	1	3	1.0	4.5
1957	1958	New York	San Francisco	1	3	1.0	2.5
1965	1966	Milwaukee	Atlanta	18	24	1.0	3.6
2004	2005	Montreal	Washington	2	7	1.5	3.0

Note: Years Before and After are, respectively, each team's final year prior to relocation and first year following relocation. Areas Before and After are self-explanatory. In columns five and six are, respectively, the population ranks and population growth rates of each team's areas the year before and after relocation. Growth rates are expressed as annual percents. The San Francisco area includes the city of Oakland, and the New York area includes the city of Brooklyn. The Montreal area ranked second in Canada.

Source: "Population of the 100 Largest Urban Places: 1870–1900," at http://www.census.gov cited 15 September 2008, and various editions of *The World Almanac and Book of Facts* (New York, NY: World Almanac Book, 1930–2008).

But in the 1885–1886 seasons, the Maroons finished eighth and then sixth in the NL while in these years, the Browns easily won AA pennants. Then in series of games between the AA and NL champions, the Browns defeated the Chicago White Stockings and declared that their ballclub should be recognized as the king of baseball. Consequently, because of the Browns' great success and the Maroons' weak performances each season, Lucas sold his franchise to investors from Indianapolis in early 1887. So in that year, a new Indianapolis Hoosiers club replaced the St. Louis Maroons in the NL.

The transfer of Cleveland to St. Louis in 1885 was the only relocation that had occurred in the NL from the mid–1880s to the early 1950s. Even so, there were movements of two clubs in the AL during the early 1900s. Besides the cost, disappointment, and risk of failing as a sports enterprise, it was the actual competition from—or the threat of invasion by—other professional baseball leagues such as the AA and UA that, in part, discouraged owners of NL teams from strategically moving their operations into new markets across the east and midwest before 1900. Then after the FL folded in 1915, there were no threats from outsiders to challenge the power of MLB teams in their local areas. Being monopolists and perhaps operating at a profit or even a loss, eight teams played games in the NL while based at their original home sites from 1900 to 1952.

Boston→Milwaukee

Between 1876—which is when Nathaniel Appollonio became the team's owner—and 1952 inclusive, the Boston Red Stockings/Beaneaters/Doves/Pilgrims/Braves franchise existed in the NL. During these 77 seasons of competition, these teams won a total of 10 NL pennants. Then in 1914, the Braves played well enough to defeat the AL Philadelphia Athletics in four games and win its first and only World Series. Despite these victories and also being a close runner-up to the AL Cleveland Indians in the 1948 World Series, the Braves tended to finish below third in the league during a majority of its MLB seasons. Consequently, these dismal performances and a series of financial difficulties caused a high turnover of sports entrepreneurs and various groups who had owned the franchise in Boston. So after a series of sales and repurchases, a syndicate headed by Lou Perini that included his brothers and a few other investors, made a bid and acquired almost 100 percent of the team in 1944. Eight years later, the Perinis bought out the franchise's co-owners and thereby achieved total ownership, and thus full control, of the Braves enterprise.[3]

During the late 1940s and early 1950s, some circumstances and events occurred that provided a great incentive and wonderful opportunity for the Perinis to shift the Braves from Boston to Milwaukee after the 1952 MLB season had concluded. First, the NL Braves ranked no higher than fourth each season in 1949 to 1952 while the Boston Red Sox placed second, third (twice), and sixth in the AL. Second, during these four seasons, the Braves' and Red Sox's average attendances for home games were, respectively, 698,000 at Braves Field and 1.3 million at Fenway Park. Third, each teams' average pre-tax profits for three years—that is, in 1948–1949 and 1952 (profits were unavailable in 1951)—were estimated at -$308,000 for the Braves and -$140,000 for the Red Sox. Thus in comparison, the Braves' clubs performed much worse and also were less popular and incurred larger operating losses, than those of the Red Sox.

Besides significant differences between these two Boston-based professional baseball franchises as revealed from the former three sets of statistics, MLB changed its rules in 1952. These changes meant that team movements (and expansions) became a concern for only the league involved and not the other league—except for invasion of another team's territory—and that the relocation of clubs required merely a three-fourths favorable vote and not the unanimous consent of its league's members. In other words, the approval for any NL and AL franchises to move from one area to another, and for either league to expand, became much easier to obtain from the decision-makers within organized baseball.

Meanwhile a new 28,000-permanent seat (or 36,000 at capacity) and publicly-funded baseball facility named Milwaukee County Stadium was completed during the early 1950s for the Milwaukee Brewers, which was the NL Braves' AAA minor-league club located in southeast Wisconsin. Thus sometime before or after the Perini brothers had received approval from MLB to relocate their franchise from Boston to Milwaukee, they successfully negotiated a sweetheart lease with government officials in Milwaukee. As a result, the Perinis received permission to rent County Stadium from the city for $1,000 per year. The team, however, agreed to amend its contract with the city and thereby accepted an increase in rent for the ballpark from $1,000 to $25,000 in 1953 and again in 1954.

In retrospect, the movement of the Braves to Milwaukee in early 1953 generated significantly more fans, revenues, and profits for the Perinis franchise. Also, it compelled the brothers to spend additional amounts of money to increase the payrolls of the team's coaches and ballplayers, and for more investment in the club's minor-league system and development programs. Invariably these expenditures resulted in a World Series championship for the Braves in 1957 and another NL pennant in 1958. Moreover, this relocation undoubtedly provided an opening and a pathway for other MLB clubs to change their locations—especially away from cities in the east into some markets in the midwest and west—and also for the expansion of teams in both leagues of MLB. In the long run, the Braves' movement caused various municipalities in the U.S. to increasingly invest public money in order to finance the construction of modern ballparks for a majority of big league clubs, especially during the mid-to late 1900s and early 2000s.

After a steady decline in attendances at County Stadium and mediocre to below-average performances of their team after its championship seasons in Milwaukee, the Perinis sold a majority of the franchise's stock for $6.2 million in 1962 to a new group that consisted of the Braves president and general manager John McHale, and also of six former minority owners of the Chicago White Sox including William Bartholomay and Thomas Reynolds, Jr. Four years later, these owners jointly decided to vacate the Milwaukee area—where the local and regional broadcast market was tiny—and move the Braves to Georgia, and then change their team's nickname to Atlanta Braves.

Brooklyn→Los Angeles

When real estate executive and practicing attorney Charles H. Bryne entered a baseball team he owned from Brooklyn into the short-lived Interstate League, it won a pennant in 1883. One year later, Bryne transferred his club to the AA where it played with such nicknames as the Brooklyns, Brooklyners, Brooks, and for the media and majority of sports fans, as the Bridegrooms. After a few seasons in the AA, the team defeated the St. Louis Browns for the league's championship. Then in a nine-game series, the Bridegrooms lost to the New York Giants, which had won the NL pennant in 1889.

When another baseball team from Brooklyn joined the newly-organized Players League in 1890, that year the Bridegrooms then moved from the AA into the NL.[4]

During the mid-to late 1890s and very early 1900s, the team's nickname gradually changed from Bridegrooms to Superbas, and then to Dodgers. These different changes in names resulted from baseball games being played at Eastern Park where several trolley lines had converged in Brooklyn. Thus, the team's name, Trolley Dodgers, evolved into merely Dodgers. Anyway, between 1900 and the early 1940s, this franchise was sold and resold, and had incurred huge debts and nearly bankrupted in 1938. Even so, it started to generate profits when Larry McPhail took over as the club's president. Then in 1942, Branch Rickey replaced McPhail while Walter O'Malley became the club's lawyer and later a minority owner of it. Before 1950 O'Malley had gained control of the franchise from Rickey, in part, by purchasing the stock of other owners.

Between 1890 and 1956 inclusive, the Dodgers won 12 NL pennants and also a World Series in 1955. Since the early 1910s, the club's home-game attendances at 31,500-seat Ebbets Field in Brooklyn frequently ranked between first and third place in the league. Then in 1954 to 1957, the Milwaukee Braves drew more two million fans each season to its home games at County Stadium. This incredible support for the Braves within a small baseball market impressed Dodgers owner O'Malley and motivated him to complain about the condition of his ballpark in the media and gripe to such officials as the commissioner of Parks in Brooklyn. In O'Malley's view, he did not receive any respect from the commissioner for demanding public land for free to construct a new facility for his team. Thus, the surge in attendance in Milwaukee indicated to O'Malley that the Braves would have enough fans, resources, and money to challenge and possibly outperform the Dodgers each season in the NL.

Besides the improvement in the Braves' environment, the Dodgers, Giants, and Yankees each played their home games within the New York metropolitan area. During 1953 to 1957, the average winning percentages and home attendances of these three teams were, respectively, .613 and 1.1 million, .497 and 814,000, and .642 and 1.5 million. Thus on average, the Dodgers teams outperformed those of the Giants in these five seasons, but nevertheless, this franchise in Brooklyn had to share America's most lucrative commercial market with its rival in the NL and also with the Yankees and local teams in other professional sports.

In the 1956 and 1957 MLB seasons, the Dodgers scheduled and played several home-away-from-home games in Jersey City's 24,000-seat Roosevelt Stadium. As such, these events reflected the ongoing dispute and bitter feud between O'Malley and a number of politicians within the local community about the proposal to allocate public land and replace Ebbets Field with a new, modern ballpark. Anyway, when his discussions with the city became hopeless, O'Malley's negotiated sincerely but hard with officials from another metropolitan area such that he was given the title to some prime real estate near downtown Los Angeles in sunny southern California. After being awarded this valuable property, O'Malley's team moved to the West Coast and became the Los Angeles Dodgers in early 1958. Based on these results, Ebbets Field in Brooklyn was then sold by the city to businessman Marvin Kratter for $3 million.

The relocation from Brooklyn to Los Angeles provided an immediate financial bonus and an excellent long-run investment for the Dodgers franchise and its various groups of owners, coaches, managers and ballplayers. While the team played four years in the city's 93,600-seat Memorial Coliseum, its attendances there increased to almost two million per season. Then in 1962, 56,000-seat Dodger Stadium opened and the club's attendances at home games zoomed to 2.2 million to 2.7 million each year until 1967. Meanwhile, different Dodgers teams played well enough to win four more NL pennants and another three World Series before 1970. To some sports economists, the move of the Braves to Milwaukee was an example of a lagging market in Boston while the Dodgers transfer out of Brooklyn occurred because of an opportunity for the team to play in greener pastures within a fast-developing and prosperous area near the U.S. West Coast.

New York→San Francisco

The New York Gothams joined the NL as an expansion franchise in 1883. Two years later, the club was renamed the Giants and then in 1890 and 1891, it had financial troubles and merged with another team from New York that competed in the PL. Between the late 1890s and mid–1950s, the Giants franchise became owned and then resold by such well-known baseball entrepreneurs as John Brush, Charles Stoneham and his son Horace, and also John McGraw. Before the late 1950s, the club had won 17 NL pennants and five World Series while, in part, playing its home games in various ballparks including different versions of the Polo Grounds. Thus, this franchise thrived while located in New York and also played competitively in regular-season games as a rival of the cross-town Brooklyn Dodgers. In fact, the Giants became a popular and successful team in the early 1950s because of the performances of such great hitters as Willie Mays, Alvin Dark and Bobby Thompson, and pitchers Sal Maglie, Johnny Antonelli, and Larry Jansen.[5]

During the late 1940s to 1951, the Giants attendances at its home games in the 56,000-seat Polo Grounds exceeded one million per season. Then between 1952 and 1957, the club attracted less than 900,000 to its ballpark each year except in 1954 when it won an NL pennant and then a World Series after defeating the AL Cleveland Indians in four consecutive games. Meanwhile, Dodgers owner Walter O'Malley had expressed a strong interest in moving his club out of Brooklyn after clashing with government officials there about having to play some games in tiny, outmoded Ebbets Field. Similarly, Giants owner Horace Stoneham began to look for another home for his team since the Polo Grounds was scheduled to be demolished and then replaced by a housing project. Supposedly Stoneham had considered renting Yankee Stadium for one or more years. Indeed this was an interesting strategy because the Yankees had played their home games in the Polo Grounds for ten years, that is, 1913 to 1922.

About the same time that O'Malley made a final decision to move the Dodgers to Los Angeles, Stoneham announced that he had received an attractive offer to transfer the Giants from New York to somewhere within the Bay Area of northern California. Because his team's attendances at the Polo Grounds fell from 1.2 million in 1954 to less than 630,000 in 1957, and due to the impending departure of the Dodgers from Brooklyn to southern California, Stoneham received approval from the league to move his club into the Bay Area before opening day of the 1958 MLB season.

After that relocation had occurred, the Giants teams played home games for two years in San Francisco's 22,900-seat Seals Stadium. Because of the anticipation, enthusiasm, and excitement of baseball fans in that sports market, the Giants attendances at Seals Stadium increased to more than 1.2 million spectators in 1958 and also in 1959. Then in 1960, a new 63,000-seat ballpark named Candlestick Park opened in San Francisco and the Giants' attendance increased to 1.7 million and remained greater than 1.5 million during most MLB seasons of the mid–1960s. Besides playing at home before large crowds, the team also won the NL pennant in 1962 after beating the Dodgers in the league's playoffs. Then in a close multigame series with the Yankees, the Giants lost 1–0 in game seven despite the powerful hitting of superstars like Willie Mays, Orlando Cepeda, and Willie McCovey.

Besides these teams' home attendances and ballparks and their amounts of revenues, two other factors had contributed to the movement of the Dodgers and Giants into California sports markets in the late 1950s. First, some members of the U.S. Congress questioned why MLB had not added new clubs and also expanded into existing or other domestic baseball territories. With at least two big league clubs playing at home in California in 1958 and more thereafter, organized baseball had, in part, responded to Congress' concerns about unoccupied sports markets within two relatively large areas on the West Coast.

Second, the longstanding Pacific Coast League (PCL) and startup Continental League (CL) were each determined to form a third major league in professional baseball. With the relocation of NL clubs from the New York area to Los Angeles and San Francisco, these actions ruined the PCL's plan whereas expansion by the AL and NL during the early 1960s eliminated the hopes of CL officials to organize and field new teams in a major league. In fact, the CL folded in 1960–1961 while being organized by attorney William Shea and future New York Mets owner Joan Payson.

Milwaukee→Atlanta

For several years after moving from Boston to Milwaukee during the early 1950s, the Braves became one of the most competitive, successful, and prosperous teams in the NL. Between 1953 and 1960, for example, the club's annual attendances at County Stadium exceeded two million during four of these years and at least 1.4 million in another four of them. Besides winning consecutive NL pennants, the Braves also defeated the Yankees 4–3 or in seven games to win a World Series title in 1957. While it existed for 13 years in the Milwaukee area, the franchise became the only team in MLB history to play more than one season and never finish with a winning percentage less than .500.

There is other noteworthy information to remember about the Braves' commercial success while operating in southeast Wisconsin. First, the club was profitable for several years because of the total revenues it had collected from paid admissions, concession receipts and parking fees at the ballpark, and also from advertising, sponsorships, and local and regional television and radio contracts. Second, some sports historians estimate that the team's arrival in 1953 generated millions of dollars in new business for local companies and furthermore, this relocation caused numerous investments within Milwaukee's infrastructure that improved the city's roads, schools, water systems, and real estate values. Third, the Braves established excellent communications and good relations with the community by contributing money and ballplayers' time to local charities, social campaigns, and many of the city's youth organizations. Indeed, these were intangible benefits and rewards, and also goodwill from the Braves that likely affected numerous people of all ages and ethnic and economic groups in the area.

After the team's huge success in the mid- to late 1950s, the Braves organization experienced some different baseball, business, and internal problems that gradually led to its final season as an MLB franchise within a sports market of southeast Wisconsin. A few of these issues had originated during the very early years of the 1960s. For example, after accumulating approximately $8 million in profits since 1953, the club incurred a financial loss in 1962 due, in part, to a 30 percent decline in attendances at its home games in County Stadium. As a result, the Perinis sold 90 percent of their franchise's stock for $6.2 million to a Chicago-based group of investors that was headed by Bill Bartholomay. In fact, this sale was the highest price ever paid for an MLB team that did not own its home ballpark.

Another issue for the Braves was that the Dodgers and Giants continued to be profitable and very successful clubs whose revenues and economic values had greatly appreciated since they had relocated to big markets in California during early 1958. Finally, some of the Braves' most talented ballplayers had aged, been traded, or retired from the game after the late 1950s. This, in turn, caused thousands of baseball fans in Milwaukee to become disenchanted and then not attend or simply ignore the team's home games after 1961.

About one or two years after the club was sold in 1962, the Braves new ownership group decided that leaving Milwaukee for another city in America was the practical and most profitable option to pursue for their franchise. They realized the geographic limitations and boundaries of Milwaukee's advertising market of 2.5 million households given the location of Chicago to the south, Minneapolis to the west, and Lake Michigan to the east. Furthermore this group was not optimistic about reviving the Braves fan base in Milwaukee, or interested in investing millions of additional dollars to sign expensive free agents from other teams and improve the competitiveness of the club, or to increase the salaries of managers and players who performed on their minor-league teams. Consequently, the Braves owners contacted government officials and business leaders in several cities of the U.S. to determine whether they would or could host their floundering Milwaukee baseball franchise.

In 1964 and 1965, there were a total of 20 MLB teams located in 17 different cities of the U.S. As such, the largest sports markets in the nation without baseball clubs—and their rankings in population during these years—were Nassau-Suffolk (9), Dallas-Fort Worth (12) and Newark (15), and then Atlanta (18), Seattle (19), and San Diego (23). After evaluating the efforts of, and negotiating with, representatives from these and perhaps other places, Bill Bartholomay's group selected Atlanta to be the next home of the Braves. The decision of the group to choose this eminent and popular southern city as a future site involved several commercial, demographic, and sport-specific matters as follows.

One, during the spring of 1964, Atlanta began to construct an $18 million, 52,000-seat ballpark to be finished and opened in early 1965. When the AL Kansas City Athletics decided to relocate to Oakland, California, in three years rather than to central Georgia, the Braves became a potential tenant of the city's new ballpark, named Atlanta Stadium. Even so, a year remained on the club's lease at County Stadium in Milwaukee and thus, this became an obstruction in the Braves plans to exist the city. Two, some important financial factors for the Braves in moving from Milwaukee into the Atlanta area included an immediate increase in television revenues of $1 million per year, more advertising income from such large corporate sponsors as Coca-Cola and local banks, and an expanded media network that extended hundreds of miles to the east and southeast coast and also to communities in the south and southwest within Florida and other southern states.

Three, Milwaukee was a city with job losses from being located within the Rust Belt whereas Atlanta had experienced economic development, employment growth, and an expanding population as workers in manufacturing and households vacated declining places in the U.S. midwest and north to live in areas of the southeast. Four, throughout the 1960s, some of Atlanta's top civic, corporate, and government leaders had established a policy many business people referred to as competitive boosterism. That is, these officials combined their knowledge, talents and resources to actively participate in luring industries and investments from other cities for the purpose of economic development.[6]

Besides the construction of Atlanta Stadium and new roads, freeways and skyscrapers, and also other complexes and facilities within the area, these individuals' activities included (a) the involvement and support of Mayor Ivan Allen, Jr., and local businessmen, (b) investments in schools of higher education such as Atlanta University, Georgia State University and Georgia Institute of Technology, and (c) a countywide mass transit system. For the most part, these improvements in infrastructure were financed primarily with local and state taxpayer money and furthermore, with donations, gifts, and grants from various corporations in the region.

Within a few months after the NL had initially approved Milwaukee's team to relocate to Atlanta, 29-year-old Bud Selig—the son of Wisconsin's biggest Ford dealer—filed an injunction in a Wisconsin court to force the Braves to play home games in Milwaukee for the 1965 MLB season. Because of various efforts from those who agreed and did not agree with the franchise's move, and due to the club's current lease of County Stadium and also the criticisms of sports reporters in the local, regional and national media, the NL reversed its decision and denied the Braves' request to relocate from Milwaukee in early 1965. So that year, the Braves finished its final season in Milwaukee by placing fifth in the league and 11 games behind the Los Angeles Dodgers. When the season concluded, Bartholomay moved his baseball team to the largest city in Georgia and renamed it the Atlanta Braves.

The final legal battle to prevent the Braves' movement to Atlanta ended in December of 1966. That is, the U.S. Supreme Court voted 4–3 against hearing this case and thus, the judges let stand the decision of the Wisconsin Supreme Court to allow the club's exit from Milwaukee. In the end, MLB and its member franchises were more prominent, prosperous, and successful during the 1970s to early 2000s because of the Braves move in 1966 from small-market Milwaukee to a fast-developing and expanding sports market based in Atlanta.

Montreal→Washington

Since its first MLB season in the NL, the Montreal Expos had struggled throughout its 26-year history to win enough home and away games to

Left: In 1936, Horace Stoneham's father died. As a result, Horace became owner of the New York Giants. Because of the dramatic decrease in his team's attendances at home games played in the Polo Grounds during the early to mid–1950s and also to continue the Giants' rivalry with the Dodgers in the California baseball market, he moved his franchise to San Francisco after the 1957 baseball season. Then twenty years later, Horace sold the team to a new syndicate of investors. [National Baseball Hall of Fame Library, Cooperstown, N.Y.] *Right:* After he had served as chief legal counsel of the Brooklyn Dodgers during the 1940s and then as the team's majority owner as of 1950, Walter O'Malley moved the franchise from Brooklyn to Los Angeles after the 1957 baseball season. Subsequent to the relocation of his club to the West Coast, O'Malley has earned a reputation for being a visionary and one of the most influential sportsmen of the twentieth century. In 1979, he died from congestive heart failure and cancer. [National Baseball Hall of Fame Library, Cooperstown, N.Y.]

qualify for the league's playoffs. Although Expos teams won two East Division titles, they normally finished with more losses than the Cardinals, Mets, Phillies, and other clubs during the majority of seasons. According to some sports historians, the franchise's decline originally began four years after a syndicate headed by John McHale and Charles Bronfman sold the franchise for $86 million to another group that included such diversified investors as a food chain and credit union, and the city of Montreal and province of Quebec.[7]

To explain this problem, in early August of 1994 the Expos had MLB's best winning percentage at .649, which placed it six games ahead of the Atlanta Braves in the NL East Division. However on August 12 of that year, a ballplayers strike occurred and that caused the teams' owners to implement a lockout and cancel MLB's regular season and postseason. As a result of that incident, baseball's reputation was damaged among fans along with the Expos' effort for the construction of a new ballpark in Montreal. Then for personal reasons, some local owners of the club decided not to invest more of their money in order to increase the team's payroll and also retain its most productive athletes. Later, owner Claude Brochu said the Expos had an excellent team that would have won an NL pennant in 1994 and then appeared in MLB's World Series. Undoubtedly Brochu's prediction was based, in part, on the performances of such Expos as Manager of the Year Felipe Alou and talented athletes as Ken Hill, Moises Alou and Marquis Grissom.

After the players strike ended in early 1995, the Expos' general manager, Kevin Malone, spent the next two years releasing many of the team's best fielders, hitters and pitchers. Besides Hill, Alou and Grissom, the other men that left the Expos in 1995 and 1996 included Larry Walker, John Wetteland, Mel Rojas, and Pedro Martinez. A few years later, American art dealer Jeffrey Loria purchased the franchise from Brochu and named his stepson David Samson

During the late 1940s to early 1950s, multimillionaire Lou Perini and his brothers gradually acquired total control of the Boston Braves and the club's ballpark from other stockholders. Unable to attract fans to its games in Boston and needing revenues, Lou moved the franchise in 1953 to Wisconsin and named it the Milwaukee Braves. Then in 1962, Perini sold the Braves for $6.2 million to a syndicate led by William Bartholomay who shifted the team to Atlanta in 1966. [National Baseball Hall of Fame Library, Cooperstown, N.Y.]

to be its executive vice-president. Then, Loria spent more than $10 million to acquire just three ballplayers. That sum, in turn, amounted to 50 percent of the club's total payroll in 1999. For that season and the next one, the Expos played well enough to finish fourth in the East Division. In short, it was the strike in 1994 that led to the team's ownership problems and the decimation of its fan base, and also to difficulties in selling television broadcast rights to local, regional and national networks, and to cable and satellite companies.

During early 2002, MLB became the majority owner of the Expos and operated the franchise while it finished second that season to the Atlanta Braves in the East Division. Then to expand the game internationally, MLB assigned the Expos to play some of its home games in 2003 and 2004 at a ballpark in Puerto Rico. As these seasons in baseball opened and closed, the league made various contacts and negotiated with them to actively move the

Expos out of Montreal to a sports market in the U.S. or elsewhere. Accordingly, MLB officials considered such domestic areas for the franchise as Charlotte, North Carolina; Norfolk, Virginia; and Portland, Oregon. Furthermore, three foreign cities that MLB likely evaluated as potential sites for the ballclub were San Juan, Puerto Rico, and Mexico City and Monterrey in Mexico. Consequently in late 2004, MLB chose Washington, D.C., as the new home of the Expos because of the area's previous experiences with professional baseball teams and also the commitment of local politicians to build the team a modern ballpark at a convenient place for sports fans to attend its home games.

In December 2004, the Expo's relocation from Montreal to Washington was approved in a 28–1 vote by the other owners of MLB franchises. Even so, Baltimore Orioles owner Peter Angelos voted against the move since his team performed at home within the area, which in his view existed as a single baseball market although there were obvious differences in cultures, populations, household incomes, and commercial activities between the two cities. Angelos, however, feared that his investment in the Orioles would decline if a competitor was permitted to enter the area. In contrast, several critics disagreed with Angelos since the Orioles had shared its market with the former Washington Senators for 18 years. This dispute, in turn, also disturbed baseball fans in Washington who remembered that the Griffith family, as longtime owners of the Senators, allowed the AL St. Louis Browns to move from Missouri to east Maryland in early 1954.

After threatening to file lawsuits against MLB and also making public announcements about protecting his franchise's territorial rights by preventing an invasion into the D.C. area from another team, Angelos and league officials successfully negotiated their dispute. Thus, the parties made a deal that ensured no financial harm would come to the Orioles from the entry of an existing baseball team from Montreal that was recently named the Washington Nationals. According to one crucial aspect of this unusual settlement, the Orioles had agreed to form a new sports network that produced and distributed games for each of these franchises on local affiliates, and cable and satellite systems. In other words, Angelos and his new network controlled the television and radio rights for broadcasting both Orioles and Nationals regular-season games. Unfortunately the network was not available for all cable providers so that Nationals' fans who lived in the D.C. area did not watch the majority of the team's games on television in the 2005 and 2006 MLB seasons.

Another short-run but controversial problem regarding this relocation was Washington mayor Anthony Williams' financial plan for a new ballpark. Initially, he had committed the city to pay a portion of the estimated $600 million or more of the cost for the facility without any subsidies from municipal or regional governments in Maryland and Virginia. After a series of proposals to amend the plan in late 2004 and throughout 2005, MLB finally signed a lease with the city in March of 2006 for a new ballpark. With respect to the lease's conditions, the league accepted a cap of $611 million to be spent for the ballpark that D.C.'s council had decided to impose; agreed to contribute $20 million to offset the stadium's construction costs; and stipulated that any excess tax revenues from the ballpark would be allocated for debt service of the bonds and also for the payment of any cost overruns. Given these three specific conditions, a contract was approved by the council to build a state-of-the-art, 41,000-seat ballpark for the team that would open for the 2007 MLB season.

A final issue concerned the sale of the Expos franchise by MLB and then choosing a new group of investors to own and operate it. Because of delays as a result of negotiating with D.C. officials and signing a lease for the new ballpark, MLB had little time to evaluate the proposals submitted by several syndicates. But in the summer of 2006, the league sold the team for about $450 million to the Lerner Enterprise Group, headed by wealthy real estate developer Theodore N. Lerner. Then in the fall of that year, Comcast Corporation committed to broadcast the Nationals' games on its cable network. For certain, this relocation from Montreal to Washington was a complicated action that involved such elements as determining the current boundaries of markets and values of professional baseball teams, as deciding how to most equitably finance and share construction costs and the overruns of a new stadium, as efficiently allocating the broadcast rights of two sports club, and as concluding the sale and purchase of an existing MLB franchise in Montreal.

To highlight this part of Chapter 4, there were six relocations of NL franchises that took place in years between the late 1800s and early 2000s. One movement had occurred before 1900 while three happened during the 1950s, and one each in the mid–1960s and early 2000s. Furthermore, three of the teams had moved from areas in the east, two from the midwest, and one from a province in southeast Canada. After relocation, the six new areas of the clubs included two each in the midwest and west, and one each in the east and south. Overall, the majority of team movements tended to be from cities and urban places in the east to others in the midwest and west.

Based on the population sizes of these areas before and after relocation, five clubs had moved from higher- to lower-ranked sports areas while one— Cleveland to St. Louis—was from an eleventh- to sixth-ranked urban place. Furthermore, four teams relocated from slow- to high-growth areas, one from a high- to slow-growth area, and another—Boston to Milwaukee—that had the same growth rate. In short, most of the six clubs had moved to less-congested and dense areas whose populations experienced relatively higher growth rates.

As a group, these six franchises relocated to other cities for several reasons. Besides differences in the sizes of areas and growth rates of their populations, other factors included the presence and performance of other professional sports clubs in a team's existing market; the opening of new baseball markets in the midwest, south and west; an opportunity to abandon an outdated facility in a city and play in a new ballpark wholly or partially financed with public money; and the potential for greater cash flows, revenues, and profits from a larger and more passionate fan base in another sports market. Finally, most of the clubs that moved had been sold to a new syndicate that consisted of wealthy entrepreneurs who invested their personal funds, or alternatively, had borrowed money from banks to own, control, and operate a franchise in big league baseball for one or more years.

Based simply on population characteristics and other factors besides team performances, the three most and least prosperous NL clubs in their markets after relocation were (and have been), respectively, the Los Angeles Dodgers, Atlanta Braves and San Francisco Giants, and for being inferior, the Milwaukee Braves, Washington Nationals, and St. Louis Maroons. When the histories of performances for each of these teams are included in an analysis, they may be considered more or less successful than indicated here. I recommend that you read the next section for information about this topic.

PERFORMANCES: NL TEAM RELOCATIONS

St. Louis Maroons

Before it moved to St. Louis, the Cleveland Blues had played for six seasons in the NL. While there, various Blues teams won about 35 percent of their games and zero league pennants (see Table 4.4). In 1880, the club attained its highest finish of third place in the NL but 20 games behind the Chicago White Stockings and five below the Providence Greys. Former Cleveland pitcher Jim McCormick had 20 or more wins each season from 1879 to 1883, and again in 1884 for the Cincinnati Outlaw Reds in the Union Association. As proof of their great performances, the Blues' Hugh Dailey became a member of the team's all-time roster while Ned Hanlon was inducted into the Baseball Hall of Fame in 1996.[8]

During two years in St. Louis, the Maroons clubs won about one-third of their 230 games and finished eighth in 1885. Then one year later, the Maroons ended in sixth place and 46 games following the champion White Stockings. The Maroons' best player was pitcher Henry Boyle, who led the NL with an earned run average of 1.76 in 1886. In contrast to the poor performances of the Blues and Maroons, the AA St. Louis Browns won consecutive pennants from 1885 through 1888 with such great ballplayers as pitchers Bob Caruthers, Dave Foutz and Silver King, and batsmen Tip O'Neill and Arie Latham.

Table 4.4 National League Teams Team Performances
Before and After Relocation, by Seasons, 1876–2008

Teams		Seasons		Win-Loss		Pennants	
Before	After	Before	After	Before	After	Before	After
Pre-1901							
Cleveland Blues	St. Louis Maroons	6	2	35.8	34.2	0	0
Post-1900		*Divisions*		*Pennants*		*World Series*	
		Before	After	Before	After	Before	After
Boston Braves	Milwaukee Braves	NA	NA	10	2	1	1
Brooklyn Dodgers	Los Angeles Dodgers	NA	11	12	9	1	5
New York Giants	San Francisco Giants	NA	6	17	3	5	0
Milwaukee Braves	Atlanta Braves	NA	16	2	5	1	1
Montreal Expos	Washington Nationals	2	0	0	0	0	0

Note: Teams and Seasons are self-explanatory. Win-Loss is the average winning percent of each team before and after it had moved. Divisions, Pennants, and World Series are the number of titles won by each team before and after relocation. The pennants of the Braves, Dodgers, and Giants in column five also include those won by these franchises prior to 1900. There were no divisions in the American and National Leagues prior to 1969. Major League Baseball cancelled the World Series in 1904 and 1994. NA means not applicable.

Source: Official Major League Baseball Fact Book 2005 Edition (St. Louis: The Sporting News, 2005); *The World Almanac and Book of Facts*, 1930–2007; Frank P. Jozsa, Jr., and John J. Guthrie, Jr., *Relocating Teams and Expanding Leagues in Professional Sport*, 1999.

Because of the vast differences in these teams' performances, baseball fans within the St. Louis market probably preferred to attend the Browns' home games rather than those of the Maroons. When the AA folded in 1891, the Browns joined the NL and then 26 years after being renamed the Cardinals in 1900, the franchise won its first pennant in the league and also a World Series by defeating the New York Yankees in seven games.

Milwaukee Braves

Prior to being renamed the Braves in 1912, the various Boston Red Stockings/Beaneaters teams were very competitive. In total, for example, they won four pennants in the NA and then another eight from 1877 to 1911 while in the NL. After becoming the Boston Braves, the club played well enough to earn a pennant and World's Series in 1914, and then another pennant in 1948. In the former World Series, the Braves beat the Philadelphia Athletics in four games, and in the 1948 Series, the clubs was defeated 4–2 in games by the Cleveland Indians. During this franchise's history from the early 1870s to 1952, these Braves clubs' greatest field managers included John Morrill, Frank Selee and Billy Southworth, and such athletes as Hugh Duffy, Kid Nichols, and John Clarkson. However, the annual attendances for games played in the South End Grounds and Braves Stadium ranged from a low of 96,000 in 1911 to a high of 1.4 million in 1948. During many MLB seasons, the Braves had small or mediocre crowds that attended its games in Boston, especially against the Philadelphia Phillies, Pittsburgh Pirates, and Cincinnati Reds.

While located in Milwaukee, the club played much better than it previously did in Boston. In each of 13 seasons, the Braves teams played at or above .500 and also, they won two NL pennants and in 1957 a World Series. Furthermore, the franchise's attendance at County Stadium exceeded one million in nine seasons and at least two million in four of them. A number of Milwaukee Braves teams won a majority of their games because of field managers like Charlie Grimm, Fred Haney and Chuck Dressen, and due to such ballplayers as home-run leaders Hank Aaron, Joe Adcock and Eddie Matthews, 20-game winners as Warren Spahn, Bob Buhl and Lew Burdette, and other athletes as Billy Bruton, Rico Carty, and Tony Cloninger.

Each of these men was popular among fans during their years with the Braves even though the team's performances and home attendances declined in Milwaukee after 1961. But certainly as teammates, Aaron and Matthews rank among the greatest home run hitting combinations of all-time while Spahn led the team in victories for ten seasons, and Adcock for two each in batting averages and home runs. Moreover, some of them were inducted later into baseball's Hall of Fame. In short, the Milwaukee Braves teams had great success in attracting fans from southeast Wisconsin to their home games at County Stadium, in winning a majority of games they played each season, in developing superstars such as Aaron and Spahn, and in promoting Milwaukee as a small but prominent baseball market for most years from the early to mid–1950s to the mid–1960s.

Los Angeles Dodgers

This exceptional franchise, whose team was originally named the Brooklyn Bridegrooms, participated in the AA for six seasons and also won a pennant in 1889 while a member of that association. Then in 1890, the Bridegrooms joined the NL. After 10 years, the club's nickname changed to Superbas and then to Dodgers in 1901. Prior to this franchise's move from Brooklyn to Los Angeles in 1958, the team had won 12 NL pennants and also a World Series championship in 1955 by defeating the New York Yankees in seven games. Before 1958, the heroes of the Dodgers' various teams included such field managers as Wilbert Robinson, Leo Durocher and Walter Alston, batters as Jackie Robinson, Duke Snider and Roy Campanella, and pitchers as Burleigh Grimes, Don Newcombe, and Dazzy Vance. In fact, Robinson and Campanella were NL Most Valuable Players (MVPs) while Newcombe won a Cy Young Award in 1956. Thus, even though the Dodgers excelled during several of the league's regular seasons and postseasons, the club was a disappointing 1–8 in the World Series it had played in between 1916 and 1956 inclusive.

While in Brooklyn, the Dodgers attendances at Washington Park and then Ebbets Field varied from a low of 84,000 in 1918 to a high of 1.8 million in 1947. But then from 1941 to 1957, attendance at the club's home games exceeded one million each season except in 1943–1944 when the U.S. military invaded Europe and also because the team had finished third and then seventh in the final standings of the league. The dominant NL team during these two wartime seasons was the St. Louis Cardinals, who appeared in consecutive World Series and also won one of them by defeating the cross-town Browns in six games.

After the franchise departed from Brooklyn to Los Angeles in early 1958, Dodgers teams continued to excel and play competitively in various MLB seasons. Between 1959 and 2008 inclusive, the Dodgers won 11 division titles, nine NL pennants, and five World Series. The team achieved these championships, in part, because of field managers Walter Alston, Tom Lasorda and Jim Tracy, hitters Tommy and Willie Davis, Steve Garvey and Mike Piazza, and pitchers Sandy Koufax, Don Drysdale, and Don Sutton. Garvey, Piazza, Koufax, and Drysdale were NL MVPs, Cy Young Award winners, or Rookies of the Year. However, the Dodgers have not won a NL pennant since 1988 despite the team's relatively high payroll and abundant revenues collected at home games played at its ballpark, which is 56,000-seat Dodger Stadium.

Since moving to the Los Angeles area, the attendances at Dodgers home games each season have ranked among the highest in the league. For example, the number of spectators amounted to more than two million in 1959 and then to three million in 1980 and during many years thereafter. The Cardinals, Cubs, and Mets are other teams in the NL whose average attendances at home games occasionally or nearly matched those of the Dodgers. In recent seasons, the differences in annual attendances between clubs in the NL West Division have tended to narrow. This has occurred, in part, because the Diamondbacks, Giants, Padres, and Rockies play at home in more modern and perhaps lucrative ballparks than the Dodgers, and also these four teams have become more competitive in regular-season games while each of them won at least one NL pennant and appeared in a World Series since the late 1980s.

The Dodgers will continue to be one of the richest franchises in MLB because of the team's location in America's second-largest populated area and broadcast market, and its history of great traditions, performances, and managers and ballplayers. With former New York Yankees manager Joe Torre currently coaching the club, the Dodgers will likely compete for a West Division title in most MLB seasons and eventually win another NL pennant and then a World Series before 2012.

San Francisco Giants

As an expansion franchise within the NL, the New York Gothams finished sixth in 1883 and then fifth in 1884. After being renamed the Giants in 1885, the club played well enough to win 17 NL pennants and five World Series between the late 1880s and early 1950s. The Giants managers who had achieved 500 or more victories while coaching a number of these clubs included Jim Mutrie, John McGraw, Bill Terry, and Leo Durocher. Some of their best ballplayers, in turn, were sluggers Larry Doyle, Bill Terry, Mel Ott, Johnny Mize and Bobby Thomson, and pitchers Christy Mathewson, Joe McGinnity, Tim Keefe, Carl Hubell, and Larry Jansen. These were popular athletes that attracted baseball fans to the club's various ballparks in New York, including three versions of the Polo Grounds. In fact, the team's annual attendances varied from a low of 299,000 in 1901 to a high of 1.6 million in 1947. But during the five years before the franchise had relocated to San Francisco, the average attendance at Giants home games fell to approximately 800,000 per season.

While based in San Francisco between 1958 and 2008 inclusive, the club's performances dramatically changed in comparison to when it played at the Polo Grounds in New York and in other NL ballparks. Although the Giants claimed six West Division titles and also qualified as a wild card in the playoffs of 2002, its teams have won only three NL pennants and zero World Series since the early 1960s. Despite such good field managers as Bill Rigney, Roger Craig and Dusty Baker, the Giants generally failed to capture a title in the league's West Division especially during the 1960s, 1970s, and 1990s. This is difficult for me to comprehend since the club had such great ballplayers as Willie Mays, Willie McCovey, Orlando Cepada, and of course, Barry Bonds. Other than Juan Marichal's excellent performances during the 1960s, a Giants pitcher became a 20-game winner only in 1973, 1986 and 1993. The lack of effective pitching, therefore, has been a primary weakness of the Giants and caused the club to finish below the Diamondbacks, Dodgers, Padres, or Rockies during a number of NL seasons.

As of the early 1990s, Barry Bonds has been the club's greatest ballplayer on offense. For individual seasons of the Giants, he set records for most home runs, total bases and walks, and also the highest slugging percentage. Although his production as a hitter had declined during recent seasons because of age and his various injuries, Barry attracted thousands of fans to the team's ballpark in San Francisco. Based on his performances as a batter, Bonds deserves to be inducted into the Baseball Hall of Fame when he becomes eligible. However, if he lied to a grand jury about consuming steroids or using other illegal substances during the late 1990s to early 2000s, Bonds will likely be denied entry in the Hall by MLB and those who vote for ballplayers.

Since 1958, the Giants played two seasons in 22,900-seat Seals Stadium, 40 in 63,000-seat Candlestick Park, and nine in 41,300-seat SBC Park. As such, the club's attendances at its home games exceeded 1.7 million in 1960 and two million in 1989. Then when SBC Park opened in 2000, more than 3.3 million attended the team's games in that MLB season and again from 2001 to 2004. Indeed, baseball fans in the San Francisco area responded to Bonds' performances but also to the Giants teams that won their division in 2000 and 2003 and also became a wild card in 2002. Six years later, however, the club's owner did not re-sign Bonds to a contract. As a result, in 2009 and thereafter, it will be a challenge for the Giants to replace superstar Bonds and his productivity as a hitter, and therefore compete against the Oakland A's and other professional teams for the support of sports fans in the Bay Area. Consequently, it may be a decade or more before the Giants win another NL pennant and play in a World Series.

Atlanta Braves

After the franchise shifted from Boston to Milwaukee in 1953 and then to Atlanta in 1966, several of the Braves teams have been very successful since the early 1990s. Because of the Braves' different locations, here is a comparison of postseason results for this franchise that distinguishes its performances in three distinct time periods and places. First, while based in Boston between 1876 and 1952, the club won 10 NL pennants and one World Series. These victories were accomplished, in part, because of such field managers as Frank Selee, George Stallings and Bill McKechnie, and outstanding ballplayers as Wally Berger, Tommy Holmes, and Sid Gordon. For its home games, the team played in Boston's South End Grounds for 39 years and Braves Field for another 38. The lowest home attendance of the Braves for any season was 85,000 in 1918 and highest at 1.5 million in 1948. During the majority of years, however, the club's attendance averaged between 200,000 and 400,000.

Second, while playing 13 seasons in Milwaukee, the Braves won an NL pennant and World Series in 1957, and then another pennant in 1958. While there, the team was led by such field managers as Charlie Grimm, Birdie Tebbetts and Bobby Bragan, and Hall of Famers Hank Aaron, Eddie Matthews, and Warren Spahn. The performances of these athletes, in turn, created big crowds at home games in County Stadium, where annual attendances varied from 2.2 million in 1957 to 556,000 in 1965. As mentioned before in this chapter, the Braves attendances at home games gradually declined after 1961 due to reasons related to the performances of the team and individual players, and to the sale of the club by the Perinis.

Third, during 43 seasons in Atlanta through 2008, the club had won five West—and also 11 East—Division titles, five NL pennants, and a World Series in 1995. The majority of these championship teams was coached by Bobby

Cox and featured such effective hitters as Chipper Jones, Fred McGriff and Andruw Jones, and control pitchers as Greg Maddux, John Smoltz, and Tom Glavine. During the 1990s, for example, Maddux earned three Cy Young Awards while Glavine won two and Smoltz one. In other years while in Atlanta, some of the Braves teams included managers Lum Harris, Joe Torre and Chuck Tanner, and well-known ballplayers as Dale Murphy, Ralph Garr, and Phil Niekro. In retrospect, it was the 13 consecutive division titles won from the early 1990s to 2000s—which was attained, in part, because of the leadership of Bobby Cox—that most highlights the Braves' 133-year history, that is, from 1876 in Boston to 2008 in Atlanta.

Between 1966 and 1991, the Braves attendances at 52,700-seat Atlanta-Fulton County Stadium were mediocre and exceeded two million each in only 1983 and 1991. When the team improved, however, a large number of fans demanded to watch the club at home and that resulted in a new attendance record of 3.8 million in 1993. Four years later, 50,100-seat Turner Field opened in Atlanta and the franchise's second-to-fifth-ranked attendance highs averaged 3.2 to 3.5 million during 1997 through 2000.

Since winning its last title in 2005, the Braves have been increasingly challenged in the East Division, especially by the Mets and Phillies. Because they each play at home in a much larger baseball market than Atlanta, the owners of the New York Mets and Philadelphia Phillies have decided to invest greater amounts of dollars in their rosters in order to sign expensive free agents from other clubs and also to retain their veterans who have performed productively in positions on the field or as batters. As a result, these two East Coast teams are now more competitive than in previous seasons. Thus, either or both of them will likely win additional East Division titles, NL pennants, and if superior, one or more World Series. In fact, the Phillies defeated the Tampa Rays 4–1 to win the 2008 World Series.

In contrast to performances of the Mets and Phillies, the Washington Nationals are less of a short-run threat to upset the Braves in regular-season games while the Florida Marlins franchise needs a brand new ballpark in the Miami area to provide enough revenues for its teams to significantly increase the payroll of players and win a championship in the league. Based on recent performances, Braves teams will unlikely ever duplicate their successful years of winning 13 consecutive titles from the early 1990s into the 2000s.

Washington Nationals

Prior to moving to Washington in 2005, the Montreal Expos played 36 seasons in the East Division of the NL. The club won a division title in 1981 but then lost in a five-game series to the Dodgers, who continued on to defeat the New York Yankees 4–2 in games of a World Series. In 1994, the Expos had the highest winning percentage of all teams in MLB after 114 games.

But following a players strike in August of that year, the league's franchise owners cancelled the regular season and postseason. Anyway, the Expos managers with more than 300 victories include Gene Mauch, Dick Williams, and Buck Rogers. These men, in turn, may have coached such excellent ballplayers as Andre Dawson, Gary Carter and Tim Raines, and pitchers as Steve Rogers, Dennis Martinez, and Jeff Reardon.

After experiencing various problems in competing against rivals while based in Montreal, MLB assumed control of the franchise in 2002, and three years later, moved the club to D.C. and changed its nickname to the Washington Nationals. Since being relocated, the team has played poorly and underperformed for four years in the league's East Division. In 2008, for example, the Nationals finished the season with 102 losses and a winning percentage of .366, which was the lowest in MLB. Unless the Nationals gradually improve and also establish a fan base in the nation's capital, it will continue to rank among the worst clubs in baseball. If the team's new ballpark becomes an attraction for baseball fans in the area, and owner Theodore Lerner invests more of his money in the franchise, then the Nationals may become moderately competitive and win more regular-season games than in previous years.

A brief statement about the different performances of six NL franchises that had moved between 1876 and 2008 reveals, in part, that some teams improved after relocation while others either played worse in regular-season games and postseasons, or else remained about the same in their results. First, the Cleveland Blues and St. Louis Maroons did not win any NL pennants and their winning percentages were nearly equal, respectively, before and after the Blues relocation. Second, the Boston and Milwaukee Braves each won, respectively, ten and two pennants and one World Series while in the league, but nevertheless, the franchise had existed for decades in Boston and only 13 years in Milwaukee.

Third, the Dodgers played marginally better after moving from Brooklyn to Los Angeles especially at winning 11 West Division titles and five World Series. Fourth, the performances of the Giants in pennant races and competing in World Series while based in New York far exceeded the championships won by the club during its history in San Francisco, although there were no NL divisions before 1969.

Fifth, the Braves had two spectacular seasons as a team in Milwaukee, but in Atlanta, the club performed very competitively for several years in the East Division and also in qualifying for the playoffs and successfully winning five NL pennants. And sixth, the performances of the Montreal Expos and Washington Nationals were each inferior to NL rivals with respect to their number of division titles, pennants and World Series, and in comparison to the accomplishments of the other four NL clubs that had moved after 1900.

NL TEAMS MARKETS

As of 2008, the NL consisted of 16 franchises. Specifically five of them played in the league's East Division six in the Central Division, and five in the West Division. In the previous sections of this chapter, the post-move area, performance, and prosperity of four existing teams were each highlighted and discussed. These included the Los Angeles Dodgers, San Francisco Giants, Atlanta Braves and Washington Nationals. In contrast, this part of Chapter 4 reveals similar but less-detailed information about the 12 NL clubs that had not moved from their original areas since being established. In other words, I will mention a few facts or other aspects about each of them relative to the quality of their market and performance in regular seasons or postseasons. Furthermore, the teams are discussed in each division from the most to least successful based on those characteristics.

East Division

Between 1883 and 1889 inclusive, the Philadelphia Quakers improved in games but not enough to win a NL pennant. Then in 1890, the club was renamed the Philadelphia Phillies. Since that year, the team has been sold and resold more than once, but in 1943, it was bankrupt and the league became the franchise's majority owner. Despite these and other financial problems, the Phillies have won eight division titles, six NL pennants, and a World Series in 1980 and another in 2008. During its history in the league, the club played at home in several stadiums, including the 43,500-seat Citizens Bank Park since 2004. At home games, the annual attendances in this ballpark and previously in 62,418-seat Veterans Stadium have exceeded one million as of the early 1970s.

To compete and win championships, the various Quakers and then Phillies teams depended primarily on managers like Harry Wright, Gene Mauch, Danny Ozark and Jim Fregosi, and some of them featured the athletic skills of all-stars such as Chuck Klein, Mike Schmidt and Richie Ashburn, and pitchers Steve Carlton, Jim Bunning, and Robin Roberts. When these athletes had retired from the game, they were replaced but not forgotten by diehard Philadelphia baseball fans. Because of its great tradition and history while in the NL, the Phillies franchise is superior to many others in MLB. Furthermore, it exists in a large sports market that also contains the NBA 76ers, NFL Eagles and NHL Flyers. Although the Eagles and Flyers are especially popular there, the Philadelphia area is an above-average baseball market that will probably host the Phillies for an additional 100 or more years. During the 2008 World Series, the area's baseball fans were excited since the team's last pennant was won in 1993. For these reasons, the Phillies' home games are a primary sports attraction in southeast Pennsylvania.

The New York Mets joined the NL as an expansion franchise in 1962. Since then, the club has won five division titles, four pennants, and two World Series. After losing 100 or more games during several MLB seasons of the mid–1960s, the club improved enough in 1969 to win its first World Series and then 17 years later, it defeated the Boston Red Sox in a seven-game series for another world championship. Between 1962 and 2008, the Mets' greatest managers have been Gil Hodges, Dave Johnson and Bobby Valentine, and such distinguished ballplayers as pitchers Tom Seaver, David Cone and Dwight Gooden, and batsmen as Mike Piazza, Darryl Strawberry, and Lance Johnson. After playing at home for two seasons in the 55,000-seat Polo Grounds, the team moved to 56,750-seat Shea Stadium in 1964. When it did, annual attendances at home games increased to one million to two million each season until the mid–1980s, after which more than two million fans watched the Mets compete each year in games at its ballpark in New York.

In recent years, the Mets' owners have significantly increased the team's payroll. For example, former Minnesota Twins pitcher Johan Santana was recently signed to a six-year, $137 million contract by the Mets, and he is expected to win at least 15 to 20 games each season. With an improved pitching staff, the Mets should win enough regular-season games to compete for a division title about every other year. Being located in a very large market means more revenues for the club from gate receipts, sales of merchandise, sponsorships, advertising, and local broadcasting contracts. Furthermore, the Mets will soon play at home in a new $1 billion ballpark which, in turn, should generate additional income that the team may use to further expand its payroll and also invest in various minor-league clubs and player development programs. Consequently the Mets will be competitive in the league's East Division after 2008, and within five years, the team will likely win another NL pennant and perhaps a World Series.

The Florida Marlins initially entered the East Division of the NL in 1993. After four below-average to mediocre seasons, the club won an NL pennant and also a World Series in 1997 by defeating the Cleveland Indians 4–3 in seven games. Then six years later, it duplicated 1997 by winning another pennant and a World Series championship, but alternatively, in a total of six games against the New York Yankees. During the franchise's relatively brief history, its most effective field managers have been Jim Leyland, Jeff Torborg and Jack McKeon, while such ballplayers as Juan Pierre, Gary Sheffield and Preston Wilson established records in batting as did Livan Hernandez, Dontrelle Willis, and Kevin Brown in pitching.

For the Marlins to win another division title and excel in the NL playoffs, the club must generate more revenues from 36,330-seat Pro Player Stadium. Without these additional funds, the club will struggle in games because many of the league's most talented players will eventually sign contracts with— and perform for—the Braves, Mets or Phillies. Since the NFL Dolphins and

NBA Heat are the most popular sports teams with the largest fan bases in the Miami area, it is difficult for the Marlins to consistently compete in the East Division without a more talented roster of athletes. If the City of Miami does not provide enough subsidies for the construction of a new ballpark, then the Marlins may soon relocate to another metropolitan area. Perhaps owner H. Wayne Huizenga will sell his baseball franchise to a new syndicate which may move it or otherwise invest their financial capital into building a new facility to replace Pro Player Stadium.

Central Division

When the AA folded in 1891, one year later the St. Louis Browns joined the NL. After being renamed the St. Louis Perfectos in 1899 and then two years later the Cardinals, this franchise has been one of baseball's all-time great organizations. Despite being sold and resold during years in several decades of the twentieth century, the club ranks only behind the New York Yankees in qualifying for—and then winning—a World Series. That is, since the mid–1920s, the Cardinals have won a total of nine division titles, 17 NL pennants, and ten world championships.

Numerous managers have successfully coached Cardinals teams to their victories including Branch Rickey, Billy Southworth, Whitey Herzog, and Tony LaRussa. To mention a few of the club's superstars, there were sluggers Rogers Hornsby, Stan Musial and Lou Brock, and such pitchers as Bill Doak, Dizzy Dean, and Bob Gibson. During the early 2000s, the Cardinals played increasingly well and won titles because of the home runs and total bases produced by Albert Pujois, Scott Rolan, and Jim Edmonds. Since the early 1980s, the team has attracted two million or more fans each season to 30,350-seat Busch Memorial Stadium in St. Louis. And in the seasons when Mark McGwire hit many of his home runs, more than three million spectators watched him and his teammates perform in home games at the club's ballpark.

Although St. Louis is an excellent baseball town, it has hosted a few NBA, NFL, and NHL clubs. Nevertheless, the Cardinals teams have been the most entertaining, popular, and successful sport enterprises to play at home in the area for fans throughout years of the twentieth and early twenty-first centuries. Thus, there is not a remote chance that the Cardinals franchise would move from its home in St. Louis, in part, because the Anheuser Busch Company owns—and therefore operates and invests in—the franchise at its current site in eastern Missouri.

Another longstanding and entrenched franchise in this division of the NL is the Cincinnati Reds. After participating as a team from 1876 to 1880, the Reds violated some NL rules that caused it to be removed from the league for nine years. But then the club returned in 1890 subsequent to dropping out of the AA. During its existence in the NL, the Reds have won nine division titles and the same number of pennants, and also five World Series. The franchise's greatest seasons in winning championships were the early to mid–1970s as a member of the league's West Division. Sparky Anderson coached the club then, but in other seasons, so did such managers as Pat Moran, Bill McKechnie, and Fred Hutchinson. Similar to the performances of various Cardinals teams, the Reds most famous ballplayers have included the great Frank Robinson, Pete Rose, and Johnny Bench. Besides these three all-stars, other Reds that contributed their skills to many victories of the team were Edd Roush, George Foster and Ted Kluszewski, and pitchers Johnny Vander Meer, Noodles Hahn, and Paul Derringer.

When 52,950-seat Riverfront Stadium in Cincinnati opened in 1970, and the Reds won its fifth NL pennant that year, 1.8 million baseball fans enthusiastically attended the club's regular-season home games. Within a few years, there were more than 2.5 million in attendance at Riverfront Stadium, especially when the club won consecutive World Series in 1975 and 1976. Fourteen years later, the Reds defeated the Oakland Athletics to win its fifth World Series.

But in the 1990s and early 2000s, the Reds teams have been less competitive against their rivals, in part, because Cincinnati is a smaller sports market than Chicago, Houston, and St. Louis. Thus, the Reds payroll has not increased in proportion to that of the Cubs, Astros and Cardinals. As a result, Cincinnati's MLB team has been struggling financially, and since 1990, to win another Central Division title. In the end, these facts suggest that the Reds will likely rank below several other NL clubs each season in attendances at home games, in revenues from 42,000-seat Great American Ball Park, and in the division's final standings.

After playing five seasons in the AA but never winning a championship there, the Pittsburgh Alleghenys joined the NL in 1887. Four years later, the club was renamed the Pittsburgh Pirates. Before 1910, the Pirates improved their performances on the field and thus won four NL pennants and a World Series. In total, Pirates teams have earned nine division titles and the same number of NL pennants, and also five World Series. Managers Fred Clarke and Danny Murtaugh each coached at least ten years and won more than 1,000 regular-season games for the Pirates while Frank Frisch, Chuck Tanner, and Jim Leyland each achieved at least 500 victories. During some of the franchise's greatest seasons, the best Pirates hitters included Honus Wagner, Willie Stargell and Dave Parker, and such pitchers as Elroy Face, Bob Friend and Sam Leever each played in games during a number of other years.

Since the early 1990s, the various Pirates teams have not won a division title. Similar to the Reds in Cincinnati, this is a very small-market team whose attendance each season at 47,970-seat Three Rivers Stadium in Pittsburgh and then at 37,900-seat PNC Park is usually below average among clubs in the NL. So without sufficient revenues from its ballpark and other franchise operations, many of the Pirates' superior players have been under-paid and under-rewarded. Therefore, these athletes are not as motivated or productive as those of equal ability on some different NL teams. If, for some reason, the league refuses to authorize an increase in the kinds and amounts of revenues shared between clubs within the biggest and smallest areas of the NL, then the Pirates teams will be inferior in their division and in some future year, its franchise owner may request a movement of the club from west-ern Pennsylvania.

Since 1876, a franchise from Chicago has existed in the NL. Originally nicknamed the White Stockings and then Colts, Orphans and Cubs, the club has won a total of four division titles, 16 pennants, and consecutive World Series in 1907 and 1908. Cap Anson, Frank Chance, and Charlie Grimm managed Cubs teams in some of their outstanding seasons while such hitters as Hack Wilson, Ernie Banks and Billie Williams, and pitchers Ferguson Jenkins, Charlie Root, and Mordecai Brown each established various records for the team. Despite decades of poor performances in its division of the league, most Cubs teams have been very popular among sports fans in the Chicago area.

During many MLB seasons before 2007–2008, the Cubs had played consistently in games for awhile but then finished in third, fourth, or fifth place in the East or Central Division. However in 2007–2008, the Cubs qualified for the NL playoffs and then lost in a series of games, respectively, to the Arizona Diamondbacks and Los Angeles Dodgers. Because the team generates a large amount of revenues while playing at 39,240-seat Wrigley Field and also from local and regional broadcasting and media contracts, the Cubs are able to sign talented free agents each year from other teams. Con-sequently, after more than 100 years since winning its last World Series, the Cubs are destined to soon compete for another NL pennant and perhaps a world championship in MLB. Furthermore, the franchise will continue to exist at its home in Chicago throughout the 2000s.

As an expansion franchise in the NL, the Houston Colt .45s (renamed Astros in 1964) has been a mediocre baseball enterprise since 1962. For its finest performances, the club has won six division titles and in 2005 an NL pennant. But in the World Series, the Chicago White Sox eliminated the Astros after playing four games. During seasons in the franchise's 47-year history, managers Bill Virdon and Larry Dierker each coached some Astros teams to more than 400 victories. Meanwhile, the most accomplished Astros players have been batsmen like Jeff Bagwell, Jose Cruz and Craig Biggio, and such pitchers as Nolan Ryan, J.R. Richard, and Joe Niekro. In fact, Ryan is MLB's all-time strikeout champion while Richard and Niekro led the club in other categories of pitching.

Houston is a relatively large-market team that initially played at home for three seasons in 32,600-seat Colt Stadium, and then for 35 years in the

54,300-seat Astrodome and nine in 41,000-seat Minute Maid Park, which was originally named Enron Field. During the 2000s, the club's home attendances averaged approximately 2.5 million to 3.1 million per year at its home ballpark since the team has won about 50 percent of regular-season games as of the early 1960s.

Because of the size and growth of population in the Houston area, and the strength and vitality of the city's economy, Astros teams are able to attract local sports fans even with competition from the NBA Rockets, NFL Texans, and MLS Dynamos. Despite an average payroll, the Astros teams usually play well enough each season to place second, third, or fourth in the Central Division, but not equal to the consistent performances of the St. Louis Cardinals. In short, the Houston area will host the Astros for many years after the 2010s.

Sixteen years after playing the Cardinals in the 1982 World Series, the Milwaukee Brewers transferred from the AL to the Central Division of the NL. In 2008, the club won 90 regular-season games, finished second to the Cubs in the division, and qualified for the playoffs as a wild card. But in a multigame series, the Phillies defeated the Brewers. Since it joined the NL in 1998, such men as Davey Lopes, Ned Yost, and Ken Macha have managed the team and coached a number of ballplayers including sluggers Richie Sexson and Jeromy Burnitz, and pitchers Ben Sheets and Geoff Jenkins. Recently the club has excelled, in part, because of Prince Fielder, Ryan Braun, and Corey Hart.

Being a small-market team that plays at home in 41,900-seat Miller Park, the Brewers struggle each season to outperform the Astros, Cardinals and Cubs, and also the Pirates and Reds. Unless the club's owner spends increasing amounts of money to acquire more productive baseball athletes who are content to live in the Milwaukee area during more than a few MLB seasons, the Brewers will not win a championship within five to ten years. However, if the star athletes on the 2008 team remain with the Brewers from 2009 through 2011, then the club may soon win some games in the league's playoffs and contend for an NL pennant.

West Division

Since becoming an expansion franchise in 1969, the San Diego Padres teams have won five division titles and two NL pennants. In World Series games, the club lost to the Detroit Tigers in 1984, and fourteen years later to the New York Yankees. The most prominent of the Padres managers have been Dick Williams and Bruce Bochy, and the team's best hitters included Tony Gwynn, Dave Winfield and Garry Templeton, and such effective pitchers as Randy Jones, Trevor Hoffman, and Jake Peavy. Furthermore, the Padres attendances in games played at 63,900-seat Jack Murphy Stadium (renamed

Qualcomm Stadium) from 1969 to 2003, and at 42,000-seat Petco Park since 2004 have been nearly the same as those of other small-market NL clubs at their respective ballparks. Therefore, San Diego's sports fans moderately support the Padres in regular seasons by attending the club's home games, especially when the team plays its division rivals.

San Diego is an inferior baseball market relative to Los Angeles and San Francisco, but somewhat comparable to Denver and Phoenix. Indeed there are some differences between the areas' populations and other demographics, and also in the outdoor activities for households and athletes to participate in and enjoy each spring, summer, and fall. So unless the Padres franchise owner spends more income to obtain some of the league's better ballplayers and the team's manager makes smart decisions in playing them at their proper field position and in the batting order, San Diego will likely contend for a division title about once every five seasons. In short, the Padres will remain a mediocre performer within the NL in 2009 and thereafter.[9]

As an expansion team in the NL, the Arizona Diamondbacks have won a majority of their regular-season games since 1998. For its performances in 11 years while in the West Division, the club was a division champion in four seasons and also won a pennant and World Series in 2001. Managers Buck Showalter and Bob Brenly had each coached the Diamondbacks to at least 250 victories, while the team's greatest batters have been Luis Gonzalez, Matt Williams and Tony Womack, and starring such pitchers as Randy Johnson, Curt Shilling, and Brandon Webb. At games in 49,000-seat Bank One Ballpark, the Diamondbacks attendances have averaged between 2.8 million and 3.5 million each year.

The Phoenix area contains a few professional sports teams besides the Diamondbacks. The NBA Suns, NFL Cardinals, and NHL Coyotes are popular clubs whose fans attend their games played at home. It is crucial, therefore, that the Diamondbacks provide entertainment for spectators in Bank One Ballpark by being competitive in games against the Dodgers and other West Division teams. Based on an expanding sports market in the southern Arizona region, there is enough businesses and households in the city of Phoenix and area to sustain the Diamondbacks for decades during the 2000s.

Since 1993, the Colorado Rockies have played as an expansion team in the West Division. In 1995, the club qualified as a wild card in the NL playoffs but lost to the Atlanta Braves in a division series. Then in 2007, the Rockies played well enough to win a pennant. But in the World Series, the Chicago White Sox defeated the Rockies in four consecutive games. Besides Manager of the Year Don Baylor, the club's most productive players during its history have been sluggers Todd Helton, Larry Walker and Andres Galarraga, and pitchers Pedro Astacio, Jamie Wright, and Jason Jennings.

Between 1993 and 1998 inclusive, the club established its five top attendance records at either 76,100-seat Mile High Stadium or 50,500-seat Coors

Field. On average, the attendance each year ranged from 3.4 million to 4.5 million at these ballparks. Since then, the team has played before 2.5 million to 3.5 million fans in most MLB seasons. Whether the Rockies will exceed these numbers after 2008 is unlikely because people in the Denver sports market also attend other professional games and support the efforts of the NBA Nuggets, NFL Broncos, NHL Avalanche, and MLS Rapids. Without a significant increase in the Rockies payroll and a sustained improvement in the team's performances, there is a small opportunity of it being a world champion in MLB very soon. Nevertheless, the Rockies will remain based in the Denver area throughout the early to mid–2000s.

SUMMARY

This chapter primarily discussed the movement of a few teams within the NL. But in contrast to Chapter 3—which focused exclusively on the AL—Chapter 4 also examined relocation among pre–1900 professional baseball groups such as the AA, UA and PL, and furthermore, within the FL during 1914–1915. For the latter four leagues, the vast majority of their inferior, weak-performing, and undercapitalized clubs did not attempt to reinvigorate or revive themselves by relocating to other urban places or cities in the U.S. Rather, they had folded, merged, or eventually been transferred into the NL. Thus, although there was entry and exit of teams between and within major leagues, these four less-prominent national baseball organizations tended to rely on expansion to replace those clubs that had problems, and also, to not attempt or support relocation as a way to improve some of their teams' on-the-field and financial performances.

Between 1876 and 2008, there were a total of six relocations within the NL. One movement occurred before 1900 while five others happened in years during the 1950s to early 2000s. On average, these clubs moved from large-to-smaller-populated areas, and from low-to-higher-growth sports markets. Moreover, four or two-thirds of the post-move cities were located either in the midwest or west regions of the U.S. Other cities that had welcomed relocated NL teams included Atlanta in the south and Washington, D.C., in the east.

For five years after their relocation, most of these teams played before more spectators in regular-season games at home and furthermore, they performed in new or renovated ballparks. Thus, their financial operations improved because of additional cash flows and revenues from such sources as gate receipts, concessions, merchandise sales, parking fees, and local television and radio broadcast rights. During postseasons, however, three clubs that moved won the same number of pennants and World Series as they accomplished at their pre-move sites.

With respect to clubs in the NL that had not relocated from their original areas, the less stable and most vulnerable of them are those who play at home in small-to-midsized markets. These franchises include the Florida Marlins in the league's East Division, Pittsburgh Pirates in the Central Division, and San Diego Padres in the West Division. Alternatively, such clubs in these divisions as, respectively, the New York Mets, Chicago Cubs, and Los Angeles Dodgers are least likely to leave their home areas for greener pastures.

In short, relocation has not been a common practice, strategy, or tactic used by the owners of franchises within the NL. Because of the numerous issues associated with such an action as experienced, for example, by the recent sale of the Expos and movement of the franchise out of Montreal to Washington, D.C., I do not anticipate any relocation of NL teams until at least 2010 to 2015.

5

League Expansion–Team Relocation Markets

LEAGUE EXPANSION

Based on the data, statistics, and other information contained in Chapters 1 and 2 of this book, there were a total of 29 new franchises that joined the American League (AL) and National League (NL) of Major League Baseball (MLB) in the years between 1876 and 2008 (see Tables 1.2 and 2.2). Seven of these teams entered the AL during 1961 to 1998, while the other 22 began to play in the NL during baseball's regular seasons that extended from 1878 to 1998.[1]

In the AL, four or 57 percent of the expansion clubs have continued to perform at home within their original markets while those in Los Angeles, Seattle, and Washington had moved to such different areas as Anaheim in southern California, Milwaukee in southeast Wisconsin, and Arlington in northeast Texas. Meanwhile, eight or 36 percent of the NL expansion teams have continued to exist and play at home within the same markets that they had competed in during their first season in the league. These franchises include the 126-year-old New York Giants and Philadelphia Phillies. In contrast, 13 or 59 percent of the NL expansion clubs ceased operating after one or more years while the MLB franchise in Montreal relocated to Washington, D.C., in 2005.

On average, an expansion has occurred in the AL and NL about, respectively, every 15 years and six years. Even so, since the AL Tampa Bay Devil Rays and NL Arizona Diamondbacks each became big league teams in 1998, there have not been any expansions in either league for 11 years. Because of the exorbitant cost and large financial risk, and also the managerial experience required for a sports entrepreneur or a syndicate of owners to successfully organize, structure, and operate a new team in the AL or NL, it will be awhile before another expansion happens in MLB.

If a current club, however, such as the AL Royals or NL Marlins fails to attract baseball fans to home games during regular seasons and cannot generate enough revenues to function as a business enterprise, and one or both of them receive approval from their respective league to leave Kansas City or Miami for another area, then MLB may decide to expand and place new clubs in these markets. Although this course of events is remote, it may occur especially for a number of baseball franchises that are currently located in midsized communities and also some within midsized-to-large urban places. In fact, replacing disbanded teams or any that had transferred to other major leagues occasionally happened before 1900 in the NL, and also it occurred among clubs in the American Association (AA) between 1882 and 1891 and in the Union Association in 1884.

Besides the replacement of teams as a strategy for leagues to expand, the following are other reasons why organized baseball may increase in size during various years of the early to mid-twenty-first century. First, AL or NL officials and franchise owners in these leagues may agree to liberalize their approval by reducing the requirement to expand from three-fourths to two-thirds, or even to a simple majority of favorable votes by the member teams. In 1952, the requirement was lowered from a unanimous to a three-fourths vote, and so after that decision, new teams were admitted into a league and thereby joined MLB.

Second, if exhibition games played by U.S.-based teams overseas—and also those played by foreign clubs in the annual World Baseball Classic—each become more popular events among baseball fans in Japan, Mexico, and in other international countries, MLB may eventually permit a new team or teams from one or more of these nations to perform in a division of the AL or NL. Realistically some places where baseball is a national sport include San Juan in Puerto Rico, Monterrey and Mexico City in Mexico, and Santo Domingo in the Dominican Republic. Perhaps America's economic, political, and commercial relations with Cuba will improve in the future such that the city of Havana becomes available as a potential site for an expansion franchise within MLB.

Third, a number of cities within the U.S. will moderately increase in population, experience above-average economic growth, and develop culturally and socially to be profitable sports markets. As a result, local government officials and some businesses may each consider their areas as an attractive site to construct a modern ballpark for the regular-season games of a new baseball franchise. These areas, in turn, will likely include small to midsized cities and also communities in regions of the southeast, southwest, and west. Of course, government officials must be able and willing to commit some or all of the public's money to build a ballpark in order to lure any new big league club into their market.

Fourth, if for some reason, baseball once again becomes the most popular team sport in North America, a few areas that once hosted AL or NL teams may qualify as future locations for an MLB expansion franchise. These areas, for example, include Buffalo, Indianapolis, and Providence in the United

States (U.S.), and also Montreal in Canada. However, for MLB to seriously evaluate any of these cities and other former places as potential expansion sites, there needs to be at least one local group of investors who could and would jointly finance, own, and successfully operate a new baseball franchise. Indeed there are well-known entrepreneurs and big businesses that have invested millions of dollars in professional basketball, football, ice hockey, and soccer clubs. As such, these individuals or groups yearn for above-average to excellent financial returns and therefore, they may agree to participate as minority owners of new MLB expansion clubs in the U.S. and foreign markets.

Fifth, although controversial and unlikely to ever be approved and implemented in the sport, there is a rule that, if changed, may further encourage the development and future growth of MLB via expansion. That is, for the current franchise owners of big league teams in Chicago, Los Angeles, New York-New Jersey, and San Francisco–Oakland to each allow at least one new baseball club to enter their sports markets. But after the difficulty experienced by MLB to persuade Baltimore Orioles owner Peter Angelos to permit the Nationals to locate and play at home in nearby Washington, D.C., the reopening of any large or relatively populated midsized market is too radical and mostly an impractical and unrealistic strategy. There would be complaints, lawsuits, and rebellion from the individuals or syndicates that partially or wholly own the Cubs and White Sox in Chicago, Dodgers in Los Angeles and Angels in Anaheim, Mets and Yankees in New York, and Giants and A's in the Bay Area. Similar to how Angelos had responded to MLB, these owners would also protect their investments as property rights and severely resist the entry of any new teams into their territories.

Sixth, expansion may occur in an area in the U.S. if various groups within a local community form an organization that promotes their self-interest in hosting a new professional baseball enterprise. Such groups may consist of leaders in government and business, of wealthy citizens and families, of civic and philanthropic institutions, and of former major and minor league ballplayers that are retired but devoted to participating in this effort. Finally, a grassroots campaign by any group or individual must involve an entire community and the media because many of these people are sports fans who will support a team whether they win games or lose them during regular seasons and in postseasons.

TEAM RELOCATION

The movements of MLB franchises in the AL and NL were each discussed, respectively, in Chapters 3 and 4. As denoted in Table 3.1, nine AL teams relocated sometime between 1901 and 2008, which indicates that at least one club moved every 12 years during the 108-year history of the league. Interestingly, six or 66 percent of the teams that relocated have continued to perform at ballparks within their post-move areas. Meanwhile the AL Browns moved to Baltimore after playing for 52 years in St. Louis, the Angels to Anaheim after competing for five MLB seasons in Los Angeles, and the Athletics to Oakland after competing for 13 regular-seasons in Kansas City.[2]

In contrast to the nine relocations that occurred in the AL, six NL teams had moved somewhere else within years between 1876 and 2008. Four or 44 percent of these clubs played home and away games in regular-seasons against other teams from the year they had moved to the early 2000s. Alternatively the NL Maroons competed for two seasons in St. Louis and then it folded, and the Braves existed for 13 years in Milwaukee but in 1966, the franchise was transferred to Georgia and became the Atlanta Braves. In short, during the league's 133-year history, a club had moved about every 22 years.

There are a number of different business, demographic, and sport-specific factors that explain, in part, why a total of 15 AL and NL franchises had moved from one metropolitan area to another since the late 1800s. One, some teams had failed to win any division titles, NL pennants, or a World Series. So because of their poor performances in several of MLB's regular seasons, local baseball fans became disappointed in them and then decided not to attend any more of their home games. As a result, the amounts of revenues that these teams collected from gate receipts, concessions, and other sources had declined and that, in turn, caused these clubs to operate at a loss and also created an increase in their debts and problems with them repaying any loans to creditors.

Two, some teams had moved from commercially-inferior and less-hospitable areas to other markets with more potential for business development and economic growth. Thus a portion of movements by franchises were from cities in the east and midwest to others in the southeast, southwest, and west. Although this strategy may have resulted in more transportation costs for teams to and from away games, the new locations provided an increase in revenues for the relocated franchises that easily offset the higher expenses to travel.

Three, a few teams were sold and then repurchased by a new syndicate of owners. Consequently, a change in ownership may have led to the relocation of MLB franchises since hometown baseball fans realized their club could or would not continue to operate as enterprises either successfully or unsuccessfully at the same location for more than a few years. In other words, the new syndicates realized that better opportunities existed elsewhere and so they did not attempt to invest more money in players or win titles and also refused to further appeal to and attract sports fans in their local market.

Four, some groups in cities had initiated promotional campaigns and marketing programs, and also used other methods to convince an existing team in MLB to move from its home and relocate to their specific metropolitan area. As a vital part of these campaigns, various committees composed of local civic leaders, government officials, and business representatives committed to build a new ballpark with public funds and negotiate a lease for that facility with owners of an incoming team.

Five, the presence of too many professional sports clubs that performed within an area may have influenced the movements of one or more big league teams from these areas during years of the twentieth century. Indeed, some athletes and households within these markets had selected basketball, football, ice hockey, or soccer as their favorite sport rather than attend baseball games in ballparks and watch them on television. Again, this may have created revenue problems for some MLB franchises and motivated owners to find other places to play their teams' home games.

Six, since the 1960s and 1970s, baseball has gradually lost market share and its popularity to other team sports across the U.S. Furthermore in recent decades, an increasing number of African Americans and some Latinos in urban places have ignored baseball while fewer of them have played the game on teams in amateur leagues and on clubs in elementary and high school, and in college. This, in turn, has somewhat diminished the demand for the sport among these socioeconomic groups at the local grassroots—and also professional—levels. As a result, many big league teams in specific cities find it increasingly difficult to market their brand to minorities and other sports fans at home, which means that relocation becomes a way for them to leave a market and revive their franchise in another city. In other words, if revenue sharing and a luxury tax were not adopted by MLB, then the movements of clubs from some markets in urban areas would have been more frequent events especially since the 1990s.

Within the previous paragraphs of this chapter I have described six each reasons or factors that, in large part, have contributed to the history of league expansions and team relocations in organized baseball. Given these dozen items, the most important of them—as cited by a majority of sports economists—is the presence, or future availability, of a brand new or renovated ballpark at a post-move site. With respect to teams in each of the leagues in MLB, this factor explains why expansions had occurred in such areas as Kansas City and Tampa Bay in the AL, and New York and Phoenix in the NL. Also the attraction of a modern ballpark with amenities within a post-move area influenced such movements as the Senators from Washington to Minneapolis in 1961 and Angels from Los Angeles to Anaheim in 1966. Besides the existence of obsolete and expensive ballparks, other important reasons for leagues to expand and franchises to relocate include areas' population and economic growth, and the numbers and types of other professional sports teams at home or in the prospective market.

SPORTS MARKETS

In this section of Chapter 5 there are three tables that, individually and in total, contain some factual data and other historical information about the distributions of areas that had previously hosted—or currently contain—baseball franchises and other teams in professional sports leagues. As such, each of these tables has been inserted here for the following purposes.

The first table indicates the number of years that teams in various major baseball leagues have occupied urban places or cities within the U.S. and Canada since the late 1800s. Then the second table reveals the number of clubs in professional sports leagues that had existed within different areas of North America during 2008. Finally, the third table denotes the number of professional sports franchises that were located in areas not occupied in 2008 by MLB teams. Consequently, the distribution of these different groups of markets—as reflected in each table—will be discussed next relative to the issues of expansion and relocation of teams within organized baseball and among other sports leagues.

Total Baseball Areas

Since the late 1800s, a few prominent baseball leagues have been based and operated in the U.S. Each of them had existed within a span of one year to decades during the nineteenth, twentieth, or twenty-first centuries. The histories of these organizations, including the nicknames and locations of their various teams, were highlighted and discussed in various sections of Chapters 1–4. However, it was expansions—if any—of these baseball leagues and also the movements of any clubs among and between them that the contents of the previous chapters had focused on and analyzed. So to revisit but primarily extend some of those contents, I reviewed all of the data available and then prepared Table 5.1.[3]

In total, this table consists of seven columns. Besides listing different cities in column one, the other columns denote how many years that baseball teams in the six leagues had played regular-season games within these sports markets. Based on this information and the ranking of populations (in parentheses), what do the entries in columns two through seven infer about the areas that were occupied or not occupied by franchises in each of the leagues, and also them as a group?

During the American Association's (AA) multiyear history, the Baltimore (7), Louisville (16), Philadelphia (2), and St. Louis (6) areas each had hosted teams in the league for ten seasons. Because some franchises existed then in the NL, Union Association (UA), or in the Players League (PL), there were no AA clubs in Chicago (4) and Boston (5). Interestingly, the AA was the only baseball league with clubs located for one year each in Rich-

Table 5.1 Major Baseball Leagues Teams
Areas Being Occupied by Number of Years, 1876–2008

Area	AA	AL	FL	NL	PL	UA
Altoona	0	0	0	0	0	1(P)
Anaheim	0	43	0	0	0	0
Atlanta	0	0	0	43	0	0
Baltimore	10	57	2	8	0	1
Boston	1	108	0	77	1	1
Buffalo	0	0	2	7	1	1
Chicago	0	108	2	133	1	1(P)
Cincinnati	9	0	0	124	0	1
Cleveland	2	108	0	17	1	0
Columbus	5	0	0	0	0	0
Dallas-Arlington	0	37	0	0	0	0
Denver	0	0	0	16	0	0
Detroit	0	108	0	8	0	0
Hartford	0	0	0	2	0	0
Houston	0	0	0	47	0	0
Indianapolis	1	0	1	4	0	0
Kansas City	2	53	2	1	0	1
Los Angeles	0	5	0	51	0	0
Louisville	10	0	0	10	0	0
Miami	0	0	0	16	0	0
Milwaukee	1	29	0	25	0	1(P)
Minneapolis-St. Paul	0	48	0	0	0	1(P)
Montreal	0	0	0	36	0	0
New York-New Jersey	8	106	2	123	1	0
Philadelphia	10	54	0	127	1	1(P)
Phoenix	0	0	0	11	0	0
Pittsburgh	5	0	2	122	1	1(P)
Providence	0	0	0	8	0	0
Richmond	1	0	0	0	0	0
Rochester	1	0	0	0	0	0
San Diego	0	0	0	40	0	0
San Francisco-Oakland	0	41	0	51	0	0
Seattle	0	33	0	0	0	0
St. Louis	10	52	2	121	0	0
Syracuse	1	0	0	1	0	0
Tampa Bay	0	11	0	0	0	0
Toledo	1	0	0	0	0	0
Toronto	0	32	0	0	0	0
Troy	0	0	0	4	0	0
Washington	2	71	0	16	0	1
Wilmington	0	0	0	0	0	1(P)
Worcester	0	0	0	3	0	0

Note: The baseball leagues and their years in operation are, respectively, the American Association (AA) in 1882–1891, American League (AL) in 1901–2008, Federal League (FL) in 1914–1915, National League (NL) in 1876–2008, Players League (PL) in 1890, and Union Association (UA) in 1884. The cities of Brooklyn and Newark are included in the New York-New Jersey area. If two or more teams from the same league occupied an area during an identical number of years, then these years are counted once and then entered into that row of a column. If these years do not overlap, then the total number of them appears in a column. The 1(P) indicates a team in the UA that occupied an area for part of a year, or a portion of this league's only baseball season.

Source: *Official Major League Baseball Fact Book 2005 Edition* (St. Louis: The Sporting News, 2005); James Quirk and Rodney D. Fort, *Pay Dirt: The Business of Professional Team Sports* (Princeton, NJ: Princeton University Press, 1992); Table 1.1; Table 2.1.

mond, Rochester, and Toledo. Furthermore, a total of 18 areas had been the home sites of teams in this league and their populations varied from 50,000 in Toledo to 1.2 million in New York. While in operation, the AA did not rely on expansion and relocation as ways to market its teams or to improve the league's overall competitiveness, power, and prosperity as an organization in professional baseball.

Between 1901 and 2008 inclusive, AL teams had occupied 19 different areas. In fact, some teams have existed for more than 100 years each in Boston, Chicago, Cleveland, Detroit, and New York-New Jersey. Since clubs in the NL and Federal League (FL) had played at home in some of these and other places, the AL avoided each of them as expansion sites but not Los Angeles in 1961. Even so, relocating AL teams did invade NL towns like St. Louis in 1902 and New York in 1903. Moreover, this is the only baseball league in the group that had placed its teams in Anaheim, Dallas-Arlington, Seattle, Tampa Bay, and Toronto. So of the 42 areas that are listed in column one of Table 5.1, AL franchises have performed in nearly 50 percent of them.

FL clubs had existed in eight different areas during 1914 or 1915. Seven of the league's teams played for two years while the Hoosiers—after winning a pennant—relocated from Indianapolis to New Jersey to become the Newark Bears. This means that 87 percent of the league's original areas had contained an FL club for two seasons. Also, because of its brief history and other reasons, the FL was the only baseball organization of the six in Table 5.1 that did not have a club that played at home for at least one season in Boston and Philadelphia. In other words, the FL was relatively stable, did not expand in size, and moved only one of its clubs, that is, from the midwest to a midsized city in the east.

In contrast to the other five baseball groups listed in Table 5.1, NL clubs had each performed in Chicago, Cincinnati, New York-New Jersey, Philadelphia, Pittsburgh, and St. Louis during at least 121 regular seasons of the league. Furthermore through 2008, NL teams had occupied 30 or 71 percent of the areas listed in column one of the table. Even such small sports markets as Buffalo, Hartford, Providence, Syracuse, Troy, and Worcester had been home to various NL teams for one or more years. Moreover several areas including Louisville and Indianapolis were sites for NL teams but not to any clubs in the AL.

After 1900 the NL expanded into the New York–New Jersey area, which then contained the powerful and popular Yankees. However, between 1952 and 2004 inclusive, five of the league's teams moved to different areas that were not occupied by AL franchises. Therefore, except for New York, expansion and relocation by the NL has not involved the territorial rights of clubs in the other leagues because, for the most part, these actions have been planned, coordinated, and approved by a 108-year-old sports cartel named Major League Baseball.

Established in 1890, the PL had its eight teams located in seven different areas within the U.S. Although two of the organization's clubs existed temporarily in the New York-New Jersey area, there were no NL franchises that played in any cities of western New York, which was the home site of the league's Buffalo Bisons. The PL, however, was the only league in Table 5.1 that did not have a team for even one season that competed in home games within the Baltimore and Kansas City areas.

If the PL had better distinguished itself among sports fans and somehow continued to operate as a professional baseball organization after 1890, it is possible that the league may have expanded into small to midsized markets that previously hosted AA but not NL clubs. These areas included Columbus in central Ohio, Richmond in southeast Virginia, Rochester in northwest New York, and Toledo in northern Ohio. Alternatively, any new or existing PL teams may also have been placed at sites where AA clubs had played ten seasons. Such cities as these were Baltimore, Louisville, Philadelphia and St. Louis. Given the location of franchises in the AA and NL, the PL was not well-organized or prepared to survive beyond one year as a baseball league.

Similar to the PL, the UA existed for one baseball season, that is, in 1884. Also, the latter league's numerous clubs performed in home games within 13 different sports markets. That distribution occurred because some of the UA's teams had played only part of the 1884 regular season in which they either dissolved, merged, or moved to another area. This group included UA franchises that were located in Altoona, Chicago, Milwaukee, Minneapolis-St. Paul, Philadelphia, Pittsburgh and Wilmington.

With respect to teams' performances, the UA St. Louis Browns won 83 percent of its total games while others in the league had finished more than 20 games behind the Browns. This competitive imbalance, in turn, discouraged many baseball fans from attending games and also, caused a high turnover of UA clubs throughout the 1884 season. It was, in part, the inferior performances of teams and their inability to attract local fans to their home and away games that determined the fate of the UA and ended its existence in early 1985.

For the group of six baseball leagues whose teams had played one or more seasons among a total of 42 different areas, the five most popular places that hosted clubs for the greatest number of years were Chicago at 244 and then New York-New Jersey at 240, Philadelphia at 192, Boston at 188, and St. Louis at 185. For the fewest number of years (but excluding parts of seasons), the five areas of teams were Richmond, Rochester and Toledo each with one season, and Hartford and Syracuse each with two of them. In other words, between 1876 and 2008, the former five areas were baseball's most superior markets while the latter five failed to host any of the leagues' teams more than one or two seasons. Even so, such cities as Richmond and Toledo have been homes to successful minor-league baseball teams at the highest or AAA level of the sport.

Four of the leagues in Table 5.1 dominated a majority of the 42 areas. For these results, AA teams played the most years in six areas including Columbus and Louisville while the AL dominated 14 of the total areas, the NL 21, and the UA two—Altoona and Wilmington. But there was no area that a team in the FL or PL had occupied for more than two seasons. Because the NL has existed for 133 years through 2008, its teams have played in and dominated more areas—as baseball markets within America—than clubs in the other five leagues. This distribution of areas, in part, is why the literature refers to the NL as professional baseball's senior circuit and the AL as its junior circuit.

CURRENT SPORTS TOWNS

During 2008, the most prominent sports organizations in America had consisted of the AL and NL in MLB and also the National Basketball Association (NBA), National Football League (NFL), National Hockey League (NHL), and Major League Soccer (MLS). As denoted in columns three through six of Table 5.2, some clubs in the latter four leagues had played their home games within 27 cities (listed in column one) that also included 30 franchises in MLB. In fact, these baseball markets were home sites to 20 or 66 percent of teams in the NBA, 25 or 75 percent of clubs in the NFL, 20 or 66 percent of franchises in the NHL, and 11 or 78 percent of teams in MLS. In other words, during 2008, each of the 30 areas in baseball also contained anywhere from one to eight clubs from leagues in the other four professional team sports.[4]

According to entries in the table, the fewest total number of clubs in the five sports had existed at two each in the Anaheim, Baltimore, Cincinnati, Milwaukee, San Diego, and Seattle areas. Furthermore, ten of the 106 teams in columns two through six played at home in New York–New Jersey while six each performed in areas of Chicago and Los Angeles. Since two MLB teams each played their home games in Chicago, New York–New Jersey and San Francisco–Oakland, any expansions within the AL or NL—or any current MLB clubs that relocate—may choose an area besides any of these nine places. Indeed the former group of areas each consists of small to midsized sports markets while the latter group of three is in large to very large metropolises. This suggests, in part, that some areas are not desirable sports markets in the future because they are undersized or oversaturated.

On average, there are approximately four professional sports franchises located in each of the areas listed in column one of Table 5.2. Consequently in 2008, a typical MLB team competed for customers in its respective sports

Table 5.2 Five Professional Sports Leagues Number of Teams, Distributed by 27 MLB Metropolitan Areas, 2008

Area	MLB	NBA	NFL	NHL	MLS	Total
Anaheim	1	0	0	1	0	2
Atlanta	1	1	1	1	0	4
Baltimore	1	0	1	0	0	2
Boston	1	1	1	1	1	5
Chicago	2	1	1	1	1	6
Cincinnati	1	0	1	0	0	2
Cleveland	1	1	1	0	0	3
Dallas-Arlington	1	1	1	1	1	5
Denver	1	1	1	1	1	5
Detroit	1	1	1	1	0	4
Houston	1	1	1	0	1	4
Kansas City	1	0	1	0	1	3
Los Angeles	1	2	0	1	2	6
Miami	1	1	1	1	0	4
Milwaukee	1	1	0	0	0	2
Minneapolis	1	1	1	1	0	4
New York-New Jersey	2	2	2	3	1	10
Philadelphia	1	1	1	1	0	4
Phoenix	1	1	1	1	0	4
Pittsburgh	1	0	1	1	0	3
St. Louis	1	0	1	1	0	3
San Diego	1	0	1	0	0	2
San Francisco-Oakland	2	1	2	0	0	5
Seattle	1	0	1	0	0	2
Tampa Bay	1	0	1	1	0	3
Toronto	1	1	0	1	1	4
Washington	1	1	1	1	1	5

Note: Area is the Standard Metropolitan Statistical Area (SMSA) that contains the number of sports teams in each league. Besides Major League Baseball (MLB), the professional sports leagues are National Basketball Association (NBA), National Football League (NFL), National Hockey League (NHL), and Major League Soccer (MLS). The movements of teams from one league to another in the same sport were transfers and not expansions or relocations.

Source: The World Almanac and Book of Facts (New York: World Almanac Books, 2007); "Baseball Standings 2008," The Charlotte Observer (1 October 2008), 4C; "NBA Today," The Charlotte Observer (29 October 2008), 5C; "Football NFL," The Charlotte Observer (21 October 2008), 3C; "Soccer MLS," The Charlotte Observer (24 October 2008), 7C; "Ice Hockey NHL," The Charlotte Observer (21 October 2008), 3C.

market with three other clubs. A few of them, however, clearly outnumbered and perhaps dominated other teams within their local markets. To illustrate, more total MLB, NHL, and MLS clubs than the others had each played at home in numerous areas including the very large markets of Chicago, Los Angeles, and New York-New Jersey. But in the NBA, two of the league's teams existed within Los Angeles and New York-New Jersey, while in the NFL, two clubs played their home games in New York-New Jersey and also in San Francisco–Oakland. Finally, 11 or approximately 40 percent of the

MLB areas contained fewer than four franchises and another eight or 30 percent of them were home to more than that number of franchises. Thus 16 or 60 percent of areas that had hosted baseball teams in 2008 were average or above average with respect to the total number of professional clubs that existed within their sports markets.

Based on comparisons between 27 cities and the teams in various sports leagues as indicated in Table 5.2, there were ten franchises in the NBA, seven in the NFL, ten in the NHL, and three in MLS that had not been included in columns three through six of the table. In fact, several areas of these other 30 teams may be potential and lucrative markets of new or existing MLB franchises. That is, such areas of NBA teams as Charlotte, Indianapolis and Portland, of NFL clubs as Jacksonville, Nashville and New Orleans, of NHL franchises teams as Buffalo, Raleigh and San Jose, and MLS teams as Columbus and Salt Lake City are each candidates as future sites of big league clubs.

After evaluating these and 18 other urban places where no MLB teams existed in 2008, it appears that the most and least attractive home sites for professional baseball teams are in, respectively, NBA and NHL cities. That perspective about locations seems reasonable because games in minor-league baseball are played by popular or semi-popular teams within or near the areas occupied by basketball and football franchises. Meanwhile, it is unlikely that Canadian ice hockey towns like Calgary, Edmonton, Ottawa, and Vancouver would support any American baseball teams given their unpredictable weather conditions and people's ignorance of the sport, and also because of the failure of the Expos and its relocation from Montreal to Washington in 2005.

Besides the previous observations from interpreting the numbers displayed in various columns of Table 5.2, there were no historical expansions or movements of AL or NL clubs into the Boston, Chicago, Cincinnati, and Pittsburgh areas. In fact, three of the original eight franchises in the NL were each established in Boston, Cincinnati, and Chicago in 1876. Then ten years after the team in Cincinnati was kicked out of the league for violating rules, an AA franchise from that city and also another team that played at home in Brooklyn each joined the NL in 1890.

So with respect to the 27 cities listed in column one of the table, 16 or 60 percent of them had hosted new baseball expansion teams while 11 or 40 percent of them were markets for one or more MLB clubs that had relocated. More specifically, two each expansions in baseball occurred in the Cleveland, Kansas City, New York–New Jersey, Seattle, and Washington areas, and also two each MLB clubs moved into the Milwaukee, San Francisco–Oakland, and St. Louis sports markets.

There are other interesting aspects to highlight about the relationships between a portion of the data in columns of Table 5.2 and the title of this chapter. Which cities listed in the table, for example, were also league expansions or relocation sites of various teams in the 60-year-old NBA, 86-year-old NFL, 92-year-old NHL, and 13-year-old MLS? For this result, I created Table A.5.1 and placed it in the Appendix. As such, this table shows the number of teams in four professional sports that in earlier years had entered one or more of the 27 areas where 30 MLB clubs had existed in 2008. Indeed these basketball, football, ice hockey, and soccer clubs had invaded baseball's current markets during expansions or by them moving from other areas in the United States and Canada. This information not only reveals the appeal, location, and quality of these areas as actual sites for other team sports, but also exposes them as current markets for games played in MLB.

According to columns two through five of Table A.5.1, the number of expansions occurred from a high of five in Minneapolis to a low of zero in Denver. By area and league, Chicago welcomed the most new teams in the NBA, Minneapolis in the NFL, Atlanta and three other areas in the NHL, and Chicago, Los Angeles, and Miami in MLS. Alternatively, 16 or 60 percent of these 27 baseball markets were not the homes of NBA expansion teams, 14 or 52 percent of them not of NFL expansion clubs, ten or 37 percent of them not of new NHL franchises, and 24 or 88 percent of them not of MLS expansion teams.

Thus a total of 50 new franchises from the other four team sports had entered the 27 markets of current MLB teams during various years before 2009. Furthermore, five or ten percent of them settled in one area (Minneapolis) and four or 8 percent in another area (Chicago), and then three, two, one, or zero of them in the other 25 areas of baseball teams. In short, each market that hosted one or more baseball clubs in 2008 was, on average, also the home of about two total professional basketball, football, ice hockey, or soccer expansion teams.

Columns six through nine in Table A.5.1 denote the number of teams in each of four professional sports that had relocated into the 27 areas listed in column one. As such, a total of five sports clubs moved into the New York–New Jersey area and also four each into Los Angeles and St. Louis. In contrast, none of the 40 non–MLB franchises that relocated between 1876 and 2008 had selected Chicago and seven other cities in the table. For the most popular destinations of franchises in each of the sports, two each professional basketball clubs had moved to Los Angeles and San Francisco–Oakland while three in football relocated to New York–New Jersey. Plus another two each in ice hockey moved to Denver and New York–New Jersey, and one in soccer immigrated into Houston. Interestingly, zero teams in these four leagues relocated to the Minneapolis and Chicago areas in which a total of nine expansions had occurred. For some reason, the potential markets of these two areas appealed only to franchise owners of some new sports teams but not to those who had existing clubs yet to be moved.

For the combined group of league expansions in columns two through five and team relocations in columns six through nine of Table A.5.1, the three most attractive locations were the New York–New Jersey area with eight, Los Angeles seven, and St. Louis six. Alternatively, the two areas with the fewest total number of expansions and relocations at one each were Anaheim and Toronto. As such, these two cities did not successfully recruit any new or relocating teams in at least three or 75 percent of the sports leagues.

But, three NFL clubs preferred to settle in New York–New Jersey, two each NBA in Los Angeles and San Francisco–Oakland, and two each NHL in Denver and New York–New Jersey. Although they were among the least desirable locations within the 27 areas, the Bengals became an NFL expansion team in Cincinnati, the MLS Earthquakes moved from San Jose to Houston, and the NBA Raptors opened its first season at home in Toronto. In short, besides those changes that occurred within the AL and NL of MLB, there were a total of 50 expansions and 42 relocations in 133 years with respect to these four professional sports leagues.

Potential Baseball Sites

Based on data organized in tables, the previous two sub-sections of this chapter discussed, respectively, where professional baseball clubs had located and played their home games during one or more years and also where clubs in MLB and four other leagues existed in 2008. Furthermore, Table A.5.1 in the Appendix revealed the areas of MLB franchises into which leagues expanded and teams in other sports had relocated. In total, this tabled information was historically significant because it applied to years between 1876 and 2008 inclusive.

Given these three tables of statistics and how they relate to various sports organizations and their markets, what are some cities that baseball officials might consider as future homes of any MLB expansion teams or that owners may choose to relocate their clubs? To identify these areas, Table 5.3 was constructed which denotes in column one the home sites of various teams that performed in four major sports leagues in 2008. Accordingly, what does this table imply about these places as potential markets for current or prospective franchises in MLB?

First, the population ranks (in parentheses) of the three largest areas in the U.S. without an MLB franchise but with an NBA team in 2008 were Portland (25), Sacramento (27) and San Antonio (29); with at least one NFL club were Indianapolis (34), Charlotte (37) and New Orleans (38); with a single NHL franchise were San Jose (28), Columbus (31) and Nashville (39); and with at least one MLS team were San Jose (28), Columbus (31) and Salt Lake City (50). Based on these results, it appears that the Portland, Sacramento, San Antonio, and San Jose areas are potentially the most attractive sports towns for any new or relocating MLB teams.[5]

Table 5.3 Four Professional Sports Organizations' Number of Teams, by Non-MLB Metropolitan Areas and Leagues, 2008

Area	NBA	NFL	NHL	MLS	Total
Buffalo	0	1	1	0	2
Calgary	0	0	1	0	1
Charlotte	1	1	0	0	2
Columbus	0	0	1	1	2
Edmonton	0	0	1	0	1
Green Bay	0	1	0	0	1
Indianapolis	1	1	0	0	2
Jacksonville	0	1	0	0	1
Memphis	1	0	0	0	1
Montreal	0	0	1	0	1
Nashville	0	1	1	0	2
New Orleans	1	1	0	0	2
Oklahoma City	1	0	0	0	1
Orlando	1	0	0	0	1
Ottawa	0	0	1	0	1
Portland	1	0	0	0	1
Raleigh	0	0	1	0	1
Sacramento	1	0	0	0	1
Salt Lake City	1	0	0	1	2
San Antonio	1	0	0	0	1
San Jose	0	0	1	1	2
Vancouver	0	0	1	0	1

Notes: Area is an SMSA in the United States, but listed as a metropolitan area in Canada. The names of the four professional sports leagues are defined in Table 5.2.

Sources: See the sources in Table 5.2.

Second, the five areas in Canada are each above-average to excellent locations for NHL clubs but not for new or existing franchises in big league baseball. The Expos moved from Montreal in 2005 after playing there for 36 years while the other four Canadian sports markets have an insufficient number of baseball fans, local sponsors and businesses, substandard ballparks, and also unpredictable climates and temperatures for playing baseball games outdoors in some weeks between March and October. So even though each of these five areas in Canada contains only one team in a major professional sport, they are not appropriate markets to host a club in MLB. Nonetheless, they may have enough people, an inadequate but local stadium, and other amenities to be the homes of clubs in minor league baseball.

Third, the areas of Memphis (41), Jacksonville (45), Oklahoma City (47) and Raleigh (59), and also Green Bay (unranked) are each simply too small as markets to host and successfully support more than one professional sports team. Some of them, however, have been outstanding home sites for years of popular A, AA, or AAA professional baseball clubs.

In total, column one of Table 5.3 lists 17 different areas within the U.S. and five in Canada which contained zero MLB clubs in 2008 but ten teams in the NBA, seven in the NFL, ten in the NHL, and three in MLS. Fourteen or 64 percent of these areas hosted one club in a professional sport while the other eight or 36 percent of the 22 were sites of two major teams. Even so, whether any of these areas would be acceptable as markets for one or more MLB franchises depends on such factors as the capacity, condition, and location of any local ballparks, and also the number of baseball fans in the city and region, quantity of sports investors within these areas, each area's population and population growth, and the existence and performances of other professional sports teams in these urban places.

To conclude this section of Chapter 5, Tables 5.1–5.3 and also Table A.5.1 in the Appendix provide some historical data and interesting relationships with respect to the home-site areas of teams in five professional sports. After carefully reviewing this information, readers of this book will appreciate and better understand how important expansion and relocation have been as interdependent strategies among franchises in MLB. Given these results, the final section of this chapter discusses the extent of baseball markets within several foreign nations and their potential as future locations of big league teams.

GLOBAL BASEBALL MARKETS

In a table within Chapter 1 of *Sports Capitalism*, Chapter 3 of *Baseball in Crisis*, and Chapter 11 of *Baseball, Inc.*, there are lists of various cities in foreign countries that rank as superior, average, or inferior baseball markets. As such, a number of qualitative and quantitative factors were used by me to intuitively measure and evaluate the popularity and prosperity of the sport within these countries' different urban places. In part, these factors included the total population of each city, competitiveness of local amateur and professional baseball leagues and their teams' accomplishments in international tournaments, number of athletes from each nation who played on clubs in MLB, condition of ballparks within the respective cities, distance from the U.S. and travel time, and the passion of local sports fans who regularly attend baseball games of their hometown teams.[6]

Based primarily on these criteria, the five foreign cities that seem to be most attractive as potential markets for any expansion or relocating MLB teams are Mexico City and Monterrey in Mexico, San Juan in Puerto Rico, Santo Domingo in the Dominican Republic, and Tokyo in Japan. Besides these five cities, other international baseball markets also mentioned in at least one chapter of my three books were such places as Tijuana, Mexico; Taipei, Taiwan; Seoul, South Korea; Sydney, Australia; Panama City, Panama; London, England; Caracas, Venezuela; and Havana, Cuba. Moreover, I did not consider the five Canadian cities listed in column one of Table 5.3 to be realistic, potentially profitable, or viable markets for any new or existing big league baseball teams.

Each of the above cities has one or more attributes—but also some drawbacks and problems—that may or may not totally qualify them as unique markets for an MLB expansion franchise or as a relocation site of a current major league team. For example, a well-established sports culture and many grassroots baseball organizations have existed for decades in communities of countries within Latin America while in Mexico baseball has flourished among the population and expanded to become the nation's most active, and popular team sport. In parts of Asia, the game of baseball is played competitively by teams in many cities and areas, and furthermore, it is participated in by numerous athletes within schools and also by those who perform on clubs in amateur, professional, and semi-professional leagues. Likewise in other populated cities of the world, there are a number of teams in local baseball leagues being enthusiastically sponsored and increasingly promoted by big businesses and municipal governments, and also being supported by sports fans and other people who attend their home games and root for them to defeat other clubs.

There are, however, a few critical issues and also significant risks that discourage or even prevent MLB officials from being more entrepreneurial and thereby approve the placement of any new or existing teams into the cities of foreign countries. One of the most difficult problems to analyze, of course, is whether any expansion franchises or relocating teams in the AL or NL can attract large numbers of fans to home games and earn enough revenues from these contests to survive more than a few years by playing in a ballpark within a city or area of a country besides the 29 in the U.S. and Toronto in Canada. This problem, in turn, involves a combination of business, cultural, demographic, economic, and social factors that relate to this sport and its history in each foreign nation. In no specific order, the following are some challenges that need to be addressed.

First, are there very wealthy individuals or well-organized syndicates within a foreign nation who each have the expertise and initiative to submit a bid for an MLB franchise and also controls a sufficient amount of financial capital to own and then successfully operate it for many years? There is information available to research about the managerial experiences and historical accomplishments of foreign entrepreneurs who have started their own businesses, and also about the performances of executives in various companies, including sports firms. If these organizations are local, regional, national, or international proprietorships or corporations that have financially struggled but nevertheless thrived despite economic recessions, this is an excellent background for the prospective owners or any ownership groups who may be awarded by the AL or NL to operate an MLB franchise. Therefore, it is commitments by franchise owners, field managers, and ballplayers to their respective team that really matters and thus attracts sports fans within a market to attend home games and passionately root for their club to compete and win.

Second, how much money and resources will a new franchise owner in a foreign country contribute to pay the construction cost of a major league ballpark at a site in Monterrey, San Juan, or in another city located overseas? Because a new facility for an MLB team will cost $100 million or more, the funds for a modern ballpark may need to be partially provided by a government department at the local and regional levels. So in relatively poor countries like the Dominican Republic and Panama, franchise owners would be expected to provide all or a majority of the financial capital for a stadium to be built in a city near its business district. Thus, this requirement is why the owners of an expansion team or a relocating MLB baseball club have not put their sports enterprises in underdeveloped countries where household incomes and business profits are below average relative to those in developed nations of the world.

Third, what is the potential size of a big league team's fan base and sports market within a major city or area of Japan, Mexico, or of other countries? Unfortunately there are no general formulas, methods, or systems of equations that accurately and precisely measure the fan base of a professional baseball team and the boundaries of its market. These areas would depend, to some extent, on the performance and popularity of a team and its players each baseball season, on a franchise owner or syndicate's ability, commitment, and willingness to expand their club's payroll and be competitive in a division of the AL or NL, on the decisions by MLB officials to increase or decrease revenue sharing and redistribute the luxury tax among 30 franchises, and on the development, growth, and prosperity of the local economy and also sports market in which a franchise is located. Consequently, a professional baseball team's fan base and the size and wealth of its market may vary from year to year based on these and other factors.

Fourth, how will attendances at—and gate receipts from—their home games, and also the revenues from other sources of any local teams in other professional baseball leagues of countries, be affected by the entry of an MLB club into their home markets? For example, the two major baseball leagues in Japan and many of their teams are in financial trouble each season because some of the nation's most popular ballplayers have immigrated into America and signed multiyear contracts with MLB clubs. Therefore, the potential entry of a new or existing AL or NL club into Tokyo or another Japanese city may be prohibited and ultimately blocked from entering any these cities' markets. Similarly, professional baseball teams in Mexico and other Latin American countries operate marginally since they generate little or no profit. As such, these clubs basically rely on admission fees from home games and small amounts of revenue from sponsors and television networks to compensate their athletes and survive each season. As a result, a new MLB club would likely be required to subsidize any domestic baseball teams that exist locally in foreign countries especially when any of them incur losses in their operations due to the competition from the entry of another professional team into their home areas.

Fifth, how many baseball seasons will it be before an expansion or relocated MLB club that had recently been placed within a foreign country become competitive enough to win a championship in the AL or NL and eventually a World Series? Indeed it may be several years or even a decade or more before a team in a foreign country is able to win a majority of its regular-season games and any series in the playoffs by defeating such prominent U.S.-based teams as, respectively, either the AL Boston Red Sox or NL Philadelphia Phillies in the East Division, AL Chicago White Sox or NL St. Louis Cardinals in the Central Division, and the AL Los Angeles Angels of Anaheim or NL Arizona Diamondbacks in the West Division.

The previous paragraph concludes this section of Chapter 5, which is titled "Global Baseball Markets." Consequently next, there is a brief summary of the chapter. Then after Chapter 5 the remaining parts of this book include an appendix and the chapter notes, bibliography, and Index.

In conclusion, I sincerely hope this book was an educational and memorable learning experience for baseball fans and also other readers. And moreover, that the topics in it—including league expansions and team relocations in MLB—contribute to an appreciation, awareness, and better understanding of how sports markets within North America have emerged, developed, and prospered for decades.

SUMMARY

The contents in sections of Chapter 5 essentially inform the readers about the different cities in the United States and Canada that have been occupied by clubs in professional baseball and other team sports during years and even decades between the late 1800s and early 2000s. Within the chapter, there are three tables of data which indicate when and where AL and NL teams had played their home games in various regular-seasons and postseasons of MLB. In turn, the distributions of these small, midsized, large, and very large urban places as prior, current, or future sports markets are organized and evaluated with respect to their being either superior, average, or inferior locations of big league franchises.

The home sites of league expansions and team relocations are each the most important topics discussed in Chapter 5. For example there is emphasis on, and an analysis of, the reasons or factors for when new franchises had entered specific areas and not others, and also for when owners of existing MLB franchises had moved their clubs into some markets and thereby, they had avoided other cities and areas elsewhere. Although the numbers of expansions and relocations among teams in MLB have not been very frequent since the early 1900s, the few of them that occurred denotes which sports markets have been the most and least popular among baseball officials in the AL and NL, and also the best and worst in sports entertainment value for local fans, businesses, and the general public.

Besides these types of issues, the chapter highlights and then evaluates some foreign cities with respect to them being potential markets for any new or relocating franchises in MLB. Despite their attributes, it is unlikely that any of these international cities will host one or more big league clubs before 2015 to 2020. So rather than locate a team in a country overseas, MLB will surely select a city within an area of the United States such as Columbus, Ohio; Indianapolis, Indiana; or Portland, Oregon. Furthermore—and other than Toronto—the five most populated cities in Canada that are each home to an NHL club have only a remote chance of being picked as a future market for an expansion franchise or current team in MLB.

In effect, Chapter 5 and the previous chapters provide an overview of how professional baseball in America has emerged, developed, and matured culturally, demographically, and economically for more than 125 years. Because cities are where baseball and other sports teams have established homes to conduct their operations, these markets play a vital role in the business success or failure of franchises and the current and future performances of their local clubs. In the end, this book retraces the history of these events and exposes their significance and impact for a prominent American sport.

Appendix

League and Team Statistics

Table A.1.1 American League Expansion Teams
Average Win-Loss and Attendance, by Seasons, 1961–2008

Teams	Seasons	Average Win-Loss	Attendance
Los Angeles/Anaheim Angels	1961–2008	49.5	1,924
Washington Senators	1961–1971	41.7	664
Kansas City Royals	1969–2008	48.5	1,669
Seattle Pilots	1969–1969	39.5	667
Seattle Mariners	1977–2008	47.0	1,827
Toronto Blue Jays	1977–2008	49.7	2,244
Tampa Bay Devil Rays/Rays	1998–2008	41.6	1,436

Note: Teams and Seasons are self-explanatory. Win-Loss is each team's average winning percent. Attendance is each team's average home attendance in hundreds of thousands. The various clubs of the Los Angeles/Anaheim Angels, for example, won an average of 49.5 percent of their games during 48 seasons and averaged 1,924,000 spectators per season at their ballpark in home attendance. The nickname Devil Rays was changed to Rays in 2008.

Source: "Teams," at http://www.baseball-reference.com, accessed 9 September 2008; "Teams," at http://www.mlb.com, accessed 12 September 2008; James Quirk and Rodney D. Fort, *Pay Dirt: The Business of Professional Team Sports* (Princeton, NJ: Princeton University Press, 1992), 483–488.

Table A.1.2 Major League Baseball Markets Population
Rank of Teams Areas, by AL Expansion Years, 1961–1998

Areas	1961	1969	1977	1998
American League				
Anaheim	–	20	18	17
Baltimore	12	13	14	19
Boston	7	8	10	10
Chicago	3	3	3	3
Cleveland	11	14	19	23
Dallas-Fort Worth	–	–	8	5
Detroit	5	5	5	9
Kansas City	21	25	29	26
Los Angeles	2	–	–	–
Milwaukee	–	–	28	–
Minneapolis	14	14	15	16
New York	1	1	1	1

Areas	1961	1969	1977	1998
Oakland	-	6	6	12
Seattle	-	19	23	15
Tampa Bay	-	-	-	21
Toronto	-	-	1	1
Washington	7	7	-	-
National League				
Atlanta	-	18	16	11
Chicago	3	3	3	3
Cincinnati	18	22	27	24
Denver	-	-	-	22
Houston	-	16	9	8
Los Angeles	2	2	2	2
Miami	-	-	-	6
Milwaukee	17	-	-	35
Montreal	-	2	2	2
New York	-	1	1	1
Philadelphia	4	4	4	4
Phoenix	-	-	-	14
Pittsburgh	8	11	13	20
St. Louis	9	10	12	18
San Diego	-	23	20	17
San Francisco	6	6	6	12

Note: The numbers in columns two through five are the population ranks of these areas. Anaheim was a metropolitan area in the late 1960s and 1970s. However, the population rank (17) of Anaheim in 1998 was based on the population of Orange County, which then equaled 2.8 million. Thus Anaheim and San Diego tied in rank. Arlington, as the home site of the AL Texas Rangers, is included in the Dallas-Fort Worth area while San Francisco and Oakland are each located in the same metropolitan area. Within Canada, the Greater Toronto Area was ranked first and Montreal Area second in population in these years. A dash (-) means that an AL or NL team did not exist in an area during the expansion year.

Sources: Official Major League Baseball Fact Book 2005 Edition (St. Louis: The Sporting News, 2005); and The World Almanac and Book of Facts (New York: World Almanac Books, 1961–2000).

Table A.2.1 National Association
Rank of Team Performances, 1871–1875

Team	1871	1872	1873	1874	1875
Baltimore Canaries	-	2	3	8	-
Baltimore Marylands	-	-	9	-	-
Boston Red Stockings	2	1	1	1	1
Brooklyn Atlantics	-	6	6	6	12
Brooklyn Eckfords	-	9	-	-	-
Chicago Forest Citys	7	7	-	-	-
Chicago White Stockings	3	-	-	5	7
Elizabeth Resolutes	-	-	8	-	-
Fort Wayne Kekiongas	8	-	-	-	-
Hartford Dark Blues	-	-	-	7	2
Keokuk Westerns	-	-	-	-	13
Middletown Mansfields	-	8	-	-	-
New Haven Elm Citys	-	-	-	-	8

Team	1871	1872	1873	1874	1875
New York Mutuals	4	3	4	2	6
Philadelphia Athletics	1	4	5	3	3
Philadelphia Centennials	-	-	-	-	11
Philadelphia Whites	-	-	2	4	5
Rockford Forest Citys	9	-	-	-	-
St. Louis Brown Stockings	-	-	-	-	4
St. Louis Red Stockings	-	-	-	-	10
Troy Haymakers	6	5	-	-	-
Washington Blue Legs	-	-	7	-	-
Washington Nationals	-	11	-	-	9
Washington Olympics	5	10	-	-	-

Notes: Team and the years 1871–1875 are self-explanatory. Rank is each team's finish in these regular seasons of the National Association. A dash (-) indicates that a team did not play in the league during that season.

Sources: "National Association of Professional Base Ball Players," at http://en.wikipedia.org, accessed 22 October 2008; "National Association of Base Ball Players," at http://www.baseball-reference.com, accessed 22 October 2008; "National Association of Professional Base Ball Players (NAPBBP)," at http://www.hickoksports.com, accessed 22 October 2008.

Table A.3.1 American League
Population Rank of Teams Areas in Relocation Years, 1902–1972

1902	1903	1954	1955	1961	1965	1968	1970	1972
2	1	1	1	1	1	1	1	1
3	2	2	2	2	3	3	3	3
4	3	4	5	3	5	5	5	5
5	4	5	6	5	7	6	6	6
6	5	6	10	7	8	7	7	8
7	7	10	11	10	11	8	8	12
13	13	11	12	11	12	11	11	13
15	15	12	17	12	15	12	12	14
				14	23	15	15	17
				21	25	18	18	20
							19	21
							26	25

Notes: The population ranks of areas of the relocation teams in each column are denoted in bold. Anaheim (ranked twenty-fifth in 1965) was not included in the Los Angeles area. Ranked sixth in 1968, Oakland is included in the San Francisco–Oakland metropolitan area. Ranked twelfth in 1972, Arlington is included in the Dallas-Fort Worth area of Texas.

Sources: Official Major League Baseball Fact Book 2005 Edition, 2005; "Population of the 100 Largest Urban Places: 1870–1900," at http://www.census.gov, accessed 15 September 2008; The World Almanac and Book of Facts, 1930–1972.

Table A.3.2 American League Teams Average Win–Loss
and Attendance Before and After Relocation, 1901–2008

Teams		Win–Loss		Attendance	
Before	After	Before	After	Before	After
Milwaukee Brewers I	St. Louis Browns	35.0	46.6	139	339

Teams		Win-Loss		Attendance	
Before	*After*	*Before*	*After*	*Before*	*After*
Baltimore Orioles I	New York Highlanders	43.6	53.8	157	348
St. Louis Browns	Baltimore Orioles II	36.5	43.0	325	934
Philadelphia Athletics	Kansas City Athletics	40.4	40.7	413	1,039
Washington Senators I	Minnesota Twins	40.3	53.6	544	1,353
Los Angeles Angels	Anaheim/LA Angels	47.4	46.6	778	1,115
Kansas City Athletics	Oakland Athletics	39.9	56.5	686	845
Seattle Pilots	Milwaukee Brewers II	39.5	43.4	677	862
Washington Senators II	Texas Rangers	44.7	43.7	742	966

Notes: The columns labeled Teams Before and After are each self-explanatory. Win-Loss is average winning percent, and average attendance is reported in hundreds of thousands. Except for the average win-loss percent and home attendance of the Milwaukee Brewers I (1901), Baltimore Orioles I (1901–1902) and Seattle Pilots (1969), the other teams' averages are reported for five seasons before and then after their relocation. The nickname of the New York Highlanders was changed in 1913 to the New York Yankees. The nickname of the Anaheim Angels was changed to California Angels in 1965, Anaheim Angels in 1997, and then to Los Angeles Angels of Anaheim in 2005.

Sources: James Quirk and Rodney D. Fort, *Pay Dirt*, 483–488; *Official Major League Fact Book 2005 Edition;* "Teams," at http://www.mlb.com, accessed 12 September 2008.

Table A.3.3 Current American League Franchises Lifetime Performances of Teams, by Division, 1901–2008

		Performances		
Team	*Seasons*	*Divisions*	*Pennants*	*World Series*
East				
Baltimore Orioles II	55	8	6	3
Boston Red Sox	108	6	12	7
New York Yankees	106	16	39	26
Tampa Bay Devils	11	1	1	0
Toronto Blue Jays	32	5	2	2
Central				
Chicago White Sox	108	5	6	2
Cleveland Indians	108	7	5	2
Detroit Tigers	108	3	10	4
Kansas City Royals	40	7	2	1
Minnesota Twins	48	8	3	2
West				
Los Angeles Angels of Anaheim	44	7	1	1
Oakland A's	41	14	6	4
Seattle Mariners	32	3	0	0
Texas Rangers	37	4	0	0

Notes: The performances of five clubs are reported, respectively, from the year when these franchises were originally named and established. That is, the Boston Red Sox as the Boston Americans in 1901; New York Yankees as the New York Highlanders in 1903; Chicago White Sox as the Chicago White Stockings in 1901; Cleveland Indians as the Cleveland Blues in 1901; Los Angeles of Anaheim as the Los Angeles Angels in 1961. Seasons are the total number of MLB regular seasons of each team. Performances include the number of these teams' division titles and AL pennants, and winning a World Series. Some clubs had won titles in two divisions. There was no World Series played in 1904 and 1994.

Sources: See the various sources in Table A.3.2.

Table A.4.1 Team Transfers Performances in American Association and National League, 1882–1900

Teams	American Association			National League		
	Seasons	Win Loss	Pennants	Seasons	Win Loss	Pennants
Baltimore Orioles	10	43.6	0	8	59.4	3
Cincinnati Reds	8	58.9	1	11	52.4	0
Louisville Colonels	10	48.2	1	8	37.5	0
Pittsburgh Alleghanys/Pirates	5	43.6	0	14	47.8	0
St. Louis Browns/Cardinals	10	63.7	4	9	37.0	0
Brooklyn Bridegrooms/Superbas	6	52.8	1	11	53.4	3
Cleveland Spiders	2	33.8	0	11	49.5	0
Washington Senators	1	32.6	0	8	37.0	0

Notes: Teams, American Association, National League, and Seasons are self-explanatory. Win-Loss is the teams' average winning percentage in each league. Pennants are the number won by teams while they played in each league.

Sources: Official Major League Baseball Fact Book 2005 Edition, 172–180; "American Association (19th Century)," at http://en.wikipedia.org, accessed 2 December 2008; Frank P. Jozsa, Jr., and John J. Guthrie, Jr., Relocating Teams and Expanding Leagues in Professional Sports: How the Major Leagues Respond to Market Conditions (Westport, CT: Quorum, 1999).

Table A.4.2 Union Association Team Relocations, Performances, and Population Ranks, 1884

Team		Performance		Population	
Pre-Move	Post-Move	Pre Move	Post Move	Pre Move	Post Move
Altoona Mountain Citys	Kansas City Cowboys	.240	.203	NR	30
Chicago Browns	Pittsburgh Stogies	NA	NA	4	12
Pittsburgh Stogies	St. Paul Saints	NA	.250	12	45
Philadelphia Keystones	Wilmington Quicksteps	.313	.111	2	42
Wilmington Quicksteps	Milwaukee Brewers	.111	.667	42	19

Notes: Team and the columns below it titled Pre-Move and Post-Move are self-explanatory. Performance and Population Rank are, respectively, each team's winning percentage and the rank in population of their urban places in the US prior to and after relocation. NA indicates that the winning percentages of the Chicago Browns and Pittsburgh Stogies were not reported separately for each club, but when combined, Chicago-Pittsburgh won approximately 45 percent of their games in the UA. NR means that Altoona was not ranked in the top 100 of urban place in 1884.

Sources: James Quirk and Rodney D. Fort, Pay Dirt, 386–388; Steve Bowles, "The Union Association: At a Glance," at http://www.baseballlibrary.com, accessed 1 December 2008; "Union Association," at http://en.wikipedia.org, accessed 1 December 2008; Official Major League Baseball Fact Book 2005 Edition, 173.

Table A.5.1 Four Major Sports Leagues Number of Expansions and Team Relocations, by 27 MLB Areas, 1876–2008

Area	Expansions				Relocations			
	NBA	NFL	NHL	MLS	NBA	NFL	NHL	MLS
Anaheim	0	0	1	0	0	0	0	0
Atlanta	0	1	2	0	1	0	0	0

Area	Expansions				Relocations			
	NBA	NFL	NHL	MLS	NBA	NFL	NHL	MLS
Baltimore	0	1	0	0	1	1	0	0
Boston	0	0	1	0	0	2	0	0
Chicago	2	0	1	1	0	0	0	0
Cincinnati	0	1	0	0	1	0	0	0
Cleveland	1	1	1	0	0	1	1	0
Dallas-Arlington	1	1	0	0	0	1	1	0
Denver	0	0	0	0	0	0	2	0
Detroit	0	1	1	0	1	2	0	0
Houston	0	1	0	0	1	0	0	1
Kansas City	0	0	1	0	1	0	0	0
Los Angeles	0	1	1	1	2	2	0	0
Miami	1	0	1	1	0	0	0	0
Milwaukee	1	0	0	0	1	0	0	0
Minneapolis	1	2	2	0	0	0	0	0
New York-New Jersey	1	0	2	0	0	3	2	0
Philadelphia	0	1	1	0	1	0	1	0
Phoenix	1	0	0	0	0	1	1	0
Pittsburgh	0	0	2	0	0	0	0	0
St. Louis	0	1	1	0	1	2	1	0
San Diego	1	0	0	0	1	0	0	0
San Francisco–Oakland	0	0	1	0	2	1	0	0
Seattle	1	1	0	0	0	0	0	0
Tampa Bay	0	1	1	0	0	0	0	0
Toronto	1	0	0	0	0	0	0	0
Washington	0	0	1	0	1	1	0	0

Notes: Area is an SMSA. The NBA, NFL, NHL, and MLS are self-explanatory. To interpret these different expansions and relocations, for example, the Anaheim Mighty Ducks joined the NHL in 1993 and the NBA Hawks moved to Atlanta from St. Louis in 1968. The transfers of teams from one league into another within the same sport as a result of mergers are not considered to be expansions or relocations with respect to this table.

Sources: Frank P. Jozsa, Jr., *Big Sports, Big Business: A Century of Expansions, Mergers, and Reorganizations* (Westport, CT: Praeger, 2006); James Quirk and Rodney D. Fort, *Pay Dirt*, 378–409; Frank P. Jozsa, Jr., and John J. Guthrie, Jr., *Relocating Teams and Expanding Leagues in Professional Sports*.

Chapter Notes

Introduction

1. For the histories of one or more of these baseball leagues and their teams, see such books as Lee Allen, *The American League Story* (New York: Hill & Wang, 1962), and *The National League Story: The Official History* (New York: Hill & Wang, 1969); David Pietrusza, *Major Leagues: The Formation, Sometimes Absorption and Mostly Inevitable Demise of 18 Professional Baseball Organizations, 1871 to Present* (Jefferson, NC: McFarland, 1991); Frank P. Jozsa, Jr., *Baseball, Inc.: The National Pastime as Big Business* (Jefferson, NC: McFarland, 2006); Leonard Koppett, *Koppett's Concise History of Major League Baseball*, 2nd ed. (Cambridge, MA: Da Capo Press, 2004).

2. Besides information reported on cities, states, and regions by the US Bureau of the Census, *Information Please Almanac*, and Statistical Abstracts of the US, there is various cultural, demographic, and geographic data about urban places and metropolitan areas in editions of *The World Almanac and Book of Facts* (New York: World Almanac Books, 1930–2007); "Historical Metropolitan Populations of the United States," at http://www.peakbagger.com, accessed 13 September 2008; and "Population of the 100 Largest Urban Places: 1870–1900," at http://www.census.gov, accessed 15 September 2008.

3. The locations, regular season and postseason performances, and other characteristics, results, and statistics for MLB teams and their ballplayers from 1876 to 2008 were confirmed in *Official Major League Baseball Fact Book 2005 Edition* (St. Louis: The Sporting News, 2005); "Teams," at http://www.baseball-reference.com, accessed 9 September 2008; "Teams," at http:

//www.mlb.com, accessed 12 September 2008; "Rodney Fort's Sports Economics: Sports Business Data," at http://www.rodneyfort.com, accessed 26 September 2008; and "MLB Franchise Chronology," at http://www.mlb.com, accessed 30 September 2008.

4. See Frank P. Jozsa, Jr., and John J. Guthrie, Jr., *Relocating Teams and Expanding Leagues in Professional Sports: How the Major Leagues Respond to Market Conditions* (Westport, CT: Quorum, 1999). An interesting online reading about these topics and their effects is Jeff Arnett, "There Used to be a Ballpark: How 50 Years of Relocation and Expansion Have Shaped the Game's Geography," at http://www.baseballhalloffame.org, accessed 15 September 2005.

5. The complete identifications of these sports books are Roger G. Noll, ed., *Government and the Sports Business: Studies in the Regulation of Economic Activity* (Washington, DC: The Brookings Institution, 1974); Paul D. Staudohar and James A. Mangan, eds., *The Business of Professional Sports* (Champaign, IL: University of Illinois Press, 1991); Charles C. Euchner, *Playing the Field: Why Sports Teams Move and Cities Fight to Keep Them* (Baltimore: John Hopkins University Press, 1993); Kenneth L. Shropshire, *The Sports Franchise Game: Cities in Pursuit of Sports Franchises, Events, Stadiums, and Arenas* (Philadelphia: University of Pennsylvania Press, 1995); and Mark Rosentraub, *Major League Losers: The Real Cost of Sports and Who's Paying For It* (New York: Basic Books, 1999).

6. Sports fans and those undergraduate and graduate faculty and students who are interested in the economics and other as-

pects of professional sports should read James Quirk and Rodney D. Fort, *Pay Dirt: The Business of Professional Team Sports* (Princeton, NJ: Princeton University Press, 1992), and their other book, *Hard Ball: The Abuse of Power in Pro Team Sports* (Princeton, NJ: Princeton University Press, 1999).

7. See note 1 above for the complete title, and the publisher and publication year of David Pietrusza's *Major Leagues*. Besides the AL and NL, his book also includes such baseball organizations as the National Association, International Association, Players League, Federal League, and Global League.

8. Some of the most interesting history about organized baseball during the late 1800s to early 1900s involves the competition and struggle for popularity and markets between teams in the "senior circuit," or National League, and the "junior circuit," or American League. This topic is vividly discussed in Warren N. Wilbert, *The Arrival of the American League: Ban Johnson and the 1901 Challenge to National League Monopoly* (Jefferson, NC: McFarland, 2007).

9. For more details about these two books, see Tom Melville, *Early Baseball and the Rise of the National League* (Jefferson, NC: McFarland, 2001), and Neil W. Macdonald, *The League That Lasted: 1876 and the Founding of the National League of Professional Base Ball Clubs* (Jefferson, NC: McFarland, 2004).

10. See Peter C. Bjarkman, ed., *Encyclopedia of Major League Baseball Team Histories: American League* (Westport, CT: Meckler Publishing, 1991), and also his *Encyclopedia of Major League Baseball Team Histories: National League* (Westport, CT: Meckler Publishing, 1991).

11. The remaining books mentioned in this section are Peter Filichia, *Professional Baseball Franchises: From the Abbeville Athletics to the Zanesville Indians* (New York: Facts on File, 1993); Lee Allen, *The American League Story* and *The National League Story: The Official History* (see note 1); and David Nemec and Saul Wisnia, *100 Years of Major League Baseball: American and National Leagues, 1901–2000* (Lincolnwood, IL: Publications International, 2000).

12. The three most prominent articles discussed in this portion of the baseball literature is James Quirk, "An Economic Analysis of Team Movements in Professional Sports," *Law and Contemporary Problems 38* (Winter/Spring 1973), 42–66; Martin B. Schmidt, "Competition in Major League Baseball: The Impact Expansion," *Applied Economic Letters 8* (2001), 21–26; and Kevin G. Quinn and Paul B. Bursik, "Growing and Moving the Game: Effects of MLB Expansion and Team Relocation 1950–2004," *Journal of Quantitative Analysis in Sports*, Vol. 3, Iss. 2 (2007), 1–27. See the Bibliography for other readings about league expansions and team relocations in the sport.

Chapter 1

1. For a history of these and other professional baseball leagues, see James Quirk and Rodney D. Fort, *Pay Dirt: The Business of Professional Team Sports* (Princeton, NJ: Princeton University Press, 1992); David Pietrusza, *Major League: The Formation, Sometimes Absorption and Mostly Inevitable Demise of 18 Professional Baseball Organizations, 1871 to Present* (Jefferson, NC: McFarland, 1991); and Roger G. Noll, ed., *Government and the Sports Business: Studies in the Regulation of Economic Activity* (Washington, DC: The Brookings Institution, 1974).

2. Some basic information about the early development and renaming of the Western League into the American League is contained in "Western League," at http://en.wikipedia.org, accessed 9 September 2008; W.C. Madden and Patrick J. Stewart, *The Western League: A Baseball History, 1885 Through 1999* (Jefferson, NC: McFarland, 2002); "American League," at http://en.wikipedia.org, accessed 9 September 2008; Lee Allen, *The American League Story* (New York: Hill & Wang, 1962); Warren N. Wilbert, *The Arrival of the American League: Ban Johnson and the 1901 Challenge to National League Monopoly* (Jefferson, NC: McFarland, 2007); and Benjamin G Radar, *Baseball: A History of America's Game*, 2nd ed. (Champaign, IL: University of Illinois Press, 2002).

3. Facts about the competition for baseball fans and markets between the AL and NL during the early 1900s are reported in James Quirk and Rodney D. Fort, *Pay*

Dirt, and in Frank P. Jozsa, Jr., *Big Sports, Big Business: A Century of Expansions, Mergers, and Reorganizations* (Westport, CT: Praeger, 2006); David Nemec and Saul Wisnia, *100 Years of Major League Baseball: American and National Leagues, 1901–2000* (Lincolnwood, IL: Publications International, 2000); Tom Melville, *Early Baseball and the Rise of the National League* (Jefferson, NC: McFarland, 2001); and Leonard Koppett, *Koppett's Concise History of Major League Baseball*, 2nd ed. (Cambridge, MA: Da Capo Press, 2004).

4. Besides the U.S. Bureau of Census, see the *Official Major League Baseball Fact Book 2005 Edition* (St. Louis: The Sporting News, 2005), and various editions of *The World Almanac and Book of Facts* (New York: World Almanac Books, 1930–2007).

5. Various business and economic aspects of league expansion and the relocation of teams in MLB are discussed in Frank P. Jozsa, Jr., and John J. Guthrie, Jr., *Relocating Teams and Expanding Leagues in Professional Sports: How the Major Leagues Respond to Market Conditions* (Westport, CT: Quorum, 1999); James Quirk, "An Economic Analysis of Team Movements in Professional Sports," *Law and Contemporary Problems 38* (Winter–Spring 1973), 42–66; Kevin G. Quinn and Paul B. Bursik, "Growing and Moving the Game: Effects of MLB Expansion and Team Relocation 1950–2004," *Journal of Quantitative Analysis in Sports*, Vol. 3, Iss. 2 (2007), 1–27; Skip Rozin, "Growing Pains: The Evolution of Expansion," *Sport* (December 1994), 10; Brian Schmitz, "Cities Adding Teams Isn't What Baseball Needs, Some Say," *The Orlando Sentinel* (11 May 2000), 1–2; and Simon Gonzalez, "Expansion Can't Explain All Big Numbers," *The Charlotte Observer* (14 July 1998), 4B.

6. To read more about the home areas, and emergence, growth, and success of one or more AL teams, there is Peter C. Bjarkman, ed., *Encyclopedia of Major League Baseball Team Histories: American League* (Westport, CT: Meckler Publishing, 1991); Frank P. Jozsa, Jr., *Baseball, Inc.: The National Pastime as Big Business* (Jefferson, NC: McFarland, 2006); and Peter Filichia, *Professional Baseball Franchises: From the Abbeville Athletics to the Zanesville Indians* (New York: Facts on File, 1993).

7. The performances of AL (and NL) clubs in MLB seasons are reported in editions of the *Official Major League Baseball Fact Book* 2005 Edition; "Teams," at http://www.mlb.com, accessed 12 September 2008; and in volumes of *The World Almanac and Book of Facts*, 1930–2007.

8. For more information about these two AL expansion clubs, see Richard E. Beverage, "Los Angeles Angels–California Angels: A Cowboy's Search For Another Champion," in Peter C. Bjarkman, ed., *Encyclopedia of Major League Baseball Team Histories: American League* (1991), 205–249; and Peter C. Bjarkman, "Washington Senators–Minnesota Twins: Expansion-Era Baseball Comes to the American League," 487–535.

9. The AL expansions in 1969 are discussed by Bill Carle, "Kansas City Royals: Building a Champion From Scratch in America's Heartland," in Peter C. Bjarkman, ed., *Encyclopedia of Major League Baseball Team Histories: American League* (1991), 183–204; and by Paul D. Adomites, "Seattle Pilots–Milwaukee Brewers: The Bombers, The Bangers, and the Burners," 422–444.

10. See James O'Donnell, "Seattle Mariners: Waiting For a Winner in Baseball's Forgotten City," in Peter C. Bjarkman, ed., *Encyclopedia of Major League Baseball Team Histories: American League* (1991), 390–421, and Peter C. Bjarkman, "Toronto Blue Jays: Okay, Blue Jays! From Worst to First in a Decade," 445–486.

11. Some interesting facts about the decisions and consequences of AL's expansion in 1998 are discussed by Albert Theodore Powers, *The Business of Baseball* (Jefferson, NC: McFarland, 2003); Frank P. Jozsa, Jr., *Baseball, Inc.*, 197–204; and "Tampa Bay Rays," at http://www.mlb.com, accessed 7 September 2008.

12. For a few readings about expansion in MLB, see Paul Attner, "How Professional Sports Governs Expansion Will Mean Success or Failure For 21st Century," *The Sporting News* (18 March 1991), 13–19; Joe Gergen, "Is Global Expansion the Wave of the Future?" *The Sporting News* (28 August 1989), 20; Martin B. Schmidt, "Competition in Major League Baseball: The Impact Expansion," *Applied Economic Letters* 8 (2001), 21–26; Jeff Arnett, "There

Used to be a Ballpark: How 50 Years of Relocation and Expansion Have Shaped the Game's Geography," at http://www.baseballhalloffame.org, accessed 15 September 2005; "MLB Franchise Chronology," at http://www.mlb.com, accessed 30 September 2008; and "Topping the Expansion List: These Four Cities Most Deserve a Major Pro Team," at http://www.cnnsi.com, accessed 12 August 2005.

Chapter 2

1. A concise reading that discusses this league's growth, professionalism, members, champions, and teams with most wins is "National Association of Base Ball Players," at http://en.wikipedia.org, accessed 22 October 2008. Also, see Benjamin G. Radar, *Baseball: A History of America's Game*, 2nd ed. (Champaign, IL: University of Illinois Press, 2002), and Harold Seymour, *Baseball: The Early Years* (New York: Oxford University Press, 1960).

2. For the history of this professional baseball organization, there is "National Association of Professional Base Ball Players," at http://en.wikipedia.org, accessed 22 October 2008; "National Association of Professional Base Ball Players—BR Bullpen," at http://www.baseball-reference.com, accessed 22 October 2008; "National Association of Professional Base Ball Players (NAPBBP)," at http://www.hickoksports.com, accessed 22 October 2008; David Pietrusza, "The National Association," in David Pietrusza, *Major Leagues: The Formation, Sometimes Absorption and Mostly Inevitable Demise of 18 Professional Baseball Organizations, 1871 to Present* (1991), 1–19; Neil W. Macdonald, *The League That Lasted: 1876 and the Founding of the National League of Professional Base Ball Clubs* (Jefferson, NC: McFarland, 2004).

3. Some important references to consult about the origin, growth, and development of the NL are David Pietrusza, "The National League," in David Pietrusza, *Major Leagues: The Formation, Sometimes Absorption and Mostly Inevitable Demise of 18 Professional Baseball Organizations, 1871 to Present* (1991), 23–41; "The First Major League (1875–1889)," at http://www.hickoksports.com, accessed 22 October

2008; Tom Melville, *Early Baseball and the Rise of the National League* (Jefferson, NC: McFarland, 2001); Lee Allen, *The National League Story: The Official History* (New York: Hill & Wang, 1969).

4. Several sources were used for data, statistics, and other information about the locations and performances of MLB's NL and AL teams. These include Frank P. Jozsa, Jr., *Baseball, Inc.: The National Pastime as Big Business* (Jefferson, NC: McFarland, 2006); *Official Major League Baseball Fact Book 2005 Edition* (St. Louis: The Sporting News, 2005); James Quirk and Rodney D. Fort, *Pay Dirt: The Business of Professional Team Sports* (Princeton, NJ: Princeton University Press, 1992); *The World Almanac and Book of Facts* (New York: World Almanac Books, 1930–2007); Peter C. Bjarkman, ed., *Encyclopedia of Major League Baseball Team Histories: National League* (Westport, CT: Meckler Publishing, 1991); "Historical Metropolitan Populations of the United States," at http://www.peakbagger.com, accessed 13 September 2008.

5. The expansion of franchises in the NL is the central topic of this chapter. For more details about it, there is Frank P. Jozsa, Jr., and John J. Guthrie, Jr., *Relocating Teams and Expanding Leagues in Professional Sports: How the Major Leagues Respond to Market Conditions* (Westport, CT: Quorum, 1999); Frank P. Jozsa, Jr., *Big Sports, Big Business: A Century of Expansions, Mergers, and Reorganizations* (Westport, CT: Praeger, 2006); Paul Attner, "How Professional Sports Governs Expansion Will Mean Success or Failure For 21st Century," *The Sporting News* (18 March 1991), 13–19; Kevin G. Quinn and Paul B. Bursik, "Growing and Moving the Game: Effects of MLB Expansion and Team Relocation 1950–2004," *Journal of Quantitative Analysis in Sports*, Vol. 3, Iss. 2 (2007), 1–27; Jeff Arnett, "There Used to be a Ballpark: How 50 Years of Relocation and Expansion Have Shaped the Game's Geography," at http: www.baseballhalloffame.org, accessed 15 September 2005; "Topping the Expansion List: These Four Cities Most Deserve a Major Pro Team," at http://www.cnnsi.com, accessed 12 August 2005.

6. For the NL's first expansion team after 1900, see "Franchise History: Major

League Baseball Comes to Houston," at http://en.wikipedia.org, accessed 2 October 2008, and John M. Carroll, "Houston Colt .45s–Houston Astros From Showbiz to Serious Baseball Business," in Peter C. Bjarkman, ed., *Encyclopedia of Major League Baseball Team Histories: National League* (1991), 239–262.

7. Information about expansion and the New York Mets is reported in "Franchise History: New York Mets," at http://en.wikipedia.org, accessed 2 October 2008; "New York Mets," at http://www.mlb.com, accessed 7 December 2008; Pete Cava, "New York Mets From Throneberry to Strawberry: Baseball's Most Successful Expansion Franchise," in Peter C. Bjarkman, ed., *Encyclopedia of Major League Baseball Team Histories: National League* (1991), 342–393.

8. The history of the San Diego Padres as an expansion team is contained in such readings as "Franchise History Pre 1970s: The Beginnings," at http://en.wikipedia.org, accessed 2 October 2008; "San Diego Padres," at http://www.mlb.com, accessed 7 December 2008; David L. Porter, "San Diego Padres: The Saga of Big Mac and Trader Jack," in Peter C. Bjarkman, ed., *Encyclopedia of Major League Baseball Team Histories: National League* (1991), 465–512.

9. Because of a higher capital gains tax proposed by United States president Barack Obama, Florida Marlins owner Wayne Huizenga intends to sell about 50 percent of his share of the NFL Miami Dolphins to the highest bidder. In fact, the tax rate may increase by 33 percent or from 15 percent to 20 percent. This action is reported in "Taxing the Dolphins," *Wall Street Journal* (30 October 2008), A18.

Chapter 3

1. For the relocation of clubs in various professional sports leagues including baseball, see Frank P. Jozsa, Jr., and John J. Guthrie, Jr., *Relocating Teams and Expanding Leagues in Professional Sports: How the Major Leagues Respond to Market Conditions* (Westport, CT: Quorum, 1999); Kenneth L. Shropshire, *The Sports Franchise Game: Cities in Pursuit of Sports Franchises, Events, Stadiums, and Arenas* (Philadelphia: University of Pennsylvania Press, 1995); and

Roger G. Noll, ed., *Government and the Sports Business: Studies in the Regulation of Economic Activity* (Washington, DC: The Brookings Institution, 1974).

2. These issues are stated in James Quirk, "An Economic Analysis of Team Movements in Professional Sports," *Law and Contemporary Problems* 38 (Winter/Spring 1973), 42–66. Two other readings related to this topic are Kevin G. Quinn and Paul B. Bursik, "Growing and Moving the Game: Effects of MLB Expansion and Team Relocation 1950–2004," *Journal of Quantitative Analysis in Sports,* Vol. 3, Iss. 2 (2007), 1–27, and Jeff Arnett, "There Used to be a Ballpark: How 50 Years of Relocation and Expansion Have Shaped the Game's Geography," at http://www.baseballhalloffame.org, accessed 15 September 2005.

3. To read more about the Western League, there is W.C. Madden and Patrick J. Stewart, *The Western League: A Baseball History, 1885 Through 1899* (Jefferson, NC: McFarland, 2002); Warren N. Wilbert, *The Arrival of the American League: Ban Johnson and the 1901 Challenge to National League Monopoly* (Jefferson, NC: McFarland, 2007); "Western League," at http://en.wikipedia.org, accessed 9 September 2008; R. Browning, "Encyclopedia of Major League Baseball Team Histories: American League," *Choice* (1 November 1991), 1.

4. The movement of the Brewers from Milwaukee to St. Louis in 1902 is discussed in "Milwaukee Brewers," at http://en.wikipedia.org, accessed 9 September 2008, and "St. Louis Browns: The Ballplayers," at http://www.baseballlibrary.com, accessed 26 September 2008.

5. For this very important relocation in MLB, see "New York Yankees," at http://en.wikipedia.org, accessed 26 September 2008, and Marty Appel, "New York Yankees: Pride, Tradition, and a Bit of Controversy," in Peter C. Bjarkman, ed., *Encyclopedia of Major League Baseball Team Histories: American League* (1991), 250–292.

6. More information about this move and later from Kansas City to Oakland is contained in Norman L. Macht, "Philadelphia Athletics–Kansas City Athletics–Oakland A's: Three Families and Three Baseball Epochs," in Peter C. Bjarkman, ed., *Encyclopedia of Major League Baseball*

Team Histories: American League (1991), 293–357, and "Oakland Athletics," at http://en.wikipedia.org, accessed 26 September 2008.

7. For the history of the Angels and the team's relocation from Los Angeles to Anaheim in 1966, see Mark Stewart, The Los Angeles Angels of Anaheim (Chicago: Norwood House Paper Editions, 2008); "Los Angeles Angels of Anaheim," http://en.wikipedia.org, accessed 9 September 2008; "Teams," at http://www.mlb.com, accessed 12 September 2008; Richard E. Beverage, "Los Angeles Angels–California Angels: A Cowboy's Search For Another Champion," in Peter C. Bjarkman, ed., Encyclopedia of Major League Baseball Team Histories: American League (1991), 205–249.

8. The failure of the AL Seattle Pilots and the team's transfer to Milwaukee in 1970 is analyzed in James Quirk and Rodney D. Fort, Pay Dirt: The Business of Professional Team Sports (Princeton, NJ: Princeton University Press, 1992); Kenneth Hogan, The 1969 Seattle Pilots: Major League Baseball's One-Year Team (Jefferson, NC: McFarland, 2006); Frank P. Jozsa, Jr., Baseball, Inc.: A Century of Expansions, Mergers, and Reorganizations (Jefferson, NC: McFarland, 2006).

9. This relocation and others in big league baseball are discussed in various essays within Peter C. Bjarkman, ed., Encyclopedia of Major League Baseball Team Histories: American League (Westport, CT: Meckler Publishing, 1991). For specifics about the Senators, see James R. Hartley, Washington's Expansion Senators (1961–1971) (Germantown, MD: Corduroy Press, 1998), and Kenneth L. Shropshire, "Washington, DC: Longing For the Senators," in Kenneth L. Shropshire, The Sports Franchise Game (1995), 52.

10. The names, attendances, and performances of various AL teams were reported in such publications as The World Almanac and Book of Facts (New York: World Almanac Books, 1930–2007); James Quirk and Rodney D. Fort, Pay Dirt, 378–408, 479–488; Official Major League Baseball Fact Book 2005 Edition (St. Louis: The Sporting News, 2005); "Teams," at http://www.baseball-reference.com, accessed 9 September 2008; "Major League Baseball League Attendance," at http://www.kenn.

com, accessed 17 September 2006; "American League," at http://en.wikipedia.org, accessed 9 September 2008; "Rodney Fort's Sports Economics: Sports Business Data," at http://www.rodneyfort.com, accessed 26 September 2008.

11. After controlling and owning the New York Yankees for 35 years, George Steinbrenner resigned in late November 2008 and was replaced by his 39-year-old son Hal. George purchased the franchise in 1973 for $10 million, and through 2008, his club had won 10 AL pennants and six World Series. Meanwhile, Hal has been chairman of the team's holding company, Yankees Global Enterprises, for the past 14 months. Hal's brother Hank will continue as co-chairman of the franchise and retain authority for baseball-related decisions. See Matthew Futterman, "Steinbrenner Passes Torch to Son Hal," Wall Street Journal (21 November 2008), B5.

Chapter 4

1. For the history of one or more of these early leagues in professional baseball, see Frank P. Jozsa, Jr., Big Sports, Big Business: A Century of Expansions, Mergers, and Reorganizations (Westport, CT: Praeger, 2006); Ed Koszarek, The Players League: History of Clubs, Ballplayers and Statistics (Jefferson, NC: McFarland, 2006); David Pietrusza, Major Leagues: The Formation, Sometimes Absorption and Mostly Inevitable Demise of 18 Professional Baseball Organizations, 1871 to Present (Jefferson, NC: McFarland, 1991); William J. Ryczek, Blackguards and Red Stockings: A History of Baseball's National Association (Jefferson, NC: McFarland, 1999); and David Nemec, The Beer and Whiskey League: The Illustrated History of the American Association—Baseball's Renegade Major League (Guilford, CT: The Lyons Press, 2004).

2. There are a number of interesting readings about professional baseball franchises and the relocation of teams in MLB's NL. See, for example, Charles C. Euchner, Playing the Field: Why Sports Teams Move and Cities Fight to Keep Them (Baltimore: Johns Hopkins University Press, 1993); Frank P. Jozsa, Jr., and John J. Guthrie, Jr., Relocating Teams and Expanding Leagues in Professional Sports: How

the Major Leagues Respond to Market Conditions (Westport, CT: Quorum, 1999); James Quirk and Rodney D. Fort, *Pay Dirt: The Business of Professional Team Sports* (Princeton: Princeton University Press, 1992); Kenneth L. Shropshire, *The Sports Franchise Game: Cities in Pursuit of Sports Franchises, Events, Stadiums, and Arenas* (Philadelphia: University of Pennsylvania Press, 1995).

3. The shift of the Braves from Boston to Milwaukee in 1953 was the first relocation in MLB since the early 1900s. Some information about this event is discussed in Lee Allen, *The National League Story: The Official History* (New York: Hill & Wang, 1969); Morris Eckhouse, "Boston Braves–Milwaukee Braves–Atlanta Braves: More Woes Than Wahoos For Baseball's Wanderers," in Peter C. Bjarkman, ed., *Encyclopedia of Major League Baseball Team Histories: National League* (1991), 20–71; "Milwaukee Braves," at http://sportsency-clopedia.com, accessed 18 July 2008; Evan Weiner, "Lou Perini Should be in Baseball's Hall of Fame With Walter O'Malley," at http://www.mcnsports.com, accessed 18 July 2008; "Braves Milwaukee," at http://www.baseballlibrary.com, accessed 18 July 2008.

4. To read about this relocation and its various business, competitive, and social effects on other franchises in MLB and also on communities, baseball fans, and the NL, there is Peter C. Bjarkman, "Brooklyn Dodgers–Los Angeles Dodgers: From Daffiness Dodgers to the Boys of Summer and the Myth of America's Team," in Peter C. Bjarkman, ed., *Encyclopedia of Major League Baseball Team Histories: National League* (1991), 72–136; Neil J. Sullivan, *The Dodgers Move West: The Transfer of the Brooklyn Baseball Franchise to Los Angeles* (New York: Oxford University Press, 1987); Roger G. Noll, ed., *Government and the Sports Business: Studies in the Regulation of Economic Activity* (Washington, DC: The Brookings Institution, 1974).

5. See James Quirk, "An Economic Analysis of Team Movements in Professional Sports," *Law and Contemporary Problems 38* (Winter/Spring 1973), 42–66; Fred Stein, "New York Giants–San Francisco Giants: A Tale of Two Cities," in Peter C. Bjarkman, ed., *Encyclopedia of*

Major League Baseball Team Histories: National League (1991), 303–341; Andrew Goldblatt, *The Giants and the Dodgers: Four Cities, Two Teams, One Rivalry* (Jefferson, NC: McFarland, 2003); "San Francisco Giants," at http://www.mlb.com, accessed 7 December 2008.

6. The concept of promoting economic enterprises—such as an MLB franchise—by organized public and private groups within urban communities is a topic discussed in a paper authored by Glen Gendzel, "Competitive Boosterism: How Milwaukee Lost the Braves," *Business History Review*, Vol. 69, No. 4 (Winter 1995), 530–566. This well-researched article gives the reasons for when and why the Braves moved from Milwaukee to Atlanta and the implications and consequences of that relocation in each city.

7. To learn about the baseball operations of the Expos or the Nationals, see Peter C. Bjarkman, "Montreal Expos Bizarre New Diamond Traditions North of the Border," in Peter C. Bjarkman, ed., *Encyclopedia of Major League Baseball Team Histories: National League* (1991), 263–302; "Montreal Expos," at http://www.mlb.com, accessed 7 December 2008; "Washington Nationals," at http://en.wikipedia.org, accessed 7 December 2008; Frank P. Jozsa, Jr., *Baseball, Inc.: The National Pastime as Big Business* (Jefferson, NC: McFarland, 2006).

8. Several sources were used to research the performances of NL teams. These included the *Official Major League Baseball Fact Book 2005 Edition* (St. Louis: The Sporting News, 2005); *The World Almanac and Book of Facts* (New York: World Almanac Books, 1930–2007); "Teams," at http://www.baseball-reference.com, accessed 9 September 2008; "World Series History," at http://www.baseball-almanac.com, accessed 8 September 2008; "Teams," at http://www.mlb.com, accessed 12 September 2008.

9. Because of troubles from an economic recession and his impending divorce, San Diego Padres owner John Moores hired a firm to explore the sale of his franchise. He purchased the club for $85 million and its value in 2008 is estimated to be $385 million. For this news, see "Padres Might be on the Block," *The Charlotte Observer* (16 December 2008), 2C.

Chapter 5

1. For more information about when and where expansions occurred in MLB and also in some other professional sports leagues, see Frank P. Jozsa, Jr., and John J. Guthrie, Jr., *Relocating Teams and Expanding Leagues in Professional Sports: How the Major Leagues Responded to Market Conditions* (Westport, CT: Quorum, 1999); Kenneth L. Shropshire, *The Sports Franchise Game: Cities in Pursuit of Sports Franchises, Events, Stadiums, and Arenas* (Philadelphia, PA: University of Pennsylvania Press, 1995); James Quirk and Rodney D. Fort, *Pay Dirt: The Business of Professional Team Sports* (Princeton, NJ: Princeton University Press, 1992); Phil Schaaf, *Sports, Inc.: 100 Years of Sports Business* (Amherst, NY: Prometheus Books, 2004).

2. The relocation of sports teams from one area to another is a topic discussed in the literature. A sample of these readings include Arthur T. Johnson, "Municipal Administration and the Sports Franchise Relocation Issue," *Public Administration Review* (November/December 1983), 519–528; Kevin G. Quinn and Paul B. Bursik, "Growing and Moving the Game: Effects of MLB Expansion and Team Relocation 1950–2004," *Journal of Quantitative Analysis in Sports*, Vol. 3, Iss. 2 (2007), 1–27; James Quirk, "An Economic Analysis of Team Movements in Professional Sports," *Law and Contemporary Problems 38* (Winter/Spring 1973), 42–66; Jeff Arnett, "There Used to be a Ballpark: How 50 Years of Relocation and Expansion have Shaped the Game's Geography," at http://www.baseballhalloffame.org, accessed 15 September 2005; Frank P. Jozsa, Jr., "An Economic Analysis of Franchise Relocation and League Expansion in Professional Team Sports, 1950–1975," Ph.D. diss., Georgia State University, 1977.

3. The histories of various professional baseball leagues and their different teams are reported in several publications. See, for example, David Nemec, *The Beer and Whiskey League: The Illustrated History of the American Association—Baseball's Renegade Major League* (Guilford, CT: The Lyons Press, 2004); David Nemec and Saul Wisnia, *100 Years of Major League Baseball: American and National Leagues, 1901–2000*

(Lincolnwood, IL: Publications International, Ltd., 2000); David Pietrusza, *Major Leagues: The Formation, Sometimes Absorption and Mostly Inevitable Demise of 18 Professional Baseball Organizations, 1871 to Present* (Jefferson, NC: McFarland, 1991); Ed Koszarek, ed., *The Players League: History of Clubs, Ballplayers and Statistics* (Jefferson, NC: McFarland, 2006); Steve Bowles, "The Union Association: At a Glance," at http://www.baseballlibrary.com, accessed 1 December 2008.

4. A number of newspaper articles reported the home areas of current teams in professional sports. These were "Baseball Standings 2008," *The Charlotte Observer* (1 October 2008), 4C; "NBA Today," *The Charlotte Observer* (29 October 2008), 5C; "Football NFL," *The Charlotte Observer* (21 October 2008), 3C; "Ice Hockey NHL," *The Charlotte Observer* (21 October 2008), 3C; "Soccer MLS," *The Charlotte Observer* (24 October 2008), 7C. For the names and locations of sports clubs that existed prior to 2008, see *The World Almanac and Book of Facts* (New York: World Almanac Books, 1930–2007); "Teams," at http://www.mlb.com, accessed 12 September 2008; "Teams," at http://www.nba.com, accessed 23 December 2008; "Teams," at http://www.nfl.com, accessed 23 December 2008; "Teams," at http://www.nhl.com, accessed 23 December 2008; "Teams," at http://www.mls.com, accessed 23 September 2008.

5. For the population of urban places and metropolitan areas in America since the late 1800s to early 1900s, there is "Population of the 100 Largest Urban Places: 1870–1900," at http://www.census.gov, accessed 15 September 2008; "Historical Metropolitan Populations of the United States," at http://www.peakbagger.com, accessed 13 September 2008; *The World Almanac and Book of Facts*, 1930–2007. Also, see various editions of the *Information Please Almanac* (Boston: Houghton Mifflin, 1985–2008); *State and Metropolitan Data Book* (Washington, DC: U.S. Census Bureau, 1979–2006); *Statistical Abstract of the United States* (Washington, DC: U.S. Census Bureau, 1978–2009).

6. See Frank P. Jozsa, Jr., *Sports Capitalism: The Foreign Business of American Professional Leagues* (Aldershot, England: Ashgate, 2004); *Idem., Baseball in Crisis:*

Spiraling Costs, Bad Behavior, Uncertain Future (Jefferson, NC: McFarland, 2008); *Idem., Baseball, Inc.: The National Pastime as Big Business* (Jefferson, NC: McFarland, 2006). Other books by this author that discuss league expansions and team relocations in professional sports are *American Sports Empire: How the Leagues Breed Success* (Westport, CT: Praeger, 2003), and *Big Sports, Big Business: A Century of Expansions, Mergers, and Reorganizations* (Westport, CT: Praeger, 2006).

Bibliography

Articles and Parts of Books

Adams, Russell. "Times Co. Seeks Buyer For Its Stake in Red Sox." *Wall Street Journal* (26 December 2008): B1.

Adomites, Paul D. "Seattle Pilots–Milwaukee Brewers: The Bombers, The Bangers, and The Burners." In Peter C. Bjarkman, ed. *Encyclopedia of Major League Baseball Team Histories: American League* (1991): 422–444.

Appel, Marty. "New York Yankees: Pride, Tradition, and a Bit of Controversy." In Peter C. Bjarkman, ed. *Encyclopedia of Major League Baseball Team Histories: American League* (1991): 250–292.

Attner, Paul. "How Professional Sports Governs Expansion Will Mean Success or Failure For 21st Century." *The Sporting News* (18 March 1991): 13–19.

"Baseball: A History of America's Game." *Publishers Weekly* (16 November 1992): 52.

"Baseball Standings: 2008." *The Charlotte Observer* (1 October 2008): 4C.

Berger, Morey. "Major Leagues." *Library Journal* (15 June 1991): 83.

Beverage, Richard E. "Los Angeles Angels–California Angels: A Cowboy's Search For Another Champion." In Peter C. Bjarkman, ed. *Encyclopedia of Major League Baseball Team Histories: American League* (1991): 205–249.

Bjarkman, Peter C. "Brooklyn Dodgers–Los Angeles Dodgers: From Daffiness Dodgers to the Boys of Summer and the Myth of America's Team." In Peter C. Bjarkman, ed. *Encyclopedia of Major League Baseball Team Histories: National League* (1991): 72–136.

_____. "Introduction—Breaking Traditions in the Senior Circuit." In Peter C. Bjarkman, ed. *Encyclopedia of Major League Baseball Team Histories: National League* (1991): 1–19.

_____. "Introduction: Historical Perspectives on the Junior Circuit." In Peter C. Bjarkman, ed. *Encyclopedia of Major League Baseball Team Histories: American League* (1991): 1–15.

_____. "Montreal Expos Bizarre New Diamond Traditions North of the Border." In Peter C. Bjarkman, ed. *Encyclopedia of Major League Baseball Team Histories: National League* (1991): 263–302.

_____. "Toronto Blue Jays: Okay, Blue Jays! From Worst to First in a Decade." In Peter C. Bjarkman, ed. *Encyclopedia of Major League Baseball Team Histories: American League* (1991): 445–486.

_____. "Washington Senators–Minnesota Twins: Expansion-Era Baseball Comes to the American League." In Peter C. Bjarkman, ed. *Encyclopedia of Major League Baseball Team Histories: American League* (1991): 487–535.

_____. "Washington Senators–Texas Rangers: There Are No Dragons in Baseball: Only Shortstops." In Peter C. Bjarkman, ed. *Encyclopedia of Major League Baseball Team Histories: American League* (1991): 535–573.

Bogey, Dan. "Baseball: A History of America's Game." *Library Journal* (1 October 1992): 95.

Bowyer, Jerry. "Sports Mania is a Poor Substitute For Economic Success."

Wall Street Journal (17–18 January 2009): A9.

Browning, R. "Baseball: A History of America's Game." *Choice* (1 August 2002): 1.

_____. "Encyclopedia of Major League Baseball Team Histories: American League." *Choice* (1 November 1991): 1.

_____. "Encyclopedia of Major League Baseball Team Histories: National League." *Choice* (1 May 1992): 1.

Burns, Jim. "Taking On the Yankees." *Library Journal* (1 August 2003): 93.

Carle, Bill. "Kansas City Royals: Building a Champion From Scratch in America's Heartland." In Peter C. Bjarkman, ed. *Encyclopedia of Major League Baseball Team Histories: American League* (1991): 183–204.

Carroll, John M. "Houston Colt .45s–Houston Astros: From Showbiz to Serious Baseball Business." In Peter C. Bjarkman, ed. *Encyclopedia of Major League Baseball Team Histories: National League* (1991): 239–262.

Catanoso, Justin. "Baseball Should Go Where the Money Is." *Business Week* (29 June 1998): 131.

Cava, Pete. "New York Mets From Throneberry to Strawberry: Baseball's Most Successful Expansion Franchise." In Peter C. Bjarkman, ed. *Encyclopedia of Major League Baseball Team Histories: National League* (1991): 342–393.

Cottrell, R.C. "Early Baseball and the Rise of the National League." *Choice* (1 September 2001): 1.

Davis, Lance E. "Self-Regulation in Baseball, 1909–71." In Roger G. Noll, ed. *Government and the Sports Business: Studies in the Regulation of Economic Activity* (1974): 349–386.

"Early Baseball and the Rise of the National League." *Reference & Research Book News* (1 August 2001): 1.

Eckhouse, Morris. "Boston Braves–Milwaukee Braves–Atlanta Braves: More Woes Than Wahoos For Baseball's Wanderers." In Peter C. Bjarkman, ed. *Encyclopedia of Major League Baseball Team Histories: National League* (1991): 20–71.

"Encyclopedia of Major League Baseball Team Histories: American League." *Library Journal* (1 February 1991): 1.

"Encyclopedia of Major League Baseball Team Histories: National League." *Library Journal* (1 February 1991): 1.

Felber, Bill. "St. Louis Browns–Baltimore Orioles: One of the Very Worst, and One of the Very Best." In Peter C. Bjarkman, ed. *Encyclopedia of Major League Baseball Team Histories: American League* (1991): 358–389.

"Football NFL." *The Charlotte Observer* (21 October 2008): 3C.

Futterman, Matthew. "As Economy Weakens, Sports Feel a Chill." *Wall Street Journal* (14 October 2008): B1, B10.

_____. "Full Count For Rays in Money Game." *Wall Street Journal* (22 October 2008): B1, B5.

_____. "Off-the-Field Losses Crimp Team Owners." *Wall Street Journal* (2 January 2009): A9.

_____. "Steinbrenner Passes Torch to Son Hal." *Wall Street Journal* (21 November 2008): B5.

_____. "Tribune May Retain Half of Cubs." *Wall Street Journal* (7 November 2008): B3.

Gendzel, Glen. "Competitive Boosterism: How Milwaukee Lost the Braves." *Business History Review*. Vol. 69, No. 4 (Winter 1995): 530–566.

Gergen, Joe. "Is Global Expansion the Wave of the Future?" *The Sporting News* (28 August 1989): 20.

Gittleman, S. "The League That Lasted: 1876 and the Founding of the National League of Professional Base Ball Clubs." *Choice* (1 December 2004): 1.

Gonzalez, Simon. "Expansion Can't Explain All Big Numbers." *The Charlotte Observer* (14 July 1998): 4B.

Guier, Cindy Stooksbury. "When the Home Team Leaves." *Amusement Business* (16 June 1997): 10–12.

Gustafson, W.F. "Koppett's Concise History of Major League Baseball." 1st ed. *Choice* (1 April 1999): 1.

Hyman, Mark. "What Does This Town Need? New Senators." *Business Week* (14 May 2001): 54.

"Ice Hockey NHL." *The Charlotte Observer* (21 October 2008): 3C.

Johnson, Arthur T. "Municipal Administration and the Sports Franchise Relocation Issue." *Public Administration Review* (November/December 1983): 519–528.

Last, Jonathan V. "Are Pro Sports Too Big to Fail?" *Wall Street Journal* (30 January 2008): W11.

Littlefield, Bill. "Baseball: A History of America's Favorite Game." *Boston Globe* (3 September 2006): D5.

Macht, Norman L. "Philadelphia Athletics–Kansas City Athletics–Oakland A's: Three Families and Three Baseball Epochs." In Peter C. Bjarkman, ed. *Encyclopedia of Major League Baseball Team Histories: American League* (1991): 293–357.

Moores, Alan. "Baseball: A History of America's Favorite Game." *Booklist* (1 August 2006): 26.

"NBA Today." *The Charlotte Observer* (29 October 2008): 5C.

O'Donnell, James. "Seattle Mariners: Waiting For a Winner in Baseball's Forgotten City." In Peter C. Bjarkman, ed. *Encyclopedia of Major League Baseball Team Histories: American League* (1991): 390–421.

"Padres Might be on Block." *The Charlotte Observer* (16 December 2008): 2C.

"Pay Dirt: The Business of Professional Team Sports." *Kirkus Reviews* (15 October 1992): 1.

"Pay Dirt: The Business of Professional Team Sports." *Publishers Weekly* (19 October 1992): 64.

Pietrusza, David. "The National Association." In David Pietrusza, *Major Leagues: The Formation, Sometimes Absorption and Mostly Inevitable Demise of 18 Professional Baseball Organizations, 1871 to Present* (1991): 1–19.

_____. "The National League." In David Pietrusza, *Major Leagues: The Formation, Sometimes Absorption and Mostly Inevitable Demise of 18 Professional Baseball Organizations, 1871 to Present* (1991): 23–41.

Pitt, David. "The Baseball Economist: The Real Game Exposed." *Booklist* (1 January 2007): 40.

Porter, David L. "San Diego Padres: The Saga of Big Mac and Trader Jack." In Peter C. Bjarkman, ed. *Encyclopedia of Major League Baseball Team Histories: National League* (1991): 465–512.

"Professional Baseball Franchises." *Booklist* (1 March 1993): 1.

"Professional Baseball Franchises." *Reference & Research Book News* (1 August 1993): 1.

Quinn, Kevin G., and Paul B. Bursik. "Growing and Moving the Game: Effects of MLB Expansion and Team Relocation 1950–2004." *Journal of Quantitative Analysis in Sports*. Vol. 3, Iss. 2 (2007): 1–27.

Quirk, James. "An Economic Analysis of Team Movements in Professional Sports." *Law and Contemporary Problems* 38 (Winter/Spring 1973): 42–66.

_____, and Mohamed El Hodiri. "The Economic Theory of a Professional Sports League." In Roger G. Noll, ed. *Government and the Sports Business: Studies in the Regulation of Economic Activity* (1974): 33–80.

Repak, Chaz. "Taking On the Yankees." *Wall Street Journal* (2 October 2003): D10.

Rivkin, Stephen R. "Sports Leagues and the Federal Antitrust Laws." In Roger G. Noll, ed. *Government and the Sports Business: Studies in the Regulation of Economic Activity* (1974): 387–410.

Rozin, Skip. "Growing Pains: The Evolution of Expansion." *Sport* (December 1994): 10.

Sanderson, A.R. "The Baseball Economist: The Real Game Exposed." *Choice* (1 October 2007): 1.

_____. "Pay Dirt: The Business of Professional Team Sports." *Choice* (1 September 1993): 1.

Schmidt, Martin B. "Competition in Major League Baseball: The Impact

Expansion." *Applied Economic Letters* 8 (2001): 21–26.

Schmitz, Brian. "Cities Adding Teams Isn't What Baseball Needs, Some Say." *The Orlando Sentinel* (11 May 2000): 1–2.

Shropshire, Kenneth L. "Washington, DC: Longing For the Senators." In Kenneth L. Shropshire, *The Sports Franchise Game* (1995): 52.

Siciliano, Ernie. "From Payroll to Playoffs." *Region Focus* (Winter 2008): 26–27.

"Soccer MLS." *The Charlotte Observer* (24 October 2008): 7C.

Spencer, Albert. "Pay Dirt: The Business of Professional Team Sports." *Library Journal* (15 November 1992): 81.

Stanley, C.V. "Professional Baseball Franchises." *Choice* (1 July 1993): 1.

Stein, Fred. "New York Giants–San Francisco Giants: A Tale of Two Cities." In Peter C. Bjarkman, ed. *Encyclopedia of Major League Baseball Team Histories: National League* (1991): 303–341.

"Taking On the Yankees." *Publishers Weekly* (21 July 2003): 186.

"Taxing the Dolphins." *Wall Street Journal* (30 October 2008): A18.

"The Baseball Economist: The Real Game Exposed." *Library Journal* (1 February 2007): 79–80.

"The Baseball Economist: The Real Game Exposed." *Publishers Weekly* (22 January 2007): 182.

"Yankees Extend Offseason Spending Spree to Get Teixeira." *The Charlotte Observer* (24 December 2008): 2C.

Zimbalist, Andrew. "New Yankee Stadium Shaping up to Offer Fans Top-Notch Baseball Experience." *Street & Smith's SportsBusiness Journal* (21–27 July 2008): 46.

Books

Allen, Lee. *The American League Story.* New York: Hill & Wang, 1962.

_____. *The National League Story: The Official History.* New York: Hill & Wang, 1969.

Bjarkman, Peter C., ed. *Encyclopedia of* *Major League Baseball Team Histories: American League.* Westport, CT: Meckler Publishing, 1991.

_____. *Encyclopedia of Major League Baseball Team Histories: National League.* Westport, CT: Meckler Publishing, 1991.

Bradbury, J.C. *The Baseball Economist: The Real Game Exposed.* New York: Dutton, 2007.

Downward, Paul, and Alistair Dawson. *The Economics of Professional Team Sports.* New York: Routledge, 2000.

Euchner, Charles C. *Playing the Field: Why Sports Teams Move and Cities Fight to Keep Them.* Baltimore: Johns Hopkins University Press, 1993.

Fetter, Henry D. *Taking on the Yankees: Winning and Losing in the Business of Baseball, 1903 to 2003.* New York: Norton, 2005.

Filichia, Peter. *Professional Baseball Franchises: From the Abbeville Athletics to the Zanesville Indians.* New York: Facts on File, 1993.

Fizel, John. ed. *Handbook of Sports Economics Research.* Armonk, NY: M.E. Sharpe, 2006.

Gershman, Michael. *Diamonds: The Evolution of the Ballpark.* New York: Houghton Mifflin Company, 1993.

Gilbert, Sara. *The Story of the Kansas City Royals.* Mankato, MN: Creative Education, 2007.

Goldblatt, Andrew. *The Giants and the Dodgers: Four Cities, Two Teams, One Rivalry.* Jefferson, NC: McFarland, 2003.

Hartley, James R. *Washington's Expansion Senators (1961–1971).* Germantown, MD: Corduroy Press, 1998.

Hogan, Kenneth. *The 1969 Seattle Pilots: Major League Baseball's One-Year Team.* Jefferson, NC: McFarland, 2006.

Information Please Almanac. Boston: Houghton-Mifflin, 1985–2008.

James, Bill. *The New Bill James Historical Baseball Abstract.* New York: The Free Press, 2003.

Jozsa, Frank P., Jr. *American Sports Empire: How the Leagues Breed Success.* Westport, CT: Praeger, 2003.

_____. *Baseball in Crisis: Spiraling Costs, Bad Behavior, Uncertain Future.* Jefferson, NC: McFarland, 2008.

_____. *Baseball, Inc.: The National Pastime as Big Business.* Jefferson, NC: McFarland, 2006.

_____. *Big Sports, Big Business: A Century of Expansions, Mergers, and Reorganizations.* Westport, CT: Praeger, 2006.

_____. *Global Sports: Cultures, Markets, and Organizations.* Singapore: World Scientific, 2009.

_____. *Sports Capitalism: The Foreign Business of American Professional Leagues.* Aldershot, England: Ashgate, 2004.

_____, and John J. Guthrie, Jr. *Relocating Teams and Expanding Leagues in Professional Sports: How the Major Leagues Respond to Market Conditions.* Westport, CT: Quorum, 1999.

Koppett, Leonard. *Koppett's Concise History of Major League Baseball.* 2nd ed. Cambridge, MA: Da Capo Press, 2004.

Koszarek, Ed. *The Players League: History of Clubs, Ballplayers and Statistics.* Jefferson, NC: McFarland, 2006.

Macdonald, Neil W. *The League That Lasted: 1876 and the Founding of the National League of Professional Base Ball Clubs.* Jefferson, NC: McFarland, 2004.

Madden, W.C., and Patrick J. Stewart. *The Western League: A Baseball History, 1885 Through 1999.* Jefferson, NC: McFarland, 2002.

Melville, Tom. *Early Baseball and the Rise of the National League.* Jefferson, NC: McFarland, 2001.

Nemec, David. *The Beer and Whiskey League: The Illustrated History of the American Association—Baseball's Renegade Major League.* Guilford, CT: The Lyons Press, 2004.

_____, and Saul Wisnia. *100 Years of Major League Baseball: American and National Leagues, 1901–2000.* Lincolnwood, IL: Publications International, 2000.

Noll, Roger G., ed. *Government and the Sports Business: Studies in the Regulation of Economic Activity.* Washington, DC: The Brookings Institution, 1974.

Pedersen, Paul Mark. *Built It and They Will Come: The Arrival of the Tampa Bay Devil Rays.* Stuart, FL: Florida Sports Press, 1997.

Pietrusza, David. *Major Leagues: The Formation, Sometimes Absorption and Mostly Inevitable Demise of 18 Professional Baseball Organizations, 1871 to Present.* Jefferson, NC: McFarland, 1991.

Powers, Albert Theodore. *The Business of Baseball.* Jefferson, NC: McFarland, 2003.

Quirk, James, and Rodney D. Fort. *Hard Ball: The Abuse of Power in Pro Team Sports.* Princeton, NJ: Princeton University Press, 1999.

_____, and _____. *Pay Dirt: The Business of Professional Team Sports.* Princeton, NJ: Princeton University Press, 1992.

Rader, Benjamin G. *Baseball: A History of America's Game.* 2nd ed. Champaign, IL: University of Illinois Press, 2002.

Rosentraub, Mark. *Major League Losers: The Real Cost of Sports and Who's Paying For It.* New York: Basic Books, 1999.

Ryczek, William J. *Blackguards and Red Stockings: A History of Baseball's National Association.* Jefferson, NC: McFarland, 1999.

Schaaf, Phil. *Sports, Inc.: 100 Years of Sports Business.* Amherst, NY: Prometheus Books, 2004.

Seymour, Harold. *Baseball: The Early Years.* New York: Oxford University Press, 1960.

_____. *Baseball: The Golden Age.* 2nd ed. New York: Oxford University Press, 1989.

Shank, Matthew D. *Sports Marketing: A Strategic Perspective.* 2nd ed. Upper Saddle River, NJ: Prentice Hall, 2002.

Shannon, Mike. *Baseball Books: A Collector's Guide.* Jefferson, NC: McFarland, 2008.

Shofner, Shawndra. *The Story of the Toronto Blue Jays.* Mankato, MN: Creative Education, 2007.

Shropshire, Kenneth L. *The Sports Franchise Game: Cities in Pursuit of Sports Franchises, Events, Stadiums, and Arenas.* Philadelphia: University of Pennsylvania Press, 1995.

Staudohar, Paul D., and James A. Mangan, eds. *The Business of Professional Sports.* Champaign, IL: University of Illinois Press, 1991.

Stewart, Mark. *The Los Angeles Angels of Anaheim.* Chicago: Norwood House Paper Editions, 2008.

Sullivan, Dean A. *Late Innings: A Documentary History of Baseball, 1945–1972.* Lincoln, NE: University of Nebraska Press, 2002.

Sullivan, Neil J. *The Dodgers Move West: The Transfer of the Brooklyn Baseball Franchise to Los Angeles.* New York: Oxford University Press, 1987.

Szymanski, Stefan, and Andrew Zimbalist. *National Pastime: How Americans Play Baseball and the Rest of the World Plays Soccer.* Washington, DC: Brookings Institution Press, 2005.

The World Almanac and Book of Facts. New York: World Almanac Books, 1930–2007.

Thiel, Art. *Out of Left Field: How the Mariners Made Baseball Fly in Seattle.* Seattle: Sasquatch Books, 2003.

Turkin, Hy, and S.C. Thompson. *Official Encyclopedia of Baseball.* New York: Doubleday, 1979.

Wilbert, Warren N. *The Arrival of the American League: Ban Johnson and the 1901 Challenge to National League Monopoly.* Jefferson, NC: McFarland, 2007.

Zimbalist, Andrew. *May the Best Team Win.* Washington, DC: Brookings Institution Press, 2003.

Dissertations

Jozsa, Frank P., Jr. "An Economic Analysis of Franchise Relocation and League Expansion in Professional Team Sports, 1950–1975." Ph.D. diss. Georgia State University, 1977.

Government Publications

State and Metropolitan Data Book. Washington, DC: U.S. Census Bureau, 1979–2006.

Statistical Abstract of the United States. Washington, DC: U.S. Census Bureau, 1878–2009.

Internet Sources

"American Association (19th Century)." http://en.wikipedia.org, accessed 2 December 2008.

"American League." http://en.wikipedia.org, accessed 9 September 2008.

"Arizona Diamondbacks." http://en.wikipedia.org, accessed 2 October 2008.

_____. http://www.mlb.com, accessed 7 December 2008.

Arnett, Jeff. "There Used to be a Ballpark: How 50 Years of Relocation and Expansion Have Shaped the Game's Geography." http://www.baseballhalloffame.org, accessed 15 September 2005.

"Atlanta Braves." http://en.wikipedia.org, accessed 2 October 2008.

_____. http://www.mlb.com, accessed 7 December 2008.

"Baltimore Orioles." http://en.wikipedia.org, accessed 26 September 2008.

_____. http://www.mlb.com, accessed 7 December 2008.

"Baltimore Orioles (19th Century)." http://en.wikipedia.org, accessed 2 October 2008.

Bowles, Steve. "The Union Association: At a Glance." http://www.baseballlibrary.com, accessed 1 December 2008.

"Braves Field." http://www.ballparks.com, accessed 22 July 2008.

"Braves Milwaukee." http://www.baseballlibrary.com, accessed 18 July 2008.

"Buffalo Bisons (NL)." http://en.wikipedia.org, accessed 2 October 2008.

"Cincinnati Reds." http://en.wikipedia.org, accessed 2 October 2008.

_____. http://www.mlb.com, accessed 7 December 2008.

"Cleveland Blues (NL)." http://en.wikipedia.org, accessed 2 October 2008.

"Cleveland Spiders." http://en.wikipedia.org, accessed 2 October 2008.

"Colorado Rockies." http://en.wikipedia.org, accessed 2 October 2008.

_____. http://www.mlb.com, accessed 7 December 2008.

"Continental League." http://en.wikipedia.org, accessed 7 August 2008.

"Detroit Wolverines." http://en.wikipedia.org, accessed 2 October 2008.

"Federal League." http://en.wikipedia.org, accessed 1 December 2008.

"Federal League Teams." http://www.toyou.com, accessed 1 December 2008.

"Florida Marlins." http://en.wikipedia.org, accessed 2 October 2008.

_____. http://www.mlb.com, accessed 7 December 2008.

"Franchise History: Major League Baseball Comes to Houston." http://en.wikipedia.org, accessed 2 October 2008.

"Franchise History: New York Mets." http://en.wikipedia.org, accessed 2 October 2008.

"Franchise History Pre 1970s: The Beginnings." http://en.wikipedia.org, accessed 2 October 2008.

Heller, Dick. "Recalling a Blacker Moment in Baseball History." http://www.sportsbusinessnews.com, accessed 29 May 2007.

"Historical Metropolitan Populations of the United States." http://www.peakbagger.com, accessed 13 September 2008.

"Houston Astros." http://en.wikipedia.org, accessed 2 October 2008.

_____. http://www.mlb.com, accessed 7 December 2008.

"Indianapolis Blues." http://en.wikipedia.org, accessed 2 October 2008.

"Indianapolis Hoosiers." http://en.wikipedia.org, accessed 2 October 2008.

"Kansas City Cowboys (Baseball)." http://en.wikipedia.org, accessed 2 October 2008.

"Kansas City Royals." http://en.wikipedia.org, accessed 9 September 2008.

_____. http://www.mlb.com, accessed 7 December 2008.

Levinson, Mason. "Sports Fans' Disinterest Grows With More Scandals, Poll Finds." http://www.sportsbusinessnews.com, accessed 15 October 2007.

"Los Angeles Angels of Anaheim." http://en.wikipedia.org, cited 9 September 2008.

_____. http://www.mlb.com, accessed 7 December 2008.

"Los Angeles Dodgers." http://en.wikipedia.org, accessed 2 October 2008.

_____. http://www.mlb.com, accessed 7 December 2008.

"Louisville Colonels." http://en.wikipedia.org, accessed 2 October 2008.

"Major League Baseball League Attendance." http://www.kenn.com, accessed 17 September 2006.

"Milwaukee Braves." http://sportsencyclopedia.com, accessed 18 July 2008.

"Milwaukee Brewers." http://en.wikepedia.org, accessed 9 September 2008.

_____. http://www.mlb.com, accessed 7 December 2008.

"Milwaukee County Stadium." http://www.ballparks.com, accessed 18 July 2008.

"Milwaukee Grays." http://en.wikipedia.org, accessed 2 October 2008.

"Minnesota Twins." http://en.wikipedia.org, accessed 26 September 2008.

_____. http://www.mlb.com, accessed 7 December 2008.

"MLB Franchise Chronology." http://www.mlb.com, accessed 30 September 2008.

"Montreal Expos." http://en.wikipedia.org, accessed 2 October 2008.

_____. http://www.mlb.com, accessed 7 December 2008.

"National Association of Base Ball Players." http://www.baseball-reference.com, accessed 22 October 2008.

_____. http://en.wikipedia.org, accessed 22 October 2008.

"National Association of Professional Base Ball Players—BR Bullpen." http://www.baseball-reference.com, accessed 22 October 2008.

"National Association of Professional Base Ball Players." http://en.wikipedia.org, accessed 22 October 2008.

"National Association of Professional Base Ball Players (NAPBBP)." http://www.hickoksports.com, accessed 22 October 2008.

"New York Mets." http://en.wikipedia.org, accessed 2 October 2008.

_____. http://www.mlb.com, accessed 7 December 2008.

"New York Yankees." http://en.wikipedia.org, accessed 26 September 2008.

_____. http://www.mlb.com, accessed 7 December 2008.

"1914–1915 Federal League." http://www.baseballhistorian.com, accessed 1 December 2008.

"Oakland Athletics." http://en.wikipedia.org, accessed 26 September 2008.

_____. http://www.mlb.com, accessed 7 December 2008.

"Pacific Coast League." http://en.wikipedia.org, accessed 8 August 2008.

"Philadelphia Phillies." http://en.wikipedia.org, accessed 2 October 2008.

_____. http://www.mlb.com, accessed 7 December 2008.

"Pittsburgh Pirates." http://en.wikipedia.org, accessed 2 October 2008.

_____. http://www.mlb.com, accessed 7 December 2008.

"Players League." http://en.wikipedia.org, accessed 1 December 2008.

"Population of the 100 Largest Urban Places: 1870–1900." http://www.census.gov cited 15 September 2008.

"Providence Grays." http://en.wikipedia.org, accessed 2 October 2008.

"Rodney Fort's Sports Economics: Sports Business Data." http://www.rodneyfort.com, accessed 26 September 2008.

"San Diego Padres." http://en.wikipedia.org, accessed 2 October 2008.

_____. http://www.mlb.com, accessed 7 December 2008.

"San Francisco Giants." http://en.wikipedia.org, accessed 2 October 2008.

_____. http://www.mlb.com, accessed 7 December 2008.

"Seattle Mariners." http://en.wikipedia.org, accessed 9 September 2008.

_____. http://www.mlb.com, accessed 7 December 2008.

Smith, B.W. "It's Time For a Relocation in Baseball." http://www.sportingnews.com, accessed 26 September 2008.

"St. Louis Browns: The Ballplayers." http://www.baseballlibrary.com, accessed 26 September 2008.

"St. Louis Cardinals." http://en.wikipedia.org, accessed 2 October 2008.

_____. http://www.mlb.com, accessed 7 December 2008.

"Syracuse Stars (Baseball)." http://en.wikipedia.org, accessed 2 October 2008.

"Tampa Bay Rays." http://en.wikipedia.org, accessed 9 September 2008.

_____. http://www.mlb.com, accessed 7 December 2008.

"Teams." http://www.baseball-reference.com, accessed 9 September 2008.

_____. http://www.mlb.com, accessed 12 September 2008.

_____. http://www.mls.com, accessed 23 September 2008.

_____. http://www.nba.com, accessed 23 December 2008.

_____. http://www.nfl.com, accessed 23 December 2008.

_____. http://www.nhl.com, accessed 23 December 2008.

"Texas Rangers (Baseball)." http://en.wikipedia.org, accessed 9 September 2008.

"The Ballplayers—League American." http://www.baseballlibrary.com, accessed 2 October 2008.

"The Ballplayers—League National." http://www.baseballlibrary.com, accessed 2 October 2008.

"The First Major League (1875–1889)." http://www.hickoksports.com, accessed 22 October 2008.

"Topping the Expansion List: These Four Cities Most Deserve a Major Pro Team." http://www.cnnsi.com, accessed 12 August 2005.

"Toronto Blue Jays." http://en.wikipedia.org, accessed 9 September 2008.

_____. http://www.mlb.com, accessed 7 December 2008.

"Troy Trojans (MLB Team)." http://en.wikipedia.org, accessed 2 October 2008.

"Union Association." http://en.wiki pedia.org, accessed 1 December 2008.

"Washington Nationals." http://en.wiki pedia.org, accessed 7 December 2008.

"Washington Nationals (1886–89)." http://en.wikipedia.org, accessed 2 October 2008.

"Washington Senators (1891–1899)." http://en.wikipedia.org, accessed 2 October 2008.

Weiner, Evan. "Lou Perini Should be in Baseball's Hall of Fame With Walter O'Malley." http://www.mcnsports. com, accessed 18 July 2008.

"Western League." http://en.wikipedia. org, accessed 9 September 2008.

"Worcester Ruby Legs." http://en.wiki pedia.org, accessed 2 October 2008.

"World Series History." http://www. baseball-almanac.com, accessed 8 September 2008.

Media Guides

Official Major League Baseball Fact Book 2005 Edition. St. Louis, MO: The Sporting News, 2005.

Index

Numbers in *bold italics* indicate pages with photographs.